Praise for Waiting for Peace

"Over the past four years, our enemies believed Israeli society would collapse in the face of their murderous attacks. The fact is that not only have we not collapsed – we have emerged triumphant in body and in spirit. The secret of our victory is found not only in the strength of our army, but in our celebration of life as can be seen by the poignant narratives offered in *Waiting for Peace*."

Natan Sharansky
Minister for Jerusalem and Diaspora Affairs

"*Waiting for Peace* is a heartfelt, intelligent and beautifully written book that takes you into the homes and hearts of the brave Israelis who have so courageously survived the terrible war of terrorism being waged against them. I hope everyone will read it."

Naomi Ragen
author of *The Ghost of Hannah Mendes* and *The Covenant*

"*Waiting for Peace* is a special doorway into the lives, minds, and hearts of a diverse group of Jews in the Holy Land.... The book is an intimate one.... respectful, revealing, and moving. *Waiting for Peace* joins in the great tradition of oral history and is a wonderful example of this art.... Most amazingly, the book is a mirror for the Jewish people and for all people. I predict that when you read this book, you will find yourself in there."

Arthur Kurzweil
author of *From Generation to Generation:
How to Trace Your Jewish Genealogy and Family History*

"*Waiting for Peace* is less concerned with the opinions of 'experts' than with the stories of ordinary Israelis who bravely endure the daily threat of terrorism and who have somehow emerged from years of war more hopeful than pessimistic. Theirs is a story not heard often enough. Anyone interested in the reality 'on the ground' in Israel should place (this) book on their reading list. (It) will give you a vivid picture of day-to-day heroism that makes up the lives of so many ordinary Israelis and provide you with more reasons than ever to 'stand for Israel."

Rabbi Yehiel Eckstei
President of the International Fellowship of Ch

"*Waiting for Peace* is a powerful, riveting, heartfelt, and eye-opening anthology of ordinary Jewish Israelis. If one book can make a difference in changing perceptions and stereotypes to the Middle East conflict, this is the one to read."

Yitta Halberstam
co-author of the *Small Miracles Series* and author of *Changing Course*

"I was deeply touched…. Now I understand (the situation in Israel) on a different level….because of your book the joy will be heightened when peace comes…hopefully soon. Every person who cares about humanity should read this book."

Rabbi Mitchell Wohlberg
Beth Tfiloh Congregation, Baltimore, MD

"Liza Wiemer and Benay Katz's journey enables us to enter the lives and hearts of every Israeli, feeling their hopes and understanding their strength, determination, and fear. A beautifully written book that truly captures the daily reality of *Waiting for Peace!*"

Pam Albert
Director of One Family, Canada

WAITING
FOR PEACE

HOW ISRAELIS LIVE WITH TERRORISM

Liza M. Wiemer
Benay Katz

ב״ה

For Marina;
        Best wishes & Many blessings.
                Liza M. Wiemer

gefen גפן
publishing house בית הוצאה לאור
JERUSALEM ◆ NEW YORK

Typesetting and Cover Design by S. Kim Glassman
Cover Photo by: Alan & Sandy Carey, Photodisc, Getty Images

3 5 7 9 8 6 4 2

Gefen Publishing House   Gefen Books
6 Hatzvi Street, Jerusalem 94386, Israel   600 Broadway, Lynbrook, NY 11563, USA
972-2-538-0247   1-800-477-5257
orders@gefenpublishing.com   orders@gefenpublishing.com

www. israelbooks.com

Printed in Israel   *Send for our free catalogue*

ISBN 965-229-343-1

Contents

Acknowledgements

These acknowledgements begin with one of several small miracles that occurred during the course of writing this book. As I explain in the introduction, I traveled to Israel at a frightening time. Terrorist attacks bombarded Israelis and news report videos were horrifying. Empty Israeli streets and hotels epitomized the fear of wary tourists and citizens. For my ten-year-old son Justin, it was too much to bear. One evening before my trip, he came into my bedroom to pour out his fears as my seven-year-old Ezra snuggled next to me. I was exhausted, my eyes spontaneously closing. I struggled to comfort Justin as he became more and more distressed over my impending trip to Israel. Ezra wanted to know why he could not come with me and stoically accepted my explanation. But Justin was terrified. We talked about God and he had many questions. How did I know God listens to our prayers? How do I talk to God? After some time, I suggested that he go back to his room and pray for my safety. Finally he calmed down enough to go to his bedroom and I drifted into a light sleep. Five or ten minutes passed. Perhaps it may be difficult for some people to believe, but I heard a voice in my head telling me to rise and go to Justin, to climb into his top bunk and to give him a hug and a kiss. The longer I wearily remained in bed the stronger the pull to fulfill the task. In the nearly five years since we bought his bunk bed, I had crawled to the top maybe once or twice. When I finally hoisted myself up, avoiding a whap from the low ceiling, Justin began to laugh and laugh. He clapped his hands out of pure joy. "What are you laughing about?" I asked. He said, "I prayed to God and said that if my mom is going to be safe, then let her come to my bedroom now and climb into my bunk bed to give me a hug and a kiss." Tears streamed down my face and I held him tight. I thanked God for this miracle. From that moment Justin knew I would be safe.

To Justin and Ezra, for being proud of me and patient when I was engrossed in this project – thank you.

*   *   *

This work came to fruition because of the hard work, generosity, and faith of so many individuals, but first and foremost I thank God for the inspiration and strength to see this book to completion.

I offer my apologies if I inadvertently miss acknowledging anyone.

Benay Katz, you are the lifeline of this book.

Jeff Katz, thank you from the bottom of my heart for your dedication, support, hard work, protection, and sharp, critical eye.

Tzviya, Lianna, Aryeh, Avital, and Eliraz Katz, your support of this project and contribution, though not visible to others, was incredible. Thank you.

Shirlee Doft, this work is as much yours as anyone's. Thank you for your impeccable editing eye and honest opinion and Barry Doft for your support and wisdom.

Rabbis Yisroel, Mendel, and Shmaya Shmotkin, Rebbetzins B. Devorah, Devorkie, and Devorah Leah Shmotkin, thank you for your guidance and faith. It is truly a privilege to know all of you and the rest of the Shmotkin family. May your lights and lifework expand one hundredfold with every individual you touch.

Peter Occhiogrosso, I could not have done this without you. Your editing skills are beyond measure, your friendship even more valued. And Lou Anne – your faith.

Lynn Wiese-Sneyd, words are not enough to express all that your friendship, talent, and guidance have meant to me. Indeed, the road has been winding and smooth. I am deeply grateful.

Devon Smullen, thank you for the incredible website. Your creative talent, vision, and generous spirit have added an important and special dimension to making this book a reality.

Alan and Cathy Goldberg, I am grateful for your love and for teaching me the value of never giving up.

Don and Barbara Goldberg, thank you so much for cheering me on and being there for each step.

Lena Goldberg; Harold, Joanna, Debbie, Nili, Mickey, Elie, and Ziona Doft; Josh, Jen, Daniel, and Zach Goldberg; Heidi, John, Taylor, Sawyer, and Katy Pence; Lynn, Jerry, Jordan, Rachel, and Aaron Schmidt; Barbara, Diana, Susan, and Jill Wiemer; Dawn and Todd Ruminski – thank you for your love and support.

Mitch Lechter, thank you so much for reading through some of the chapters and sharing your valuable skills and opinion.

Martin F. Stein, you have been a light. Your philanthropy inspires me and your devotion to the Jewish people and the world even more so.

Ilan Greenfield of Gefen Publishing, thank you for believing in this project, and Smadar Belilty and Michal Avrahamy for seeing it through.

Rachel Feldman, Gefen's expert editor extraordinaire, thank you so much.

* * *

There have been so many others who have made a tremendous impact either through support or because I interviewed them for this book. To explain their impact would take another book. I list them with my deepest gratitude, in alphabetical order:

Einat Achituv Du-Nour, Judith Antonelli, Shahar Argaman, Tirza Ashkenazi, Darawshe Aziz, Paula Balzer, Robin Barasch Permut, Yehuda Beko, Momy Ben-Simon, Dubi Biran, Steve Bojan, Richard Braehr, Jenni Chudnow, Carrie Codell, Shana Cohen, Debbie Drori, Ofer Du-Nour, Ruth Eglash, Mazal Emek, Rabbi David Fine, Joe Freedman, Sue Freedman, Dafna Gaizman, Alex Gan, Shlomit Gan, Leah Glaser, Marcia Glaser, Rabbi Yom Tov Glaser, Sam Glaser, Effy Glick, Hayah Goldlist, Marcia Goldlist, Jill Goldstein, Mark Goldstein, Elise Gould, Shayna Gould, Eileen Graves, Glenn Graves, David Green, Orit Gressel-Raz, Shlomo Gurevich, Orly Hadad, Douglas Handelman, Laurie Handelman, Ze'ev Jabotinsky, Audrey Kadis, Betsy Kaplan, Martin (Moshe) Katz, Sari Katz, Sarah Kealy, Dov Kempinski, Moshe Kempinski, Iris Klein, Stuart Krichevsky, Omri Krongold, Renana Laish, Jeff Langer, Orna Lapid, Shmuel Lapid, Eran Lerman, Michael Lerner, Hana Levy, Ling Lucas, Meirav Moyal, Daniel Nachshon, Marion Nachshon, Freda Naftali, Yaffa Perez, Jonathan Perlman, Maria Permut, Micha Piran, Dr. William Rabenn, Mary Reilly, Ron Rosner, Lior Sadan, Fred Safer, Rena Safer, Arik Schahaff, Gary Schutkin, Jon Schutkin, Rhonda Schutkin, Adina Shamri, Moshe Shohat, Michael Shumacher, Shevy Shumacher, George Strick, Moshe Tamari, Jessica Vilnitzky, Esther Virany, Orly Virany, Josh Weinberg, Barbara Weiss, Dr. Stanley Weiss,

Jim Wellman, Mary Wellman, Rabbi Yisroel Wilhelm, Rebbetzin Leah Wilhelm, Amnon Yarkoni, Yehuda Zach.

*   *   *

Most of all my deepest gratitude to Jim. I accomplished this because of your unwavering support and love.

   Liza Wiemer

Introduction

On a spring dawn in early April 2002 I awoke from a restless sleep at 4:00 a.m. My mind turned to thoughts of Israel and I said to myself, "I feel helpless and hopeless and I don't know what to do." The day before, I had received a phone call from my aunt, Shirlee Doft. "Do you know about the bombing in Haifa?" she asked. "Go turn on CNN." I sprinted to the family room. My children, Justin and Ezra, who at the time were ten and seven, found me in front of the television staring at the gruesome images with tears brimming in my eyes. I quickly turned the channel and put on a happy face as if everything in the world was okay. But it wasn't. My heart ached. The children killed in the suicide bombing felt like my children; the grandparents, like my own.

This was not the first time I had watched with horror the images on the screen, and unfortunately not my last either. Each bombing brought panic and a speed-dial call to Benay Katz, my friend, my blood in Israel. "Is everyone okay?" I would ask. Thank God, she and her family were safe. Palestinian suicide bombings and terrorist shootings, one after another, plagued Israelis. The videos of the suicide bombings shown on news shows haunted me. I had silently sobbed in front of the TV, wondering, "Why would a human being blow himself up and kill innocent people? Why? Why?" The bloody wounded carried off on stretchers, the row of dead laid out on the street, the twisted metal of the burned buses and restaurants, the shocked looks of bystanders, and meticulous, dedicated medical staff working to save lives.

As I sat in bed replaying these images in my mind, the hopelessness of the situation overwhelmed me. Then a thought came to me. "I should go to Israel and interview people about what living with terrorism is like." Not politicians, army generals, or "experts," but varied groups of average

Israelis who experience terror every day. Where do they get their strength to survive, to endure such a life?

I got out of bed and called Benay to get her opinion on this idea for a book. She was enthused. After listening to nearly two years of political spin doctors sharing their opinions on news shows and talk radio, we would do something to balance what we perceived as skewed perceptions hostile to Israel. We would provide an intimate, personal, Jewish account of the intifada. I use the term "intifada" because it has become a colloquialism. But the Palestinian suicide and terrorist attacks since September 2000 have not and never were a simple intifada, "an uprising." As defined by Dr. Eran Lerman, a retired colonel who was in the core of Israeli intelligence, Palestinian terror has been a calculated and planned warfare aimed at the destruction of the State of Israel. His interview is in Chapter 3.

Before my trip at the end of April 2002, hardly a day went by without a Palestinian terrorist attack against Israeli citizens. These ruthless bombings and shootings raised the anxiety level of many who were concerned for my safety, my children included. Friends and family agonized over my well-being, some my sanity. A few begged me to cancel the trip. "How can you go? Don't you have a responsibility to your family?" they would ask. My answer was always the same. "What kind of message would I send my children if I do not stand up for what I believe in? This is who I am. These are my people." I quoted Hillel, the scholar: "If I am not for myself who will be for me? But if I am only for myself, what am I? And if not now, when?"

To say that I was not a little apprehensive, however, would give a false impression. I was. Some of the opposing phone calls shook me to the core, especially those who brought up the subject of my children. But encouragement from the majority of family and friends negated the naysayers and my apprehension. My husband, Jim, knew my heart and though concerned for my safety, he certainly didn't show it. Instead, he was my champion. He too received calls asking how he could permit me to go. He never wavered.

Before I arrived in Israel, Benay and her husband, Jeff, worked tirelessly to arrange interviews with Jewish Israelis from all walks of life. Our schedule was packed with back-to-back interviews. On the Sabbath we rested, but once the last rays of the sun vanished it was full-force work. Bus drivers and computer programmers, students and principals, the wounded and the doctors, the political left and the political right, the religious and the nonreligious, social workers and hotel managers – we interviewed them all. We heard the hopes and fears of a new army recruit and the stories of veteran fighters. A trip to the West Bank on a bulletproof bus brought us to four individuals living in the heart of a war zone. Their emotional stories illuminated a brutal reality. These people presented a surprisingly different picture of relationships with Palestinians before and during the intifada.

Some people Benay and Jeff knew personally, but many we met through small miracles. Twenty-two-year-old Orly Virany was one of those encounters. Two blocks from Rambam Hospital Benay received a call on her cell phone from the father of a wounded soldier we were to meet. The young man was in the process of being transferred to a rehabilitation hospital in Ra'anana and therefore had to cancel the interview. Benay looked at me and said, "What should we do?" "Let's go to the hospital anyway," I replied, "and see what happens." We walked into the office of Yaffa Perez, Assistant Hospital Administrator, who then introduced us to Orly Virany, a survivor of the Matza Restaurant bombing in Haifa. Orly's powerful, gripping story of loss and hope epitomizes the essence of Jewish survival.

In all, over seventy-five individuals were interviewed, a few only briefly for a specific area of expertise or perspective. Ultimately some individuals who so generously gave their time were not included in the book because the conversations either diverged from the overall purpose and direction or were similar to others. Indeed, these were difficult decisions. In addition, a few names have been altered to protect their privacy and are indicated by an asterisk.

When I returned home from Israel in May 2002, the arduous work of transcribing, conducting research, follow-up interviews, and writing began. Over the next two years Benay Katz was an integral part of the process providing an Israeli heart and soul to my American "eye." On November 11, 2004 Palestinian Chairman Yasser Arafat died – a key obstacle to Is-raeli/Palestinian peace. Benay and I decided to keep all comments about Arafat in the present tense, retaining the authenticity of the interviewees' words and the time period. Arafat's death brings a renewed hope among Israelis for peace. Though terrorism continues to be a reality, one lesson is certain – Israeli society will not cave into terror.

An interview with Benay concludes the book. I believe this is a fitting end to a journey that began with the dream to bring ordinary Jewish Israeli voices to a world where sixty-second media bytes cloud our views. Our hope is to make a difference.

Esther and Orly Virany

Simcha and Yaffa Shumacher

Chapter One
Triumph Over Terror: Survivor Stories

At about 2:45 on a quiet Sunday afternoon in Haifa, the last day of March 2002, Karen Moshiyof answered the telephone. "Hi," said her husband, Arnon. "Did you hear about the Matza Restaurant bombing?" Karen froze as panic and fear swirled in her head. Stunned silence led to hysterical tears. Karen screamed, "Orly is there!" Arnon assured her that he would come home immediately. Their two-and-a-half-year-old son sat quietly staring at Karen.

Half an hour before the call, Karen had declined to join her sister, Orly Virany, at a mall in Haifa, not far from their home. Suicide bombers were targeting malls and Karen had promised her husband she would stay away. Orly decided to play it safe too, and made a quick change of plans. "I'm going to eat at Matza with Danielle and then I'll come to you," she told Karen.

Twenty-two-year-old Orly was born and raised in the hills of Haifa, near the magnificent Mediterranean Sea. When she was four years old, her parents divorced and her father moved to Germany. During a six-month stay with her father in 2001, Orly decided to attend a local college for foreign students. Lacking the required math needed to enroll, Orly returned to Israel in January 2002 to complete her math studies and take the matriculation exam. It was in the math class at Ankori high school that she forged a bond with a twenty-two-year-old fellow student named Danielle Manchell.

"We were in tenth and eleventh grade together, and we didn't say hello, not even once," Orly said. "Then in our senior year she left and went to another school. When I started the mathematics course, Danielle came in, looked at me and said, 'You're here too?' I responded, 'But of course.'"

Their friendship bloomed. Daily phone calls and eating at Matza after their Sunday and Wednesday math class became part of their regular routine. Long and rectangular, Matza looks like a typical family-style restaurant, dwarfed by the hills of Haifa. A gas station and convenience store share its parking lot off a twisting, hilly thoroughfare. The Adawi family, Arab Israelis who own Matza, probably never imagined that their restaurant could become a target for a suicide bomber. After all, it is a local favorite for both Arabs and Jews. They had not hired a security guard.

Perhaps the crowded restaurant attracted the bomber, or maybe he saw the sign, Matza, which had significance, because the attack took place on the fourth day of Passover. Jews eat matza (or matzo), unleavened bread, during the holiday of Passover to commemorate the Israelites' hasty exodus from Egypt. Had the bomber been thinking in symbolic terms?

Orly Virany and Danielle Manchell sat in Matza talking and enjoying each other's company. Orly was about to light a cigarette when the bomber, Shadi Abu Tubasi of Jenin, also twenty-two years old, walked to the middle of the restaurant and detonated the bomb strapped to his body. In half a second an enormous gaping hole appeared in the roof. Shattered glass and bloody, twisted metal exploded in every direction – reaching as far as the road, the gas station, and the convenience store. The wounded began to scream and moan.

Despite the intense force of the explosion, Orly never left the seat of her chair. At first, darkness surrounded her. Then the thick black smoke cleared enough for Orly to see the suicide bomber's decapitated body in front of her. The grizzly scene overwhelmed her; all she could do was raise her eyes to the ceiling and stare at the sky.

Ironically, only five minutes before the explosion, Orly had said to Danielle, "Do you know that this month alone, seventy people were killed from bombings?" Several minutes after the bombing the paramedics arrived. Erez Geller, the rescue worker in charge at the scene, grabbed Orly and threw her over his shoulder like a ragdoll. Her left arm throbbed with excruciating pain. Orly glanced at Danielle. She was sitting on her chair, her head resting on her chest. Orly thought, "What the hell? Why is she staying there? Someone take her out of here!" With the intense, sharp pain Orly was too dazed to speak.

Orly was terrified to close her eyes, afraid that if she did she might never open them again. "I don't want to die at the age of twenty-two," she told the paramedics. Her head thrashed from side to side and her rescuers implored her to lie still. They tried to place an oxygen mask on her face, but Orly grabbed it and pushed it off. Patiently, they placed it back on. Back and forth, on and off, Orly struggled with the mask. Wide-eyed, she remained conscious. In the emergency room Orly began to scream, "It hurts! It hurts!" Still conscious, she was wheeled into the operating room.

Shortly after Orly's sister, Karen, received the phone call from her husband, she regained enough composure to dial the dentist's office where their mother, Esther Virany, worked as an office manager and assistant. "Mom, Orly is at Matza! Orly is at Matza!" she cried. Esther had not heard the news and even after Karen explained how she knew that Orly was at the restaurant, the words did not register with her. "It can't be possible," Esther responded. "Orly's at school."

"*No*, she's there!" Karen screamed into the phone.

Orly had taken Esther's car that morning, so she called a taxi and within ten minutes had arrived at Matza. The police kept everyone away from the scene. Still, Esther wanted to be there, to see if Orly was there, to hold her hand, anything. She didn't find her. Esther and her children Karen and Erez separated and for two hours went from hospital to hospital throughout Haifa. Still no Orly. Then a social worker at one of the hospitals said, "Rambam Hospital has the hard cases and we know there are five women in surgery who have not been identified yet. So if you want to look for somebody who is not on the list of the wounded, look there."

Esther met Karen and Erez at Rambam Hospital. They asked if Orly's name was on a list. "We're sorry," the woman said, "we don't have her name here. Maybe she's in surgery and we'll look." Esther asked the staff to look for a small lizard tattoo on Orly's right wrist as a way to identify her. They did not find her. One of the five young women came out of surgery, then the second, third, and fourth. A social worker said, "One Orly, Orly Ofir, is out of surgery. Your Orly is not there." Orly Virany's family grew grimly certain that she was dead. By around 6:30 P.M. the searching was over. Their hope extinguished, they remained at the hospital waiting to identify her body. Fifteen minutes later, the social worker assigned to the Virany family approached them. With a calm expression she took Karen's hand and said, "Karen, we found your sister and she's alive!" Hugs and tears of joy and relief were exchanged.

But with Orly's rebirth, death came to another young woman. Orly Virany had been mistaken for sixteen-year-old Orly Ofir. For two and a half hours, Orly Ofir's father had waited for his daughter to come out of surgery. In the ICU he looked at Orly Virany and said, "This is not my Orly." Orly Ofir had died soon after arriving at the hospital.

"It was awful for the father," Esther explained, her eyes brimming with tears. "When he said, 'This isn't my Orly,' the staff looked at the tattoo on Orly's wrist and understood their mistake." The paramedics had been able to make out only Orly's first name, so the confused identity followed both Orlys to the hospital.

Thirty-one days after the bombing, I met Orly and Esther Virany at Rambam Hospital. A flushed, youthful glow illuminated Orly's freckled face, which bore no makeup. Wire-rimmed glasses highlighted her hazel eyes and blond streaks accented her short, reddish-brown hair. Dressed in black jogging pants, a loose-fitting white T-shirt, and a gray sweatshirt against the chill, Orly lugged a ten-pound metal brace screwed into her left arm. Tied around her neck, a beige cloth sling supported her left wrist and held her arm out at a ninety-degree angle.

Fifty-two-year-old Esther, who had emigrated from Romania at age eleven, wore dark slacks with a long-sleeved blouse of burnt orange, pale yellow, and olive green flowers. Her dyed-auburn hair was streaked with strawberry blond highlights. Mother and daughter shared the same compelling eyes, thin-lipped mouth, and nose. We sat down to talk in the hospital's common room. A stenciled band of flowers on the blue and yellow walls improved the dreary scene. Patients relaxed, engaged in chitchat, or ate a meal at the long formica table. Doctors and nurses, Arabs and Jews, the sick and their loved ones walked in and out through a squeaky door that banged shut repeatedly with an annoying high-pitched whine. At one point, a friendly Arab Muslim woman dressed in traditional garb walked to the water fountain, which was situated on the wall near my chair. She greeted me with a nod and said in Hebrew, "Hello, how are you?" I returned the salutation with a smile.

Orly rested her braced arm on a pillow. With slight amazement she said, "I just realized yesterday that I was at the Matza Restaurant bombing. For a month my stories were about some girl who was there." Orly laughed at this revelation and proceeded to explain her arduous, painful recovery. Reunited with her family, Orly spent five days in intensive care, heavily sedated, unable to feel her legs, tubes attached for life saving measures. Although she remembered little from those days, she did recall repeatedly asking three questions: "Am I going to die? Am I paralyzed?" And, "Is Danielle dead?"

The doctors and Orly's family avoided answering her last question until she was ready to leave intensive care. Danielle had died instantly when a screw from the suicide bomber's exploding belt hit her heart. Three screws had struck Orly. The first shattered the humerus bone in her left arm; the second lodged in a lung; and the third was removed during the initial life-saving surgery to repair her shredded intestine. It was found lodged in tissue near her spinal cord. The doctors saved that screw and gave it to Orly as a keepsake. Miraculously, Orly regained all feeling in her legs and has no residual problems. The doctors had expected to surgically remove the screw from her lung – a dangerous, complex procedure – but the lung healed by itself and there the screw will remain.

Although medication reduced her suffering, the intestinal problem persisted for three days. The doctors talked about the possibility of performing surgery, but once again her young, strong body healed. "I didn't eat solid food for a month," she told me. "Yesterday I ate my first toast, bread with cheese, and vegetables with Thousand Island dressing and it was the best thing!"

The physical pain was gone, but emotionally Orly was a wreck. Psychiatric treatment began three weeks after the bombing. Although she often woke up crying, the tears did not last long. Relieved to release her emotions, she was also grateful to be alive and recognized the need to go on. Yet fear crept into her life. "In a few days I will leave the hospital for home, and it is very scary," Orly said. "I don't know how I will get through the gate of the hospital, to my car, and then home. I don't know if I am ever going to go to the mall, if I am ever going to go out of the house. No one can help me feel safe."

Orly recalled the first moment she stepped out of the hospital walls for a breath of fresh air. "The other day I was sitting outside in the sun. The feeling was great, but I was looking around, checking, my heart was beating fast. I asked my mother, 'Is the security here okay? Did the guards check the Arabs well?' What can I say? I am scared. I don't want to be in another bombing. I think it's going to be very, very hard for a long time."

Orly and Esther are not religious Jews. They do not attend a synagogue on a regular basis, but they believe in God. Esther said, "I am sure that there is something there, something that is keeping us alive. Something guides us along the way from the moment we are born until we are dead. I am sure of it."

Orly agrees. She is certain that God was listening when she said over and over again, "I don't want to die." She also believes that her strong will, youth, and physical strength made a difference. Esther's motto could also have made a difference. "Be happy and do no wrong to anyone," she said. "Perhaps this helped us as a family to get Orly back."

Gradually our conversation turned to the Palestinian people. Do Orly and Esther hate them? Are they angry? Is there a political solution? Anxious to share her thoughts, Esther began, "They have to give the Palestinians a country and shut the border. A border we can watch. They will live their lives and we will live our lives. Only this will make things better. The Palestinians are very poor. They don't have money. Their lives are shabby and I think that they are very angry. If I were living like that I would be angry too, but I wouldn't go there and blow them up."

Occasionally Orly wakes up and thinks, "I can't believe that man did this to me." But her anger is directed at the terrorist and not the Palestinian people. "We don't hate the Palestinians," she added, "but we don't understand them. How can a man go inside a restaurant and blow himself up when people are just sitting and eating lunch? Or celebrating the Passover holiday? I can't understand that. How can there be no value to life?"

The answers to these questions do not come easily to Orly and Esther. Instead, they focus on the positives and are grateful for the warm wishes of family, friends, and strangers. Esther received over five hundred phone calls from well-wishers. Flowers, chocolates, baskets of food, and cards filled every corner of Orly's hospital room. Orly was on a first-name basis with her nurses and doctors. They were her saviors and best friends.

Although Orly left the hospital a few days after our interview, her recovery continued to be a long one. Her arm remained in a sling, at a ninety-degree angle, for five months. In July 2002 she returned to Rambam Hospital, where doctors removed a bone from above her buttocks and used it to replace a part of the humerus bone in her left arm. A metal rod with screws now holds the bone in place. She spent five days in the hospital and nearly a month unable to sit or stand without pain. Her arm no longer straightens and it occasionally aches.

Fear continues to grab hold of Orly. A noise, a word, an image can bring the nightmarish memories flooding back. She rarely ventures out and is terrified to be alone. During the day she often will stay with Karen or go to work with Esther. "It's very hard for me now," Orly said. "I don't need anything but to have my life back. No one can help me with that but me. This is not life. You wake up in the morning and you just want to go to sleep again. You want the day to end. Before the bombing I was very happy, funny, and had lots of fun, just like Danielle."

As Orly waited for some sense of normalcy and joy to return, she sought a reprieve from her fears by taking trips to the United States and Thailand. She plans to visit her father in Germany and possibly study journalism at a university near his home. The stress of living in Israel under a constant cloud of terror has been almost too much for her to bear. "I would very much like to study in Israel and stay and raise my family, but the way things are now, it's not going to happen. Maybe running away to Germany is the easy way out, but things definitely need to change, and fast. It is incredible how many people have died on both sides. It shouldn't be that way."

A few days after meeting Orly and Esther, I visited the Matza Restaurant. An Israeli flag billowed proudly from the rooftop. Inside carpenters worked diligently to prepare for its reopening. Resting against the stone exterior wall, a dried wreath with wilted flowers was the only reminder of the terrorist attack.

The cleanup at Matza immediately following the explosion had been swift and thorough. The Orthodox ZAKA volunteers were some of the first people on the scene. ZAKA is an acronym for *Zihui Korbanot Ason*, which translates as Identification of Disaster Victims. Their job is to gather all human body parts. The commandment of *halvayat hamet*, or attending the dead, is a sacred component of Jewish life. Those who fulfill this commandment show *chesed shel emet*, "true kindness," because their careful attention to the dead is selfless and without ulterior motive.[1] The sanctity of each human being is so important in Judaism that ZAKA volunteers collect every last bit of human remains; even drops of blood are carefully wiped onto clean cloth. Unidentifiable parts are buried together. Once the ZAKA volunteers finish their holy task and the authorities complete their assessment of the damage, rebuilding begins immediately. On May 9, 2002, five weeks and four days after the Matza bombing, the restaurant reopened its doors.

Orly and Esther attended the somber ceremony to commemorate Matza's reopening, but did not stay for long. It was too emotionally painful for Orly and she has no plans to return any time soon. An orange and yellow metal sculpture in the shape of a flame with a plaque attached to the stone wall memorializes the fifteen people, including Danielle Manchell, who died in the bombing. They ranged in age from sixteen to sixty-seven. Over forty others, like Orly, continue to live with the physical and emotional wounds of that fateful day.

* * *

Perhaps it is Israel's size, about the same as New Jersey, or perhaps it is the frequency of the Palestinian terrorist attacks. Maybe it is a combination of both. No matter the reason, wherever I traveled in and around Israel and with whomever I spoke, everyone had some connection to a terror victim. And I mean everyone. Statistically my sampling was admittedly small, only seventy-five people out of a population of 6.5 million, but still, I had expected that at some point someone would have said, "No, I don't know anyone who has been injured or killed in a terror attack." But that did not happen. The stories included a girlfriend's cousin who was injured in a bus bombing; an orthodontist's brother who was killed by a sniper's bullet while driving home; and a daughter caught sitting in a restaurant. Obviously, the physical, emotional, and spiritual impact of terror changes dramatically depending on one's connection to an individual who was involved in an attack. A distant relationship, such as the brother of your orthodontist, may bring feelings of sadness, sympathy, and compassion. But as terror strikes closer and closer – an acquaintance, a friend, a family member, yourself – the impact intensifies.

Terror is a source of such sudden and almost inconceivable pain and suffering that survivors' responses can vary drastically. Where it destroys one person's resolve even to go on with life, it may strengthen another's determination to stay in Israel. Most families touched by terror display a number of often-conflicting emotions that include nuances of fear, anger, resignation, despair, paranoia, courage, sympathy, determination, and compassion.

In order to understand where responses come from, we have to look not only at the often disturbing details of terrorist attacks, but also at the profound effects they can have on terror survivors, their families and friends. In the dynamic of those familial support groups often lie the differences in survivors' responses. Therapist Jonathan Perlman related the following story about teenager Yaakov Samuels.* "Yaakov's stepsister was killed when a terrorist hijacked a bus and drove it into a crowd at a bus stop. His stepsister was in the crowd," Perlman said. "The stepfamily refused to mourn the death and tried to return to normal functioning as soon as possible. Yaakov was depressed and barely functioning when he came to Natal, a trauma center for Israeli victims of terror and war, for therapy. After a year in therapy along with medication, the anxiety that Yaakov experienced disappeared. He returned to his high school studies and started a job, planning to save money for a vacation prior to his army service."

Support also comes from a vast network of groups and individuals that has developed since the beginning of the intifada to help Israelis cope with the overwhelming devastation that often follows an attack. As with the survivors of any war, the physical, emotional, and even spiritual scars will remain with survivors of terror to their dying day. What can we learn from them? On the surface, their stories show the obvious horrific impact that terror has on life and society. On a deeper level, we find compassion, generosity, and love shared by the best of civilization – those individuals who care passionately for people who are suffering, and who choose to make a difference.

* * *

Too many days have been scarred by the evil of terror, a stark contrast to the sanctity of the ancient Holy Land that has deep religious significance for all three monotheistic traditions. This dichotomy was on my mind as I traveled through Jerusalem on my way to the town of Ma'aleh Adumim, where I would meet the Shumachers, another family touched by terror. Ma'aleh Adumim, with a population of approximately thirty thousand, is surrounded by magnificent, treeless desert hills that reflect yellow in the bright sun and glow a spectacular red at sunset. To drive from Jerusalem to Ma'aleh Adumim, the road cuts through an intersection at French Hill in northern Jerusalem, the site of several bombings. The road then stops briefly at the Green Line[2] checkpoint and continues to roll through the Judean desert where terrorists have ambushed vehicles as they travel to Ma'aleh

Adumim. Although the thought of a murderous sniper wasn't far from my mind, the breathtaking view captivated my attention.

On this pleasant, sunny morning in May, I sat down to talk with Michael and Shevy Shumacher in their immaculate living room. Shevy's kind eyes occasionally showed a haunting glimpse into the fear, loss, and worry that her family has endured. Though she does not perceive herself as physically or emotionally strong, there is no doubt that her love is the glue holding her family together. And just as her love for them gives sustenance, it is their love that sustains her. Her home, shades drawn, is her sanctuary from the world of terror outside.

Forty-six-year-old Michael exudes emotional strength, expressed through compassion and concern for victims of terror. He does not forget that God has spared his family not once, but twice from death's door. Wearing a knitted kippah, glasses, and with a neatly groomed beard and mustache, Michael shared his family's story in an orderly manner. Intensity and passion powered his voice, especially when he discussed the need for support of terror victims.

The Shumacher story begins in early August 2001, when Michael and Shevy flew from Israel to Toronto to spend time with Shevy's father, who was dying of cancer. Leaving behind their self-reliant children was not easy, especially because of the mounting terrorist attacks in Israel. But they knew that Ze'ev, 23 and married to Chani; Meira, 21; Simcha, 19; and Yaffa, 15, would look after each other.

At around 7:30 A.M. on August 9, Michael received a phone call. Soon after, his mother-in-law found him collapsed near a chair in her Toronto home. "Shevy, Shevy!" she screamed. "He's on the floor!" While Shevy called for an ambulance, Michael regained consciousness. He choked, "Yaffa was in a terrorist attack and we have to go home!" It was Ze'ev who had phoned just a few minutes before to tell his parents that Yaffa had been wounded in the Sbarro Pizzeria bombing in Jerusalem.[3] In a state of shock, Shevy and Michael packed their bags and made arrangements to take the next flight out of Toronto; an El Al plane was leaving in four hours.

Yaffa had left her sister-in-law Chani near the Sbarro Pizzeria on the corner of King George Street and Jaffa Road in the heart of Jerusalem. From there, Yaffa joined two of her best friends at Sbarro's for lunch. As they stood in line to pay for their meals, the bomber entered the restaurant carrying a guitar case filled with explosives. Within a few seconds he ignited the bomb, killing himself along with fifteen people, including five from the Schijveschuurder family, and injuring 130. As Yaffa waited for help, she heard Mordechai Schijveschuurder, a forty-three-year-old husband and father of eight, ask his family to recite the Shema with him, a prayer declaring the belief in one God. This most holy of prayers is recited twice a day by observant Jews and if one can, in times of distress and before death. Soon after, Mordechai passed away. His wife and three of their children also perished. Two daughters survived the attack and the three oldest sons were not at the restaurant.

Within minutes of the bombing, paramedics were on the scene. So were CNN reporters and cameramen. One captured Yaffa, grimacing in pain, covered in blood, and burned. She screamed from the stretcher, "Don't film me! Don't film me!" Despite her extensive injuries and blinding pain, she did not want her parents to see her on the news and worry. Within minutes Yaffa and one of her girlfriends were taken to Shaare Zedek Hospital. Surprisingly, Yaffa's cell phone was with her instead of in her purse, which had been blown across the street. A social worker was able to contact Yaffa's siblings by speed dialing their numbers programmed into the phone. Within a short time they were at Yaffa's side.

By cell phone Michael spoke with a close friend on the staff of Shaare Zedek Hospital as he boarded the plane in Toronto. The doctor updated him on Yaffa's condition, alleviating some worry. During their agonizing ten-and-a-half-hour flight, Michael recited Psalms and Shevy sobbed and occasionally watched inflight movies. Periodically the pilot radioed the hospital for updates on Yaffa's condition.

It took doctors six hours to repair her shattered elbow. Another operation stabilized a broken femur, and a third fixed a fracture to her left arm and hand. The doctors also removed shrapnel from her body. Yaffa needed three transfusions and her condition remained stable. Michael said, "We were with Yaffa around the clock for the twelve days in the hospital. Knowing she was with people all the time made it so much easier for her to deal with the emotional trauma. The first person Yaffa held onto for support was the rabbi at her school, who came and sat with her a number of times. They talked in a way that we didn't speak. She felt comfortable with him. That was Yaffa's way of dealing with the bombing: her faith and talking. I know Yaffa also talked with her girlfriends those first few days, particularly at night when no one was around."

Yaffa could not walk for two months after she returned home. A special wheelchair helped her descend and climb the twenty-three steps to the Shumacher home. She needed assistance using the bathroom because her burned hands were bandaged.

One week after Yaffa's homecoming, Shevy's father passed away. Michael and Shevy were hesitant to leave the country to attend the funeral, but their children insisted. Michael explained, "I couldn't have gone if it hadn't been for our children, the most amazing people. They've proven their potential many times over. I returned home after a few days. Shevy stayed until after shivah (the seven days of mourning) and then the September 11 attacks in New York grounded her for a few more days.

Soon after their experience with terror the Shumachers felt the need and responsibility to visit other victims and their families. Yaffa, along with her two friends who were with her in the attack, felt that they could provide perspective that would help others get over the trauma and begin to heal. Both Michael and Shevy are amazed at Yaffa's inner strength. Shevy explained, "The first thing Yaffa said to me when I walked into the recovery room was, 'Mom, don't cry.' That is Yaffa. She gives me the strength to go on. If she had to get it [strength] from me she would be in trouble. She likes getting on with her life. Screw you, Mr. Terrorist!" Shevy laughed. "Even though I am her mother," Shevy added, "I have to say that Yaffa is also an exceptional child. The attack didn't make her fall down. But each new terrorist attack takes a little chunk out of her. The worst one was on Ben-Yehudah Street in December[4] because so many kids were killed. I will never forget, she was lying beside me watching TV and Michael was in Toronto. Her body was there, but her mind was away some place else. I could just tell that she had drifted back to that horrendous feeling again."

The Sbarro bombing was not the Shumacher family's only horrifying encounter with terror. Seven months later, on Thursday, March 7, 2002, around 11:00 P.M., their youngest son, Simcha, was studying with 120 young men at the pre-military religious academy in Atzmona, a Jewish community in the Gaza Strip. A Palestinian gunman snuck into the school and began his bloody shooting spree with eight or nine magazines of machine-gun fire and six or seven hand grenades. He went into one of the dormitory rooms, opened fire, and threw a grenade. A boy was killed instantly. The dormitory room caught fire and charred the student's body. In another room boys quickly turned off the lights and one young man stood on the inside holding the door closed as the terrorist passed by. Many students ran to the *bet midrash*, the main study room, which was also a sheltered area. The terrorist killed two boys and wounded several others as they fled for their lives. One of the boys had eighteen or nineteen bullets riddled throughout his body. The murderer then threw a couple of grenades into the *bet midrash*, killing several more terrified, defenseless eighteen-year-olds.[5] Shortly after the brutal attack, the Shumachers heard personally from Simcha that he was okay. He was in one of the side rooms and was not in the direct line of fire.

The shooting spree lasted approximately five minutes. A career soldier and resident of Atzmona heard shots, raced to the school, and killed the terrorist. At the time of the attack only civilians were present at the school. They had no weapons to defend themselves. Since then, the situation has changed.

Five eighteen-year-old sons were killed that night; twenty-three were injured and taken to hospitals in Beer Sheva and Ashkelon. Simcha accompanied one of his injured friends in an ambulance, and Michael met Simcha at the hospital. They stayed there overnight and spent the next day attending three of the five funerals. The other two funerals took place in different parts of the country at similar times, so logistically they were unable to attend.

Michael explained the impact of this attack on both Simcha and their family. "Simcha seems to show amazing strength and character. Someone asked him a day or two later, 'How are you?' He answered in Hebrew, 'Strong in body and spirit.' When Simcha said this he didn't realize how much he had said to me. We have been exposed to terror and after twenty-four years of living in Israel it just strengthens our determination, our cause, and our way. There are those who are less fortunate than we are, those who lost loved ones and whose tests have been more difficult. The reconfirmation, the purpose of our being here, our ideology, our faith are the anchors to deal with these events. We live a lifestyle that is very closely identified with personal commitment to our Yiddishkeit [Jewishness], to faith, and a commitment to the community. Yes, we had to put those tenets to the question. Do we reaffirm them? Do we accept them? Do we throw them out or question them? The answer is that we do what we are doing [visiting victims of terror and making shivah calls]. We continue to do. I think that the fact that we're out here doing is in itself a statement. It is our way of dealing with it. Why were we saved? I don't get into theological issues."

Michael continued, "The Sunday night after the Atzmona shooting, Simcha and I were at a memorial for a friend of his whom I had never met before. The boy's father was from Toronto. Simcha and I both cried, we both hurt and I kept saying, 'Why am I fortunate that I am sitting here with my son when this young father is mourning his son's life?' I mean the fate that put him in Toronto and then here. Who's to know? I just think that since we have been so closely exposed and spared we can't be indifferent and live life like before. I am very driven by what I feel is morally correct to do. It's taken over my life.

"I think of Yaffa, 'Please, God, let her return to as full a life as possible.' She will be limited. She won't be 100 percent. She will deal with it. People have dealt with worse things. Parallel to our personal life and our family we have to do for others. Why were we saved if not to make a difference, to make a change?

"What will happen in five years' time? I think it would be good if we could fall back into some of the routines from before. I don't think it is normal either to be so possessed by what's going on. It's another extreme. It has to be balanced with the other side."

Shevy shared her perspective on how terror has affected her life. "It is hard, very hard. It gets worse. For me at least, it doesn't get better. I don't feel like it has passed over. I feel like I am very much sunk into it. I am more nervous now than I ever was. Every time the children move in the wrong direction it's, 'Where are you going? How are you going? What are you doing?' Not that anybody really goes anywhere. I make them all really nuts. I haven't gone to Jerusalem where I used to go out to eat, go shopping. I went to my dentist who happens to be in the middle of Jerusalem. Otherwise, I don't think I would have been there at all. I work in Ma'aleh Adumim so I am lucky I don't have to travel. I feel like I am in prison. I am still nervous at home. I pull down all the shades because you hear about terrorists coming into houses. I lock the doors all the time. The kids make fun of me, 'Why are you locking the door all the time?' I try to be in control, but it doesn't always work all the time. It's not over for us."

So what has life taught Shevy? "Not to cry," she said. Michael responded, "I think crying is good."

Before we parted, Michael and Shevy brought out a heavy, thick scrapbook, placing it on the coffee table before me. It contained numerous newspaper articles with photos of Yaffa after the bombing. There were pictures of her in the hospital with family, many visitors, and her two girlfriends who survived with her.

Yaffa also had her blood-stained, slightly torn prayerbook. Someone found it across the street from Sbarro's sometime after the explosion. Because "Shumacher" was written on the inside cover, it was returned to her. In a small glass jar Yaffa keeps a melted piece of metal shrapnel that had been removed from her body.

Since the bombing, Yaffa has had surgery to remove the hardware implanted in her body. She still faces additional delicate surgery to repair nerve damage. Michael said, "Yaffa is doing better. She hopes to be able to attend school on a regular basis." Shevy added, "She is trying to make her life as normal as possible, but it doesn't always work that way. I can see that she's moved past the 'I am a victim of terror' stage. She just wants to be sixteen again."

Michael has come up with a list of suggestions to aid victims of terror. "People can help by offering financial and emotional support: 'adopt' a family, or write letters to victims and politicians. Open your pocketbooks. Make sure your money gets to the right causes and does not get lost in the organizational overheads. Let victims know we are brothers and that you feel our pain."

Amnon Yarkoni

Freda Naftali and Yehuda Beko

Mazal Emek and Debbie Drori

Chapter Two

Targets for Terrorism: Kadim – A West Bank Community

With the encouragement of low-cost loans from the Israeli government, five families established the West Bank community of Kadim in February 1984. At its peak, forty-two families lived there. Twenty-four remain today. Kadim is in the north central area of the West Bank, within walking distance of the Palestinian town of Jenin.

For years the residents of Kadim lived peacefully with the Arabs around them. The Jews and Arabs worked together, shopped in the same stores, and traveled on the same roads. No longer. Jenin, Kadim, and the surrounding areas became a war zone when the intifada reignited in September 2000.

I traveled to Kadim to get a small glimpse into the lives of those living in the heart of conflict. It was a dangerous adventure. Jeff Katz, a tour guide and former artillery officer with a 9-mm Smith & Wesson handgun in a royal blue front pack strapped to his waist, accompanied me as both protector and interpreter. Although we could have taken a private vehicle to Kadim, we agreed that a bulletproof bus would be the safest choice. We caught the bus at the Afula main terminal, the site of several suicide bombings. The timing of our arrival at the station was crucial. Too early and we would be potential terrorist targets – sitting ducks milling about in a crowd; too late and we would miss our bus. Because public transportation attracts the masses, suicide bombers target the highly populated central bus stations. Amnon Yarkoni, a driver with twenty-five years of experience, expected us.

The head of the Kadim council had called to inform him that we would be on the 2:30 P.M. bus.

We sat down in the high-backed, multicolored fabric seats of our coach, similar to those found on Greyhound buses, and our journey began. Peering through the two-and-a-half-inch-thick bulletproof windows, my sense of anxiety rose. My life in Wisconsin is filled with the usual worries of any mother of two young boys; a late bus or a call from the school nurse after a playground fall can provoke concern. But nothing could have prepared me for the on-edge sense of danger that bulletproof glass and an armed escort can stir up. We wove our way through the Jezreel Valley, in and out of small flat-farming communities. In all, we dropped off and picked up just a handful of passengers and within twenty minutes arrived at the heavily guarded border checkpoint. An armed Israeli soldier, clad in an olive green uniform and essential protective gear, waved us into the West Bank. If not for the barrier, crossing the Green Line would have gone unnoticed. For seven long minutes we sped through the sparse, rolling countryside. Scraggly green brush, sporadic clumps of yellow wildflowers, and an occasional cypress tree grew among the protruding, sun-bleached rock.

Shortly before arriving in Kadim, Amnon told us to look out our right window. The Palestinian city of Jenin, the site of intense fighting and death, was within view. The road made a ninety-degree left turn and cut through the jagged rock. A standard green road sign in English, Hebrew, and Arabic announced Kadim, Ganim, and Jenin. An arrow pointing to Jenin alerted drivers to the sharp right turn leading to the Palestinian city. Boulders blocked its entry. Less than one minute later, perhaps half a mile away from our position, we saw the Israeli community of Ganim (a sister community to Kadim). Soon after, the bus slowed down and Amnon gave two short horn blasts. A Kelly green electrified steel gate opened at the guard post of the Israeli community of Kadim. Amnon was smiling. How could he grin under life-and-death circumstances? Later he said, "This is the way I am. I love this work and I love this area."

Forty-seven-year-old Amnon is a descendent of Iraqi Jews; his parents immigrated sometime in the 1940s. Born and raised in Israel, Amnon continues to volunteer in the Israeli army reserves, even though he is no longer required to do so. His graying hair is still cut to military length along with a neatly trimmed gray mustache. His solid build provides a commanding presence. He wore a dark blue button-down shirt opened to a sharp v, khakis, and dark sunglasses. Several Israeli flags hung from his rear-view mirror and a window shade near his captain's seat. When I took his picture he wanted to make sure the flags were within the shot.

Amnon moved to Kadim in 1984 and continued living there until 2000 as the head of the local council. "When we lived in Kadim before the intifada," Amnon began, "it was great fun. It was a pleasure. We lived very nicely with the Arabs. My wife even took her driver's test in Jenin, where we had many friends. I used to get them jobs, a lot of work. We lived well."

Soon after the intifada broke out, however, Amnon moved with his wife and children to Afula. "We left," Amnon said, "because of the poor security situation. The main thing was to move to a safer place for the children's sake." And yet, because he knows Kadim and its people, he continues to work on the Afula–Kadim bus route, even though he could have changed. "My wife and children were putting pressure on me, so I stopped driving this route for a month," he said. "They saw that when I stopped, I became very depressed, because I had driven this route for sixteen years." And so he returned to it. "The children are angry that I work here. But I explained to them that there have been terrorist attacks in Afula too, and I hope that they understand. I believe in God, and so I believe that what is written on high is what will be. If it's written that something will happen to me in Kadim, it will happen. If it's written that it will happen in Afula, then it will happen in Afula."

Until April 2003 Amnon drove his own unarmored vehicle to Kadim on a regular basis. Now he will only travel in his protected bus. The area has been extremely dangerous since the intifada started, due to the frequent terror attacks, but more recently violence has intensified. "There have been numerous shootings on the road leading to Kadim," Amnon said in a follow-up phone interview. "Between April 27 and 29, 2003, my bus was shot at twice by terrorists. They missed, but it is much too dangerous now for ordinary vehicles to drive on the road leading from the border checkpoint to Kadim. I am concerned for the safety of the children. Just the other day at the checkpoint there were several cars waiting to drive to Kadim in convoy with an army escort. I saw that there were children in the cars, so I got out of my bus and told the parents that I would drive the children free of charge. The parents then followed me in their vehicles until we reached the community safely."[6]

If Amnon sees that no military jeeps are patrolling the road or that Palestinians are going back and forth over the border without being supervised, he immediately reports this to the army over an army radio on the bus. "Besides being shot at on this road while in the bus, I've already gone by two roadside bombs. One I passed and the bomb exploded thirty meters behind me. The second time the back of the bus was damaged, but no one was hurt. The terrorists place the bombs and activate them by cell phone. When I drive fast, it's hard to catch me at the right moment. Even when I'm traveling with an escort, I drive quickly. I'm driving eighty kilometers an hour right now." Under normal circumstances Amnon would drive no faster than fifty kilometers an hour on such an urban road.

"I was at the Afula bus terminal when a terrorist disguised as a soldier opened fire.[7] He was shooting three meters from me. I got on the armored bus and drove away. I didn't have a weapon on me and I had no choice but to get out of there. On another occasion I was about thirty meters away when there was an explosion at Afula's central bus station.[8] I saw the severed head of the terrorist on one of the seats of the bus. But it didn't stop me from sleeping. However, my wife, who didn't see it but only heard about it, couldn't sleep. Maybe it's something that you force out of your mind."

The moment Amnon heard that a few Israeli Arabs had collaborated with the terrorists, he was deeply upset. "My feelings toward the general Arab population changed," he said. "Everything changed. When you know that an Israeli Arab living near Afula drove a terrorist into Afula so that he could hurt us, of course your attitude toward him changes. But I don't worry about my Arab coworkers. I know the drivers and I don't believe that any Arab Israeli who works for Egged would commit any terrorist activity."

Amnon happily continues to work with Arab bus drivers who are members of the Egged Bus Cooperative, acknowledging, however, that when there is a terrorist bombing it is not a comfortable situation for them, either. "Relationships between Arab and Jewish bus drivers are very good. We socialize after hours in each other's homes and talk. When there has been a terrorist attack you try to pretend that nothing has changed, but it's not true. If I say that nothing has changed, then I'm lying. The day of a terrorist attack and the following day, the Arab bus drivers feel very uncomfortable and they try to avoid their Jewish coworkers. I try to pretend that everything is okay and that our personal relationship hasn't changed, but I keep my true feelings of being upset inside. These feelings are not personal or directed toward them as individuals. After a few days things get back to normal. We've sat and talked about the terrorist situation here in Israel and my Arab coworkers have voiced their strong rejection of these attacks. Everyone agrees that Israeli and Palestinian leaders need to sit together and talk in order to reach a peace agreement."

Amnon has police authorization to search any passenger who looks suspicious, and he will do so without hesitation because it can mean the difference between life and death. "I examine every passenger who gets on, and if a person looks even a little bit suspicious, I get off the bus and I don't hesitate to stop him from getting on. I ask him to open his bag and make sure he doesn't have a weapon or bomb in it. Then, when everything has checked out okay, he travels on the bus. He sits nearby and it is unpleasant because he looks at you in a certain way. My only consolation is that I don't have a choice. We have to search passengers and we do it. When I approach a bus stop, I slow down and look all around. If I see that there is someone suspicious there, I don't stop. I continue to drive and report him to the police."

There are many suspicious behaviors that signal bus drivers to be leery of an individual. Inappropriate dress for the weather conditions, nervous, fidgety behavior, awkward hand positions and, for drivers familiar with a route, a new face in the crowd or a person standing alone at a stop rarely used during that particular time of day or night. One afternoon at a bus stop on Amnon's route, an Arab man carrying a bag with a radio stepped onto his bus. With a quick scan Amnon noticed what appeared to be wires hanging from the radio. Instantly he pulled on the bus hand brake and using both hands he grabbed the man and removed him from the bus. Amnon called a soldier who happened to be a paid passenger to assist him. "I took the man around to the back of the bus," Amnon said, "and the soldier and I searched the bag. It turned out the radio had some harmless strings tied onto it. I spoke to the man in Arabic, apologizing for the manner in which I took him off the bus. We then got back on and continued our journey. This Arab man sat in the seat next to me and we spoke during the rest of the trip. I said to the man, 'You must understand why I did this. With the security situation as difficult as it is, I thought you might have a bomb.' The man was not upset and he said, 'It's okay. I don't want to take a chance when I am on a bus either. I ride the bus all the time. *Kol hakavod*.'" The phrase means "Great job!" or "Way to go!"

A day does not go by when Amnon does not think about the possibility of a terrorist act. "Every day we wait for an explosion, an attack or something to happen," he said. "When there isn't anything, we are happy. You have to continue to live here. There's nothing else to do. My wife's family is begging me now to go to New York and to take the family. My mother-in-law already has a green card. And there are the family unification laws, so we could go. But no way! I won't leave Israel. There's a song, 'I was born here. / My children were born here. / I built my house here with my own two hands.' I really hope that we will be able to live quietly and in peace. I don't think there is anyone in Israel who doesn't want peace. I have a large house, a huge villa, in Kadim, but I am willing to give up the house for peace, if it will be a real peace."

As we stepped off the bus, several soldiers with bulletproof vests and helmets were mingling by the circular commons of Kadim. Red, white, and yellow flowers graced the circle's edge. From this area, paved streets branched off in various directions. Spiraling barbed wire attached to wooden, γ-shaped, twenty-foot poles with taut wire surrounded the community. It occurred to me that a terrorist could cut through the wires and enter at any time. We walked slowly to the Kadim office, looking at the environment around us, and I was aware of my own anxiety and the need to keep it under control. We passed several mobile homes, and Jeff mentioned that each had an exterior water tank and a generator. A young boy rode his bicycle nearby. He stopped as soon as he saw us and stared at us with suspicious, nervous eyes, then immediately disappeared from sight, leaving behind him an eerie silence.

Inside the trailer office we were introduced to four people: Mazal Emek, Freda Naftali, Yehuda Beko, and Debbie Drori. A long table with chairs on either side filled the room. Near the back of the trailer and almost touching the table stood Mazal Emek's desk and telephone. Large aerial photos of Kadim and the surrounding area hung on one of the walls. Cigarette smoke choked the room and the tiny slotted windows offered little fresh air. Though Jeff asked them not to smoke, we soon realized that this was an impossible request. Smoking is their release from stress and the more they talked about living with terror, the more they smoked.

Mazal Emek works as the head of the council in Kadim, somewhat similar to the position of mayor. She moved to the community from Tiberias ten years ago with her husband and three infants. "I came here because it was a beautiful place and I wanted our family to have a good life," she said. "It was safe and quiet, and everyone was like family to my children. It was very important to me that they grow up in a place where there were no drugs, no scary people, and everyone knew each other. I didn't think about our Palestinian neighbors. Now, living here is different." Mazal, thirty-five, was sitting behind her desk, on which she banged occasionally when making a point. Her short, dark brown hair was dyed auburn. She wore black slacks and a V-neck button-down cotton sweater with blue, black, and white stripes. The long sleeves were pushed up to her elbows.

Freda Naftali, fifty-two, was born in Haifa but moved to Upper Nazareth after she married. In 1985, when her eldest daughter was fifteen, she decided to move to Kadim. "I was looking for quality of life and fresh air. I don't want to sound anti-Arab, but there were too many young Muslim Arabs hanging around the street where we lived. Groups of four or five young Muslim Arabs would come to the area, park their cars, and harass the young Jewish girls as they walked to or from their apartments. One of my eldest daughter's girlfriends returned home a little after midnight with her boyfriend one night, and they were physically attacked by these Muslim Arabs. This was the point of no return for me – my red line. I was afraid for my own daughters' safety. So we decided to come to Kadim."

Freda is no longer working, but before the intifada she chauffeured passengers with her own van. When driving became dangerous, however, she would have had to buy an armored car to keep her customers, and she couldn't afford it. "I used to drive through Jenin when I chauffeured a school principal. Two months before the current intifada started, my husband asked me to stop driving through Jenin. So I had to drive for forty-five minutes to get to the school instead of the regular twenty minutes through Jenin." Freda was smoking more heavily than the others in the room and she and Mazal were the two who most often raised their voices when they disagreed with each other. But soon after, they would smile and tease one another like old friends. When Freda mentioned her wedding anniversary, Mazal quipped, "Poor guy! Thirty-three years." Freda responded, "She feels sorry for my husband! You see, where else can you find such a sense of humor. We care about each other and sometimes we want to break each other's necks.

We fight; we have arguments. That's normal – and then we go out and have fun together." Freda smiled, her blue eyes reflecting mischief.

Yehuda Beko moved to Kadim five years earlier on a trial basis. "We saw this beautiful place and fell in love with it," he said. "I didn't come here because of ideology. I came here for quality of life. We also had friends among our Arab neighbors. They were, in fact, the building contractors for our home. We got along with them nicely until this whole mess began." At thirty-two, Yehuda was the quietest of the group. He did not smoke and several times made sure our glasses were filled with water. He wore a gray sport shirt with the number 3 centered on his chest. His graying black hair and weathered skin perhaps reflect the trying life he has faced. Sitting back in his chair, he listened to the women tell their stories.

Mazal described the situation in Kadim with brutal succinctness. "We live as if in a prison," she said. "An army escort comes to the Green Line checkpoint and then we drive the car in to the West Bank. Some of us are braver than others and drive alone. Some of us wait to share a ride so that we are not in the car alone. But we all drive with an escort."

"Let me put it this way," Freda said. "No one is going to disturb the way I'm used to living. If I have to go to Afula, I will go to Afula, even if bullets are flying all over. It all depends on the person. I am not a hero. There are moments when I am afraid for myself also, but I don't let it disturb me. Bullets used to fly over the houses. We'd feel them hit the roofs and the walls. They also went through the houses."

It is the children who suffer the most from the constant anxiety associated with terror. "Though my children are grown now," Debbie said, "I know that some of the kids living here wake up in the middle of the night because of nightmares. They are afraid. If they play outside, they stay in their yards or go to a neighbor's house." The settlement once had a kindergarten and a nursery school, but there is no longer a need. The older children take armored buses to school in Shaked, a forty-five-minute drive, while the younger children go to Moshav Gan Ner, twenty-five minutes away. Because of the constant risk of terrorist attacks on the way to and from school, the emotional stress has caused some of the children's grades to suffer. The parents also feel tremendous tension while their children are gone. "When I wake up in the morning and I send my children to school," said Mazal, "I always, always check to make sure that they get to the bus stop and that there is a soldier on the bus who will take care of them.

When they are on the bus for Shaked, I call my older son and ask him if everything is all right. When they are on their way back home, I call the bus driver to find out when the children will be coming home. And when they arrive back at Kadim, if I am in the office, I always have to see them before they go home."

"The most difficult part of the day," added Freda, "is when the children are out and you know that at a certain hour they should be coming home and they are late. Then the heart stops pumping."

"But that is not the scariest part of the day," Mazal said. "The scariest part is when they have to be alone in the house." Most of the parents work outside of Kadim and can't always be there when the kids come home from school. "When you realize that anyone can come in here, do whatever they want and then just disappear – the scariest part is knowing that something may happen and you cannot help them."

And yet, Yehuda refuses to give in to fear. "You don't abandon a house when the situation gets a little difficult," he said. "This is our home and we live here and we will continue to live here even during these hard times. We will continue to live here even if we have to travel to Afula and back with weapons on our laps, or even if when my son is a bit late we have to call to find out if something happened. I don't know how others feel, but I know that you don't abandon your home when the going gets a bit tough."

Debbie Drori, forty-six, moved to Kadim eighteen years ago. She is married with three children – a son of twenty-six and daughters of twenty-one and seventeen – and is the office administrator for Kadim. She wore a red T-shirt, blue jeans, and sneakers. Her dark wavy hair hung two inches below her shoulders. Debbie has strong opinions, but a more laid-back approach than the other women. Her youngest daughter wants her to build a second story onto their house for her and insists she is not afraid.

But Mazal's eleven-year-old son is afraid to be alone in the house or in his room. He is afraid to sleep in the dark. "He has a lot of animals in his room," Mazal said. "Not stuffed animals, live animals – a hamster, a dog, and fish. He thinks that if a terrorist comes to his room, all the animals will scare him away. When he is on the bus going to school and he hears a noise like gunfire, he sits on the floor of the bus because he is afraid of bullets. That's his life. This is very sad for me and this is why I'm not going to live here anymore. I'm going to leave this place in another month.

Nothing is worth that, not the land, not the country, not the people, and not the government.

"My oldest son, who is fourteen, is always watching TV or playing on the computer because there are no children his age to play with. One night he told me that he wants to sleep with a slingshot. I asked him what he would do with it. He said that if someone comes to the window, he would scare him. I said nothing to him. My youngest child likes to live here because she has friends. But she knows that if I go outside and call her and she doesn't answer, I will become very paranoid. So, every five to seven minutes she comes to say she's all right."

Yehuda works night shifts at a factory and often doesn't get back home to Kadim until 2 to 4 A.M. He does not want to leave his home, and said that he gets his strength from his children. "It's true that I'm not safe driving on the road when terrorists place bombs or shoot at the car. When all the trouble began, I told the kids I wanted to move to Afula because of the shooting. They said, 'Dad, what's the problem? Because of a little gunfire, we're going to give up? We're not leaving!' This is our home even if we are the last ones to stay. The good conditions we have here we won't have in any other place. Each child has his own room with his own TV. My youngest son, who is eight years old, cries that he doesn't want to come back into the house when I call him in at eight or nine at night. Of course, he knows at his age what bullets, jeeps, and tanks are. A child in Afula or somewhere else doesn't know these things."

I asked Mazal why she felt uncomfortable with her children playing outside when Yehuda's boys were allowed to play into the evening. "The main difference is that his children came from the city," she said. "All of a sudden they have a house and a yard, wind in four directions, a place to play. Our children have lived here since they were small and only know this way of life. We don't see a house on a plot of land as something that you have to hold on to."

Freda acknowledges the other prices they have to pay to live where they do. She does not see her grandchildren, because her eldest daughter, who is thirty-two, doesn't come to visit. "Neither does the rest of my family," she added. "No friends. No one. Sometimes, when people from Afula hear that we are from Kadim, they say, 'Are you nuts? Don't you have anything else to do with your life?'

"But if we won't live here, the Arabs will live here. And when the Arabs are here, Afula will not sleep quietly. And it is not only Afula, the same goes for the surrounding Jewish villages."

Freda's eldest daughter left Kadim after serving in the army and did not return, because she felt there was nothing for her to do there. Her middle daughter also moved away after she finished serving, to be able to work and earn a living. "My nineteen-year-old daughter, the youngest one, is still with me, but leaves the house all the time. The problem is that if she wants to go to a disco, or to a movie, or to friends, she has to stay overnight outside Kadim. On Friday she leaves and comes back on Sunday."

Security isn't the only problem associated with living in Kadim. The wells have begun to dry up, something Mazal believes the government knew about seven years ago. "But they didn't think that Kadim and Ganim would still be on the map, so they didn't look into the problem." Now the army brings in water tankers to supply the community. It's unclear how long the residents will be able to stay.

Debbie believes that Kadim will still exist in twenty or thirty years; Freda gives it a maximum of two years. "If the government decides that it doesn't care about us," Mazal said, "everyone will leave without government support."

Like the bus driver, Amnon, Debbie would be willing to leave her home in Kadim in exchange for peace, but she does not believe that peace will come. She said, "If I would know that my being evacuated from Kadim would ensure peace, then I am prepared to call myself a victim of peace. But it's bullshit! Nothing like that will ever happen."

It is not easy for any of them to imagine giving up their homes, giving up their dreams. They do not want terror to win, but sometimes it is more than anyone can endure.

Mazal has had several close calls with terror already, including an incident in which she was driving on the road one evening. "My husband was driving the car behind me with our elder son. In front of me was a bus. The bus went over a bomb and exploded. Terrorists began to shoot at us. I looked around and saw my son and knew that there was nothing I could do to help him. There was a soldier at a distance who began shooting at the terrorists, but I couldn't do anything. It's like having a very sick child and you cannot help him. It is a horrible feeling." In the end nobody on the armored bus was hurt, although the tires were blown out. The army chased off the terrorists, but it was the fourth time something like that had happened. "We laughed a lot because we had to let our son feel that nothing happened," Mazal said. "We joked that if something would happen to me, my husband could pay off the mortgage with the life insurance money. He would buy the kids more clothes and more candy. That is the only way to cope.

"Once, I was driving home and a woman who had lived in Ganim, but who had moved away because she was scared, was driving the car behind me. I started to hear a noise. I looked around and I noticed that she had lost control of the car. And then I realized that someone was shooting at her. I was not scared because I was too worried about her losing control of the car. I didn't realize that they were also shooting at me. When we got near the gate at Kadim she couldn't control the wheel anymore and she froze like a block. She just held onto the wheel." The woman eventually stopped her car safely and no one was hurt, but the memories are hard to erase.

Debbie told of driving home from work at 11:00 P.M. in a convoy of three cars. "There was an explosive device planted by terrorists on the road. The road was very narrow and we could not turn around without the possibility of ending up in the ditch. We all had to drive in reverse for miles back to the intersection. After the explosive device was removed, we were able to continue home, but it was already 1:30 A.M."

Freda recounted another terrorist attack, this one with fatal results. "There was a woman from Ganim named Katya, who was shot to death in her car. She left a baby boy and a husband." During the same attack another woman, in the car behind Katya, was shot in the leg. At the time, Mazal was on a bus full of children on their way to Shaked for a party. The woman whose leg was injured telephoned for help. She called the first number that appeared on the speed-dial list of her cell phone. It was the bus driver's number. Her voice came over the bus's loudspeaker and the children heard her crying, "They're shooting at me! I've lost my leg! They are killing Katya!" The children began to cry because they didn't know what to do. The woman was still in the hospital ten months later.[9]

If dealing with terror is not stressful enough, those living in Kadim face another problematic challenge: medical care. They have no doctors or ambulances. Freda has a heart condition and several times has needed immediate help. Once, Debbie sped to the army checkpoint with Freda, where they waited for an ambulance to come. Another time a military ambulance came to Kadim and drove Freda to the hospital. As Freda discussed these obstacles a pained look crossed her face. It was clear that there had been close calls, and I could not help but wonder if she was worrying about a future need for emergency assistance.

Our conversation shifted to their relationships with the Palestinians. It was during this part of the interview that voices grew louder, fists banged on the table for emphasis, and I sat back listening, a little perplexed as to when to call for a truce. As it turned out, they found some points to agree on and the tension dissipated.

Freda began. "We had a good, normal relationship with the Palestinians, especially with Jenin's former mayor. Jenin was the last place that the intifada started. We used to go there to buy all our groceries, shoes, clothes, and everything we needed. We had Arab friends and they used to warn us half an hour to an hour before stones were going to be thrown. I am sure that the Jenin merchants are weeping now, because they earned a lot of money from us.

"The Palestinians wanted [coexistence] because they had a very good life. They went to Haifa, Tel Aviv, and to Tiberias to swim in the sea. Israelis came from all over to buy in Jenin, in Kalkilya, and everywhere else in the West Bank. You have no idea how much money they made. The Arab shop owners in Nazareth cried. They said that they were losing money. The Arabs of Nazareth and the surrounding villages left them and came to the West Bank to shop."

"But it's not like that," Mazal responded, her frustration rising. "Even if they say they want to live peacefully with us and that everyone just wants to make money, the Arab people are bound to the land. They feel deeply about the land, and they don't want to see us living on the land."

"That is why I haven't gone into Jenin since the first intifada,"[10] Debbie interjected. "I don't shop there at all. The Arabs are a people who cannot be trusted. Ideologically, I don't believe in one country for two nations. If we go back in history three thousand years, we will see that when there were two nations anywhere in the world on one piece of land, there were wars and nothing could prevent them. I should let the Arabs benefit from my shekels? I haven't done that for fifteen years. I have no faith in them, nothing."

Freda pointed out that there was a Palestinian man living only a short distance away who used to work for Kadim. "He was very loyal to us. This man, though, is not the problem. Someone from Hamas or Islamic Jihad

can take one of his six children hostage and tell him that if he doesn't plant
a bomb for them, they will kill his child, or maybe his whole family. The
army would not allow him to continue working here. He and his children
were hungry. He called my neighbor and told him that he had no food to
give his children. The man was crying. The neighbor brought him food
with an army escort."

"We do not hate the Arabs," said Mazal. "This man knows 'Hatikvah,'
our national anthem."

"He would go on field trips with us," said Freda. "He would put up flags
for us on Independence Day. He and his family would come and celebrate
with us. He respected us. You cannot be indifferent to such a person."

"He ate matza on Passover," Mazal said. "He went to all the weddings
and bar mitzvahs."

"But," Debbie said, "he is only one."

"No," Mazal said, "it is a whole family."

"Okay," Debbie agreed, "But it is only one family."

Freda pointed out that any Palestinian who wants to live among and
have a good relationship with Israeli Jews will be considered a collaborator,
and his life will be in danger.

"So they should object," Debbie said. "They should fight against terrorist organizations like Hamas and Jihad." Mazal agreed and once again
the tension mounted.

"You are forgetting one thing," Freda added. You grew up in a democratic country. You can stand up on your own two feet and say what you
want."

"This legitimizes crime?" Mazal's frustration flared.

"It's not written on their foreheads who is good and who is bad," Freda
answered. Calmly, Debbie interjected, "Let's take the example of the Palestinian child who is a first grader. We all know what math books were found
in the West Bank. In first grade he has to solve the problem: Dad goes out.
He sees three Jews. He kills two. How many are left?"

"But as a mother, if I know that this is the book my children are learning from, I won't send them to school," Mazal said, still upset. "If you are
a good person, you have to make changes for your children's sake in your
home. After that you have to make a political change."

"As I said, you grew up in a democracy," Freda responded. "I am not
defending them. If one thousand, even two thousand Arabs stand up and

say that they want peace they will be slaughtered! But if they number two or three million Arabs, they cannot slaughter three million."

Turning to me, Mazal said, "If I just take Freda's opinion and think like her, there will never be peace. You can never make peace with people who are afraid to say what they think."

Debbie saw the situation from a different angle. She was born on a moshav near the Palestinian town of Tulkarem. There was terrorism while she was growing up and nothing has changed. She does not see terror ending in the future.

As this discussion came to an end, I asked the group if living in Kadim was worth giving up their lives. The question evoked intense emotion. Debbie began by explaining that her son is a disabled ex-serviceman. "He never asked me why I sent him to the army," she said. "And I never complained to my mother asking her why she came here from Europe. My father-in-law was a Lehi[11] resistance fighter who was sentenced to death and sat in the jail in Akko[12] with eighteen or nineteen other boys. He also fought for Israel. Nothing has changed in the last fifty or sixty years."

Yehuda repeated that he came to Kadim not out of ideology but for a better quality of life. "Of course I don't want something to happen to my children because I live here. So if they say tomorrow that they're closing up Kadim and we all have to leave, I will leave. But, until someone says that, I'm staying."

"It's a difficult question," Freda answered. "And I'm going to be very truthful to myself. The price is too high to pay. Because the moment you lose someone dear to you, you have no life. You don't care what will happen. Lose someone from my family? No!" And yet, Freda admits that she hasn't left because she loves the place and has been there for eighteen years.

Mazal responded in quite a different way. Her voice rose almost to a shout. "I am very angry you asked this question! As a mother you can never ask someone something like that. *Never!* It's like asking what price you are willing to pay for losing a child. This is the difference between a mother from Jenin and me. She is willing to send her children to die. I am not." The tension and dangers that mark living in Kadim have compelled Mazal to leave. She has given herself a month to find a home inside the Green Line. "There used to be an element of safety in Kadim," she said, "because we truly believed that Sharon[13] would make a difference, that he would make us feel more comfortable. But he didn't do this. After the April 2002 operation in Jenin,[14] we realized that the country doesn't think about us. Nobody really cares about us.

"Now we realize that it is very scary to live here. We didn't know that before. We knew soldiers would take care of us. And if we didn't have water, it wasn't that bad because we had water in the tanks. Neither did it matter that we had to drive on the road with an escort. But now we know that nothing is going to prevent the coming danger, not the escort and not the army. Jenin is full of terrorists with a lot of weapons and the motivation to kill the people from Kadim and Ganim. *We* had thought that they were good people just waiting for peace. Now we know that they are terrorists just waiting to kill us. That is what made me decide to leave now."

What has life taught them? There was a brief pause. Freda lit another in a seemingly endless chain of cigarettes. "I do not want to end as a line in the newspaper that tomorrow will be used to wrap fish. I feel sorry for the poor Palestinians. But we are ordinary people with feelings, with loves and hates. If they stab us, don't expect us to turn around and kiss them. This is a daily fight for our lives. Our children are suffering. So we suffer also. We don't hate the Arabs. On the contrary, they hate us. I want people to imagine going out and having a good time. You want to celebrate thirty-three years of your marriage, to sit in a coffee shop, to go to a fancy restaurant, and you don't know if you'll come back home or if you will be blown up. I want people to understand, to imagine if they can, what it means to take a bus or taxi ride, to be an innocent bystander and to get hurt only because you are Jewish. This is what I want people to think about. I do not want people to judge us. First you have to be in our shoes and feel what we feel. The Americans did after September 11. It was a terrible ordeal. And they know exactly what I am talking about."

"It's very hard to be a young mother and have to work for a living," Mazal added. "But that's not the reason I am feeling down now. The reason is that someone else decides whether I live or die. The person doesn't have to be large, smart, beautiful, or intelligent. Just one Arab can wake up now and decide that he wants to kill me. He goes out of his house and goes to the community's fence and shoots. One person, one little child, can change my life forever. And I can't do anything about it. No one can help me. No one can promise me that it will not happen. This is the basic fear we live with every day."

"My parents are Holocaust survivors from Auschwitz," Debbie said.

"They had to fight hard. They stayed alive so that we would live. Unfortunately, we have to keep living and fighting for our children, grandchildren, and great-grandchildren so that there is a place for us to live here, not in Europe, the U.S. or any other place. Jews have only one country."

Yehuda, who had sat patiently through most of the interview, had a surprising, but understandable answer. "Maybe I should not have come here. From the beginning I knew I was coming to this kind of place in the Territories. I was looking for a cheap place. I would not have been able to afford to build a house like I have here in Afula. But it has cost me a lot more because of the situation, so maybe I made a mistake. This house is worth nothing now. My considerations were not the wisest."

The interviews came to an end and Jeff and I had an hour to spare before the return bus arrived. So we walked around. Soldiers wearing camouflage army gear drove through the deserted streets in military trucks. Many patrolled the grounds on foot. Three small boys played basketball in the gymnasium with a few off-duty, uniformed soldiers.

It is easy to imagine what Kadim once was: a thriving community with children laughing on the playground, neighbors talking as they cared for their lawns, teenagers hanging out in the park. Reality, however, has erased those happy images. Spindly, snarled weeds that towered above my 5' 3" frame surrounded abandoned homes. Broken shutters dangled from windows and gutters hung from the edges of red clay-tiled roofs. Some of the deserted homes around the community had become army quarters for the soldiers guarding Kadim.

Near the gymnasium a plethora of army equipment stood ready for action. Just fifty feet away from there was a watch tower (I could not tell if it was occupied) that stood amid the barbed wire fence that surrounds Kadim. I stopped and looked nervously toward the sparse, sloping, rocky landscape on the other side of the penetrable barrier. Could a terrorist be hiding behind a boulder just waiting to take a shot? My heart pounded. This was way too close to the edge for me. With my eyes still darting at the fence, I backed away. A tall, sweet-faced, and soft-spoken nineteen-year-old soldier wearing a *kippah* approached Jeff and me. I don't think it was common practice for residents to stand so close to the Kadim perimeter. We quickly explained why we were there.

Suddenly, short, crackling sounds of gunfire could be heard coming from Jenin. My heart crashed against my chest, and the anxiety I had been doing my best to manage came boiling to the surface, worse than ever. There was no doubt in my mind that I was ready to leave. I fought back my urge to run. As Jeff and I walked back to the bus stop we saw a woman watering her manicured lawn. I wondered why she bothered. Perhaps this was her way of retaining a sense of normalcy despite the terror.

Jeff and I sat in the three-sided wooden bus shelter near the circular commons and waited. I hugged my knees up to my chest, so that no terrorist would see my feet dangling from behind and take a potshot at us. I was certain that the wooden enclosure would not be adequate protection. If Jeff was nervous, he did not show it. His feet rested on the ground. Army vehicles continued to stream in and out of Kadim. Could a person get used to this kind of life? I thought about the young soldiers stationed to protect the remaining families of Kadim. I thought about terrorism and the Palestinian man on the other side of the barbed wire fence with starving children. I thought about Mazal and Debbie and Freda and Yehuda. This was no longer some distant place, faceless and nameless. These were regular people struggling to survive. I wondered whether peace would ever come to this land. I was grateful when Amnon's bus finally pulled into Kadim and we sped off into the West Bank countryside with an army escort. Once through the checkpoint, I started to breathe a little more easily.

But back at the Afula bus depot, I started to shake all over. Ironically, I was relieved to be back at the bus terminal, the site of several suicide bombings. I guess I felt safer there, safer than being the potential object of daily target practice for terrorists shooting in the West Bank. For a short time we stood talking to Amnon. The terminal was deserted, except for the three of us. Empty vendor stalls, stark cement walls, and unused metal tables and chairs were all that could be seen in the ghostly area. As we walked through, Jeff received a call on his cell phone, so we paused for a moment. Against a wall nearby, a table caught my eye. It was filled with holy tefillin,[15] waiting for men to approach and wrap the leather straps with their small black boxes around their foreheads and arms. Prayerbooks lay next to the tefillin, a photograph of the late Rabbi Menachem Mendel Schneerson, the Lubavitcher Rebbe, graced the wall, and a video was playing of the Rebbe delivering a message in Hebrew. Given the horrendous murderous acts that had occurred within this bus depot's walls, to me this scene symbolized Jewish survival. After all, archeologists have found tefillin that date back two thousand years. Jeff's call ended and we walked out of the bus depot into Afula's bustling downtown. I took a long, deep breath. Though terror can occur any time and any place, it was a little too close in Kadim.

Dr. Eran Lerman

Ofer and Einat Du-Nour

Ze'ev Jabotinsky

Chapter Three
Political Reality: Three Views

The phrase "You can't take the politics out of the Israeli" is a truism throughout the Holy Land. And Israelis certainly do not adhere to the saying "Avoid talking politics, race, and religion." Everyone in Israel seems to have a political position they believe will counteract today's acts of terror. Terrorism affects so many aspects of Israeli life: first and foremost peace and security, and then such issues as the lack of government resources for education, healthcare, and social services. A political solution to the crisis is the subject of debate, agreement, disagreement, protest, support, and even family breakups. Finding the resolution is both complex and challenging. This chapter offers perspectives from those who have intimately participated in the political process, whether in government, through protests, or in the representation of a Zionist legacy.

Forty-five-year-old Dr. Eran Lerman has spent the majority of his adult life as an intelligence officer conducting analyses for the Israeli government. His resume is impressive: a bachelor's degree from Tel Aviv University in Modern Middle Eastern History and General History, a Ph.D. from the London School of Economics, and a third degree from Harvard University's Kennedy School of Government. In the Israel Defense Forces (IDF), Eran rose to the rank of colonel and was at the core of intelligence until his retirement from active service on November 1, 2001. He had an integral role in the Multilateral Peace Process from 1992 through 1995, discussing arms control and regional security issues. Eran's insider position provides a window into the Middle East conflict.

"I refuse to use the term 'intifada,'" he said. "I know it has become as common as throwing around the word 'fundamentalism,' which is another mistaken concept. An intifada is an uprising, literally a camel rising on its hind legs. You can legitimately describe what had happened from December 1987 to mid-1989 as an uprising by the Palestinians against Israel. The situation that began in September 2000 is, from the outset, entirely a terror campaign organized by small groups of politically committed Palestinian activists with Arafat[16] himself being involved. It is the result of the choices that Arafat made. This was and still is an armed struggle. Abu Mazen, the former Palestinian prime minister, for example, talked about the mistake of militarizing the uprising. In other words, the choice was made to go into an armed conflict instead of a civil or popular uprising. The way the conflict was switched to an armed battle was another indication that this was almost entirely a Palestinian leadership-controlled activity, a conflict organized from above and not a popular uprising from below. The term 'uprising' indicates a grassroots activity. This wasn't. In fact, I think that Arafat chose the weapon of terror, the return to the so-called armed struggle, or in other words terrorism, because he realized that there was not enough commitment and support on the popular level to take any other option. Most people would not go to the streets for him.

"The great majority of the Palestinian people have been sitting this conflict out. This is a point that is often lost on right-wing Israelis, left-wing Israelis, and left-wing supporters of the Palestinians. This fact confuses the political situation, and choices are made by a small group of Palestinian leaders regarding the positions, needs, and legitimate grievances of the majority of the Palestinian people.

"I saw where Arafat was heading when we [Israel intelligence] predicted back in early 1999 that there would be a major conflict either in the third or fourth quarter of 2000. We were not off the mark. We did make two mistakes, which I remember presenting to the Mitchell Commission when I testified. The first was that we thought Arafat would use the UDI, the Unilateral Declaration of Independence, which was scheduled for September 13, 2000. Arafat was to declare unilaterally a Palestinian state, abrogate the Oslo process,[17] and then basically use this to ignite conflict. He didn't do it. After the failure of Camp David,[18] Arafat went around the world. He found out that because he declined Barak's[19] offer, a good offer supported by President Clinton, none of his friends in Europe, the Third World, or other people he counted on and trusted all these years to support him would recognize a unilaterally declared state. He would have been made a total buffoon by the international community if he did so.

"Arafat was out searching for a cause of conflict the moment Camp David failed and was prepared for it. Sharon's visit to the Temple Mount provided him with the excuse. So, our mistake was that we had thought Arafat would go for the UDI, but by September 13, 2000 he already knew if he did declare statehood he would not be recognized. This is the history and this is why Arafat was looking for another excuse to move for violence. The signs that violence of a certain kind would come were in place for two years prior to the outbreak. Intelligence recognized it and ultimately this is what happened.

"Arafat's choice of violence, a return to terrorism, became more of a real possibility after Israel's withdrawal from Lebanon. Our withdrawal in May 2000 was presented in the Arab world as being a victory for Hezbollah and Hezbollah tactics. This was pushing the young Palestinian leaders like Marwan Barghuti into a very dangerous direction. They were telling themselves, 'Look, Hezbollah pushed Israelis out of Lebanon,' misreading Barak's decision, which had more do with the Syrians and the Syrian-Israeli relationship. Realities don't matter here, only the spin. Only the virtual reality produced on Arab TV stations and radio stations matter. We saw the Palestinian government preparing the youth in summer camps, we saw the propaganda, we saw the language they were using in the public media. There was no question: They were not preparing the Palestinian people for the possibility of an agreement reached through compromise. There was no question of compromise at any point.

"Our second mistake was that we thought that essentially Arafat would above all appeal to the international community. At the end of the day, he was hoping to create such a destructive storm of violence that the international community would be drawn in Kosovo-style and would impose a solution under which control of the entire territories would become Palestine. Once the UN became involved, Arafat hoped that the UN would define the mandate as the 1967 lines,[20] including Jerusalem. To a large extent this remained and may even remain today as his strategy. However, there are two ways of doing it. One is to appeal directly to Western opinion through images of Palestinian suffering and misery, which was done. But this is not the mainstream of his effort. The main effort was to appeal to Arab opinion through images of Palestinian heroism and suffering. We saw this in Jenin.

When Arafat spoke about Jenin, the obvious appeal to the West was that there was a massacre. Of course, there wasn't a massacre. But this was not his choice. He would have preferred a massacre. Still, he spoke about images of Stalingrad, images of resistance, of heroism. The reason for this talk was that he hoped to inflame the opinion of young Arabs, students, popular activists across the Arab world against their own governments, destabilize the region, and then frighten the American administration and the West into supporting his demands. Otherwise the whole Middle East would be on fire. I am making these points based on very close knowledge and understanding of the way Arafat's mind works. He was hoping for international intervention, but he wanted to bring about this international intervention through conditions that would inflame the frustrated, socially destabilized, and economically weak Arab world. He felt that there was a population out there that would be easily swayed by the set of images that he would provide and this would force the West, and ultimately the United States, to intervene and impose a solution on Israel along the lines of his demands.

"Of course, that's not what happened. I thought at the time that Arafat had miscalculated. We had some arguments about it in the intelligence community. It is one thing to say, 'I think looking at the special relationship between Israel and America and the role of American Jewry that Arafat has miscalculated the situation.' At present, it is easier than it was then to make the judgment that Arafat is playing with forces he doesn't understand and ultimately he's going to end up holding the short end of the stick. That was my opinion looking at the entire picture. Analytically, when you look specifically at his mindset, it was too clear that his main interest is in having piles and piles of dead Palestinians. Palestinian blood matters more to him than Israeli blood. This may sound crass, but this I have heard from Palestinians. Arafat is called 'the blood merchant.' I have heard this from the mid-level Palestinian officials, those who know how Arafat's mind works. If you read very carefully what former Palestinian Prime Minister Abu Mazen has said publicly, it is obvious that he thinks Arafat made a catastrophic set of miscalculations, even though he never mentions Arafat by name.

"Arafat does not hold the strings to terrorist organizations like Hamas and Palestinian Islamic Jihad, but he holds the strings to the jail gates. He threw open the Palestinian jails in October 2000 and it was within a matter of weeks that Hamas and Islamic Jihad started putting together bomb factories, mortar factories, and Qassam rocket factories. Arafat does not control

Hamas or the Palestinian Islamic Jihad, but he definitely can control their leaders who could control them [the movements], if Arafat wanted them controlled. He didn't and doesn't. It's as simple as that. He does control the Tanzim completely and the interactions between the Tanzim and the other terror organizations. The point is that Arafat only needs to do two things: Send a whole set of signals through the Palestinian media – what is good, what is bad; he says, 'We like what is going on, we like the martyrs, we honor the martyrs.' As a second step, he tells the preventive organizations, such as the Palestinian police force, to do nothing."

Eran continued, "I don't buy the slogan of the Israeli Right: "Who gave the Palestinians guns?" because their guns don't matter. The point is not that they have guns. The point is that Arafat has forbidden the General Security Services, the largest armed element in the Palestinian system, to use their guns against terrorists. Nominally, they are police or security, but they are the Palestinian Army. It is commanded by officers who have been brigade commanders for the Palestinian Liberation Army abroad. People like Abd al-Raziq Majaida in Gaza and Haj Ismail in the West Bank. Now these people have literally tens of thousands of people under arms. They could smash the Hamas and Palestinian Islamic Jihad infrastructures easily, overwhelmingly. They were told not to do so essentially by Arafat and we have heard this from the best of sources. He would tell the Israelis what he was going to do and behind our backs he was winking to his people to go on with the killings. Basically Arafat undercut anyone who tried to bring things back under control. So in that sense, yes, he controlled and controls the strings. He still pays for the Tanzim and some of the terrorist infrastructures. There is now a serious effort finally to take the money away. It is going to take time."

Eran put the political situation into historical perspective. "Because of certain historical equivalence it is understandable but wrong to put the Israel story, the Zionist story into the colonial gestalt, or framework. This is not the same as the colonialists in Kenya or the French in Algeria. You can make an equally powerful story of the People of the Land who have been dispossessed for two thousand years returning to their own land. This is not unlike what the Palestinians themselves expect. If they are arguing that they have the right of return because they were exiled for a period, well we have a right. We have been exiled for a longer period, but does the length of time matter? The deeper issue is that when the Zionist movement was established as an attempt to organize the Jewish people for return to their ancestral homeland, there was not a political entity or even a national identity claiming the same land as a separate political unit. There simply wasn't. Any Palestinian who tells you that there was an organized Palestinian people, who were conscious of there being such a separate Palestinian people in 1897, is simply lying. They were there as individuals holding land in some places, but they were there as Arab residents of the Ottoman Empire, no different from Arab residents in other parts of the Ottoman Empire. This land was just a tiny part of the Ottoman Empire that the Jews wanted to reclaim as their ancestral homeland. In other words, we are not talking about a colonial effort here. We are talking about two peoples with a conflict over land, an ethnic conflict more like the sorts of things you have seen in the Balkans, in various parts of Europe, and in other parts of the world over the years. Just because the majority of Zionist activists came from Eastern Europe doesn't mean that this is a European colonial story. In the context of what was happening nationally across Eastern Europe in the late nineteenth century, everyone was organizing along national lines, from Poles, to Romanians, to Slovaks, to Serbs, to Jews. This was the natural outcome of the rise of Nationalism. Zionism is the national liberation movement of the Jewish people. If you don't accept that basic framework then we have a problem. You have to look at this from that angle.

"There's another question. The events that led to the very real dispossession of individual Palestinians in their hundreds of thousands in 1948 were not initiated by the Israeli side. The war was, by the Palestinians' own admission, launched in response to the UN decision for partition and with the purpose of eliminating both that decision and the Jewish population. People tend to forget that the Arabs' purpose of what we call the War of Independence in 1947–48 was exterminatory. I would define it as the last campaign of World War II and the first Arab campaign of the Arab-Israeli conflict. It is the tragedy of Palestinian history because this conflict was not inevitable. We were not predestined to fight each other. There were Arab leaders, not Palestinians, who were willing to recognize the Zionist endeavor, particularly the Hashemite family and some of the Egyptian nationalists. Then there were Palestinian leaders who were willing to support partition in the 1930s. The Nashashibi family, the opposition Palestinians in the 1930s, was willing to support the proposals by the British government for a partition that would have involved the establishment of a Jewish state. The dominant element on the Palestinian street at the time was the Mufti of Jerusalem, and his supporters slaughtered the Nashashibi side. They virtually wiped them out in some places. They broke their [the family's] back. And then, of course, the Mufti was wanted by the British government for the rebellion he organized against the British government. The Mufti fled to Hitler and became a Nazi collaborator. He was sent to the Balkans to help organize the Muslims of Bosnia and mobilize them for the SS. If you go to Yad Vashem [The Holocaust Martyrs' and Heroes' Remembrance Authority in Jerusalem] you can see him surveying the troops raised on behalf of Hitler. He returned to the region after all of this and became the leader of the Palestinian people once again. In 1948, 600,000 Jews in the *yishuv*, the Jewish community in Palestine, faced this man and his so-called Army of Salvation [Jaysh al-Inqaz], who came directly from the side of the Nazis. Their intent vis-à-vis the small Jewish community in the Land of Israel was exterminatory. We tend to let all of this drift by us as if it didn't happen and start mourning what happened to the Palestinians afterward. But this is the story.

"Now, more recently, there have been some sober voices in unexpected quarters who have come to the same conclusion. Joschka Fischer, the foreign minister of Germany, said, 'I am the son of refugees.' He was born in Hungary. His family was driven out along with ten million other Germans at the end of World War II. The whole German population living east of the Oder–Neisse line was literally pushed westward or killed. The Federal Republic, when it was established in 1949, had ten million refugees to handle. People tend to forget this. Fischer said that the question of the rights of the German refugees in the postwar period can no longer be raised as a political question in Europe. If we do raise it we will throw all of Europe into chaos. Much the same is true in the Palestinian case. This is a war they initiated with exterminatory intent as a direct follow up of the Nazi attempt to put an end to the Jewish people. They failed, many of them fled, some were driven out in that conflict. To now try to undo this is to throw the entire future of the Middle East into extreme violent uncertainty, because the Jews will not leave.

"I have a good story about this. Two Israeli generals, one of whom I know, told me the story. They went to Vietnam of all places on their leave. They wanted to see Vietnam. Because they were senior officers they asked if a meeting could be arranged for them with Vo Nguyen Giap, the general who commanded the Northern Vietnamese forces. To their great surprise he not only agreed, but spent the whole day with them. At one point Giap said quite frankly, 'You know, the Palestinians also come to see me and they always ask me the same question. They've said to me, "You're a great hero. You drove out the French, you drove out the Americans, how do we drive out the Jews?" I always give them the same answer: "The French went back to France. The Americans went back to America. You're not going to drive out the Jews because they have nowhere to go."' If the greatest strategist Vietnam has ever produced understands this, it's about time the Palestinians and the world understood this too.

"If there will be peace, it will be because a good number of Palestinians have come to understand that their leaders and the terrorist organizations made a terrible miscalculation. They thought they could break a soft, squishy Israeli society on the wheel of terrorism. They did exactly the opposite. The way I put it is that democratic societies are a bit like eggs. They get harder when they are boiled. The Palestinian leaders and terrorist organizations boiled Israeli society. They have made a catastrophic miscalculation in respect to the basic question: Will Israeli society break or consolidate? There is no question by now, anyone who reads our story or has lived through this period knows that Israeli society has consolidated and certainly has not and will not disintegrate. The same happened to American society after September 11. Such catastrophic miscalculation by terrorists is perhaps the leading issue here.

"The average Palestinian will tell you, if you take him aside, that corruption destroyed any hopes that they had, how Camp David was a terrible miscalculation, and how he feels Arafat betrayed the Palestinian people as the Mufti betrayed them in the 1940s. I met directly with this approach from a Palestinian who was strongly supportive of the Palestinian cause whenever he had a Western audience. Then, one evening we talked about a paper he had written in which he said that Israel should recognize the horror of what we did to the Palestinians in 1948. I said, 'Well maybe we should recognize that once you recognize that the Mufti was a Nazi collaborator and his intent was exterminatory.' He said, 'You know, the Mufti murdered half of my family and he's not half as bad as Arafat.' That's somebody who understands the language and understands what really is going on.

"You take an innocent American journalist whose heart is bleeding for an occupied people, a suffering people, and you manipulate it because it is a weapon of war. Because the Palestinian people are really much poorer than us, their suffering is greater. It is not as if I am not sorry about this. I wish there were no suffering at all. We *are* stronger and they made a terribly stupid mistake thinking a much stronger power would disintegrate. It didn't. It is understandable that the people in the West can only process so much suffering – so they process the Palestinians' instead of ours.

"The crucial element in dealing with this feeling of empathy is a separation of people and leadership. We recognize the Palestinian people are really suffering. What they are going through is really terrible. The blame is nearly 100 percent on the shoulders of their own leaders who brought it on them. Every American would understand this concept if it happened to him. It is patronizing and to some extent racist to take the position that the Palestinians are like children; that they want revenge; they're angry; they don't understand that their leadership betrayed them; that all they understand is that they are here and there is a wall there and the Israelis are on the other side. In the assumption that they are stupid, childlike people driven by basic emotions like revenge is an undercurrent of racism that fails to recognize the difference between the people and their leadership and the very strange kind of discourse that takes place in a society that is not essentially free.

"The basic thing that most people don't notice about the Palestinian people is that they've been sitting this conflict out – 80 to 90 percent of them. In three years of conflict about fifty Palestinians, maybe one hundred were arrested for terrorist activity in Jerusalem. How many Palestinians are in Jerusalem? About 250,000. Less than 1 percent has had anything to do with terrorism. They work, they live, they go about their daily business. There are no barriers. There are no walls within the city. If they had wanted to make sure that Jerusalem could no longer be managed as it is managed now, there is no way any degree of police oppression or military oppression could have stopped them. If they didn't, it is because they didn't want to.

"The great majority of Jordanians are Palestinians. Do they want to bring over to their side of the river the kind of government that they see in the West Bank? No, they want peace and quiet. Jordan has been remarkably stable against the expectation of my best friends in the CIA and some of my best friends in the Israeli intelligence community. Why? I think most Palestinians are sensible people. Most of them know what Arafat did to them and now they have voices. You meet with somebody like Finance

Minister Salem Fayed. He says, 'Corruption? Corruption you have in Chicago. This wasn't corruption. This was total rot.' The whole system was wired to fail from day one. The whole thing was rotten. There was nothing right with the Palestinian system of government. You know how they paid their soldiers in Gaza? An officer would come with a plastic bag full of wads of Israeli money. In the midst of all this, the only currency in the Palestinian economy is the shekel. The officers would take out money and give it to the soldiers and put some in their own pockets. That was the system. Today they get their paychecks in their bank accounts like clockwork. It's because they switched the finance minister to somebody who is a good egg according to the Israeli government, the u.s. government, and in my personal impression of him.

"The whole thing is about leaders. You have to keep drawing that line between the Palestinian people and their leadership. I think the mistake of the Israeli Right is that they blame 'the Palestinians' for what is going on and the mistake of the Israeli Left is that they condone people like Arafat because their heart bleeds for 'the Palestinians.' You always have to keep drawing the line: politics aside and people aside.

"The same has happened in Iraq. American soldiers have been killed by 5 percent or less of the Iraqi people, the thugs who want their power back. You find in the papers, 'The Iraqi people are against us.' Sixty percent of the Iraqi people are Shi'i. They have nothing to do with the Sunni triangle, where all these murders are taking place. Twenty percent are Kurds who are fully incorporated in the administration, who fought shoulder-to-shoulder with the 173rd Brigade in the north during the war. So, 80 percent of the Iraqi people are, to begin with, on the side of the administration. Reading the papers you would think that Americans are being killed by the Iraqi people; that Americans are invaders. This constant confusion is the same as regards to the Palestinian issue."

The conversation turned to whether or not Eran believes that the majority of Palestinians want to have a peaceful coexistence with Israel. He said, "The Palestinian people have been indoctrinated not only by their own government, but by the Arab public domain at large – by television stations from Al-Jazeera to the Egyptian state television, which are paid for by their government and which receive money from the u.s. taxpayer. At the end of the day their position on Israel remains exterminatory. It's not just Hamas and Islamists.

And yet, despite all this, the overall situation is complicated, never black-and-white. Let me be clear. If the Israel Defense Forces and the Shaldag[21] go into a house in Tulkarem and arrest a young woman who is already strapped with a bomb, it was not because of divine revelation. It was probably not SIGINT (signal intelligence), even though terrorists will talk on the phone and give themselves away. In all likelihood a Palestinian tipped the IDF off. This is happening more and more because some Palestinians have a feeling that these terrorists bring disaster upon themselves, their families, and their society."

Even with some Palestinians who recognize the harm suicide bombers cause, there are still many who support Hamas and other terrorist organizations. The question is why? Eran answered, "Partly because they have been so brainwashed by this culture of worshipping the martyr. The second reason is that the Palestinian Authority (PA) is so corrupt that those people look for some other leadership to latch on to. They want somebody whom they can admire, somebody clean, outsiders. Hamas are honest. They don't steal the peoples' money. The PA stole the peoples' money in such amounts that it was mind-boggling. Hamas gave Palestinians money to eat and to buy what they need for Ramadan,[22] whereas the PA completely failed as a social network. That leads to the third reason, that Hamas has been able to bring in money and offer social services.

"The kind of support that Hamas receives is broad, but very shallow. If you change these three elements of the equation, I think the terrorist organizations' power would be considerably reduced, if not eliminated. The entire current effort by the Israeli and American governments is based on the assumption that you can take away this commitment to support terrorism that is expressed by a broad number of Palestinians. The support for Hamas and other terrorist organizations is shallow because it is not based on the profound support for the struggle, but on brainwashing by television and terrorists' financial support for some of the basic human needs. When the PA begins to be run by more honest people and you take away Hamas money and supplement it with PA money – which is what the U.S. government is doing when it gives money to Salam Fayed to manage – then things will change. It might change significantly. I have seen some indications that the balance is already beginning to change. It doesn't happen overnight.

"The Palestinians are the largest recipients in the world of aid per capita even now. But they're not getting the money. A lot is stolen, but still, enough trickles down that there is no starvation. There is deprivation. There is frustration. There probably is some malnutrition. There are also some Israelis who suffer malnutrition because their families cannot afford a balanced meal. There are Ethiopians and Russians in Israel whose immigrant parents are laid off or cannot find a job. There are Israelis of Moroccan heritage in development towns who are suffering. But the question remains, What are the avenues of politics and social action through which you can work to fix this? In a democracy they are different than in an authoritarian system."

Eran offered a powerful message on how the United States must continue to be strong against terrorism. He said, "The ultimate weapon against terrorism and suicide bombers is the resilience of the targeted society. Let me put it this way, it is an aphorism, but it is useful: How do you deter a suicide bomber? You cannot tell her or him, 'Look, you're going to die.' They figured that already. They're going to die, straight to heaven and to awaiting virgins. The message is, 'You are going to die for nothing! Because two weeks after the bombing there are going to be people drinking coffee in Cafe Moment,[23] in ten days people are once again going to play the sax in Mike's Place,[24] and the Hebrew University[25] is going to continue as if nothing happened. But your family will have to live on the street. Even though individual Israelis will suffer terrible agonizing pain, society at large will come out stronger and more determined. So if you think you are dying for something, somebody is telling you a lie.'"

As the interview came to an end, Eran said, "I'll be very blunt with you. I think that the outcome of the Middle East conflict depends on American success in Iraq. If the war in Iraq comes to be perceived as a general failure by people in the Middle East, there will be total collapse of the current effort to bring change to the region as a whole. People like Arafat, and worse, will be greatly encouraged. We will go very quickly into the abyss. On the other hand, if the American effort is perceived as gaining ground and stabilizing the Iraqi situation despite the losses and the pain, then we have solid foundations for a better Middle East. Why? For various reasons, ranging from Syria to Egypt to Saudis to the role of Iraq itself, to their stabilization, and the power of the Jordanian regime, to Salam Fayed and Abu Mazen. It is all part of the larger picture. Success rests on the stability and transition of the Iraqi system, the ability to transfer some authority to local hands, the creation of components of civil society, a burst of economic activity that will engulf Iraq, Jordan, and those Palestinians and even Israelis who will wish to participate. You can create a whole zone of cooperation and economic activity. All of these things are building blocks for a better future. It all depends at end of the day on whether or not people in the region come to recognize American authority as dominant."

* * *

Protesters shouted, "*Shalom Achshav! SHALOM ACHSHAV!*" ("Peace Now! PEACE NOW!") Nine-month-pregnant Einat Achituv Du-Nour walked with her fellow demonstrators along the Ben-Yehudah pedestrian mall in Jerusalem on February 10, 1983 protesting the IDF's presence in Lebanon. Counter-demonstrators' hostilities grew and the crowd became unruly and violent as they made their way toward the Prime Minister's Office.

Though over twenty years have passed since Einat struggled to get away from the demonstration, she remembers the experience all too well. "I was beaten," forty-seven-year-old Einat said. "Not on purpose, but I was pushed and people were pushed into me. It was not that easy to get out of the crowd. No one was letting me through. Some of my friends started to scream, 'A pregnant woman needs to get out!' Somehow I found my way out."

Einat met up with her husband Ofer, who at the time was studying at the Hebrew University. They then went to a play. Einat said, "When we left the theater we heard that as the demonstration was coming to an end, a right-wing activist threw a hand grenade killing Peace Now protester Emil Grunzweig. Nine others were injured. Our friends were worried because they couldn't get hold of us. After we heard the sad news of Emil's death, we felt we had to do something. We decided to drive from Jerusalem to the Tel Aviv city hall, where we participated with twenty to thirty others in an all-night vigil in memory of Emil."

The Israeli government called the war in Lebanon, "Operation Peace for the Galilee." Between 15,000 and 18,000 Palestinian Liberation Organization (PLO) forces were attacking northern Israel from inside Lebanon.[26] "At the time the Israeli government decided to go into Lebanon we already understood that the war was a quagmire," Ofer said. "We went into Lebanon and we didn't know how to get out. It was wrong. Today it's very popular to say we shouldn't have been there."

Sitting in their living room on their burgundy couch, Einat and forty-six-year-old Ofer reminisced about the Peace Now protests in which they participated and how important they felt it was to voice their political opinions. The Du-Nours' demeanor remained solemn. "Einat and I were considered Leftists and were activists in Shalom Achshav, the Peace Now movement," Ofer said. "We believed we should live in peace with the Arabs. We understood that if Israeli citizens and soldiers remained in the West Bank and Gaza it would not be good. Arabs are a majority there. It's a demographic problem. The nation was divided between those who said we should be in the West Bank and Gaza and those who said we shouldn't. The religious in Israel thought we should stay there because of biblical and religious connections. But I see that Israel has two options. It's very simple: You either take the Arabs out of there or you go out of there yourself. Morally, I don't think it's right to transport the Arabs, and technically, I don't think it's possible to do that. So, the only option is for Israel to leave."

Ofer paused and shifted his position on the couch as he reflected upon the problem. He continued, "The demonstrations were usually quiet and people brought their children. People who were not protesting came to us and asked, 'If you demonstrate for peace and the Arabs talk war all the time, why are you demonstrating? There is no one to talk to!'"

Ofer admitted, "This was pretty much true. But what we were saying was important, upholding the belief that a person is a person. It didn't matter if he was a Jew or an Arab. We had interactions with Palestinians. They were people who had the same aspirations and dreams as us. People who wanted to raise a nice family and go to work, nothing more than that. It's very important to let the Palestinian people know that Israel is willing to try for peace, because in a situation like today's intifada you get to the point where nobody believes anybody. It was important for us to say that Israel is a democratic country, which is not the case with the Palestinians. In a democratic country you can say, 'This is how big the population is. This is how many people in Israel believe in peace. So when you are ready, at least know that there is a counterpart on the other side.' That is the reason we demonstrated and supported Peace Now. Of course, we felt that it is very important to influence our own society. It's not because we liked the Arabs, not because we thought they were suffering too much, which is true. That's not the reason we were demonstrating. We were demonstrating because we felt we should influence Israeli society. We believed that leaving the West Bank and Gaza and staying within the borders of 1967 was in Israel's best interest. Israel's interest is not to have two million Arabs living within the Jewish nation.

"Unfortunately, we are in a situation where many Israelis say, 'Why should I deal with the Palestinians? They are bad. They want to get me. They just want to throw the Jews into the sea.' If you listen to the stories on the Palestinian side you hear the same things. 'The Jews are bad. The settlers are coming to take our homes and our children.' There's no end to it.

"I believe in a Jewish state. And I believe that Israel should stay Jewish. I don't think it can stay a Jewish nation if 50 percent of the population is non-Jewish, unless you make it an apartheid state, and that never succeeded in any government. You could run a country with a minority of Jews, but only with a lot of discrimination while forcing the rest of the population to be second-class citizens. At a certain point it comes into conflict with your ideals of equality and human rights. These are the reasons why we were politically active even when we didn't have a counterpart leader on the other side. It is also the reason why we kept on going.

"And then Oslo came. This was what we were striving for all our lives. This was what we were hoping for. We said, 'Here, peace is coming! Now we can talk about the rest of the problems in Israel.' One of the things that always frustrated us was that the Israeli-Palestinian conflict consumed all of our country's energy. We have so many other problems in Israel – economic, educational, and social. The fact is our nation is always concentrating on this one issue because it is a matter of life and death. You want to say, 'Enough is enough. Fifty years we've been dealing with this. We've got a lot of other issues.'

"I think what happened since Oslo was like climbing up a pole, almost touching the top, and then falling all the way down. You think, 'Should I start to climb up again? What should I do?' You see the confusion all over, left wing, right wing. What is interesting today is that most of the Israeli population politically thinks the same way. Right now most Israelis think there is nobody to negotiate with on the Palestinian side. Once the intifada is over I'm sure the Left and the Right will go back to politics as usual. The political arguments and separation will come up again. On one hand, almost everybody is united around the same idea: Israeli citizens must have security. But on the other hand, everybody is confused because how to go about obtaining security is not so clear, not for the Left and not for the Right.

"Personally, I feel a little bit betrayed by the Palestinians. All my life I believed we were talking on a personal level, person-to-person, and what we got was murder after murder. It takes me back many years, when it was very clear, when it was black-and-white. The PLO and Arafat were the bad guys. The Israelis were the good guys. The news on April 27, 2002, from Adora, where the terrorists killed a five-year-old girl in her bed, brings me back to 1979 with what happened to Smadar Haran in Nahariyyah,[27] a coastal town not far from Lebanon. It's the same thing. The Palestinian terrorists come into the house and kill people cold-bloodedly. From Oslo until the intifada started I think average Palestinians were trying to get back to their lives and build some kind of a nation. With the intifada, all of a sudden you find yourself going back to seeing everyone as 'bad guys' or 'good guys.' It's not so easy because you know it's so much more complicated. That's why I feel there is great confusion.

"What is most upsetting is that we'll fight each other for I don't know how many years and the end solution will be the same. There will be a Palestinian state. Everybody knows it. The Arabs know it and we know it. That's why it looks so macabre. We are fighting and everyone knows the end will be the same."

Einat supports the Israeli government's decision to fight terrorists. She said, "We had to do something. From a psychological standpoint we can't put up with the bombs and the slaughter anymore. I support the government decision to go into Arab cities to try and catch terrorists and their weapons. But it isn't going to solve anything. You can never end terrorism by force. History shows us this. For the short term we had to do something. We have to be strong and we have to show force. We have to defend our lives. But there must be other kinds of efforts, political efforts. We have to try to negotiate again. This is the most frustrating thing because I no longer believe or trust, because Arafat is a terrorist. You have to have a great character to transform yourself from a terrorist into a leader of peace. Arafat is not great enough to do it. He remains a terrorist and he will die a terrorist."

"I know the minds of Palestinians are being poisoned against us and they are told stories about massacres and other bad things, which are mostly lies," Ofer added. "You don't know if they are supporting Arafat because they really support him or because they are afraid of Arafat's security forces or of their society."

Ofer relayed the following as an example of the fear Palestinians experience within their home environment: "Omar is one of my Palestinian friends. A mutual Jewish friend called him on his cell phone the other day. Omar answered the phone and immediately hung up. When my friend called again, Omar didn't answer. Half an hour later my friend called a third time. This time Omar answered and said, 'You know what happened? I was in the middle of a store in Jenin and if I had talked to you in Hebrew, people in my village would have killed me thinking I was giving you directions for an air raid. There was no way I could answer your call.'

"A few days later I had the opportunity to talk to Omar about this conversation. I said to Omar, 'Look what your people are doing.' Then he told me stories of corruption in Arafat's organization and how its officials don't really care about what's going on with their own people. I asked Omar, 'Why don't you stand up and say something about it?' He answered, 'We are afraid.' My conversation with Omar showed me that you can't really believe what the Arabs say in public because they are too fearful to speak the truth."

Another of the Du-Nours' Palestinian friends, Nabil, left for the United States in 1998. "Nabil is a Muslim Palestinian who was born on the Arab side of Jerusalem," Einat said. "He left Israel because he just couldn't stay here anymore. Mentally he was closer to his Jewish friends than to Palestinians. The fact was that he didn't identify with the Palestinian mentality of violence. He believed in peace and hated Arafat more than we do." Ofer added, "He has a very interesting story. He was born in Wadi Joz, which is an area in Jerusalem below Mount Scopus, where the Hebrew University is. When he was a child he would look up the hill and see the university. He would say, 'That is where I want to go to get an education. If I want to be someone in the world and not just a simple person working at a car garage, I should go to university.' His parents were not rich. But Nabil pulled himself up, went to a university in Lebanon, and then earned a second degree in criminology from the Hebrew University. He worked on the streets with gangs of youngsters. He was a very charismatic guy. He said that while living among Jews he started to understand the meaning of democracy, the meaning of equality, and the meaning of women's lib.

"He had a Jewish girlfriend, a good friend of ours, and that's how we came to know him. After two or three years together he understood that he could not marry her since he had aspirations to be a Palestinian leader. He had all these ideas about an independent Palestinian state, and a Jewish wife would not be accepted in Palestinian society. So he left our friend. Of course, Nabil stayed our good friend. He tried to find a Palestinian wife, but it wasn't so easy for him. Muslim women whom he dated from the university seemed, at least from the outside, to be more advanced and reformed, but it was only on the surface. When he'd go a little bit deeper under the surface, he'd come back to the same traditional wife, a wife who should stay at home. Once, he wanted to go to a movie with a woman and he had to go with her cousins! I mean we are talking about the 1980s! He had lived with his Jewish girlfriend and it was very difficult for him to go back to traditional society.

"At one time, he was nominated for a position in local management. The Israeli municipality had decided to divide Jerusalem into quarters and he became the manager of one of the Arab quarters. He told us that he was not able to do anything in the position. There was a balance of forces in the Palestinian society between pro-Jordanian Palestinians [people who sought to increase Jordanian government influence and involvement in the West Bank] and Fatah [PLO] supporters. It was a forced balance. If you belonged to either of the sides nothing would happen to you. But if you didn't you were in no-man's-land and anybody could hurt you. If he belonged to the Jordanian supporters' side he could not move one step without getting permission from Jordan to do so. He could not install a sewer pipe, open a school, nothing. Everything had to go through the elders. Everything to be done was seen with some sort of political agenda behind it. It wasn't enough that Nabil just wanted to build a new sewer because it was needed. He began to worry that he was in danger. Arabs started to kill each other if they thought a person was cooperating with Israel.

"The Shabak,[28] the Israel Security Service, didn't know how to read him and he was under investigation. He told us that the Shabak took his aged father and hit him. The Shabak investigator, who was trying to get information, said to Nabil, 'We know if we torture you, you are not going to say anything because you are a strong young guy.' Nabil told us that at this point he fell apart and he started to hit the Shabak investigator. Lately the High Court of Justice put such investigations under supervision and put more restrictions on them. There are all kinds of rules now regarding how to conduct investigations.

"Afterward Nabil left for Los Angeles and sometime later he was walking on a beach in Los Angeles where he met the same Shabak investigator. The investigator apologized to him because at that point he understood that our friend was not from Fatah and wasn't dangerous."

Like so many other Israelis, Ofer and Einat dream of peace and a better future. They do their best to create a sense of security for themselves, their two sons, Omri, nineteen, and Ido, sixteen, and daughter, Attar, eleven. Reality, however, is not so easy to face. Einat explained, "We live in a small and safe place with breathtaking views of the Jezreel Valley. Bedouins surround us and we go to their villages quite often. But after giving it a second thought our sense of security is an illusion. We are a fifteen-minute drive away from Afula, which is not a safe place. We do not try to blow this illusion of security, however. It is convenient and necessary for all of us to preserve it." The Du-Nours hope that their illusions will become reality.

* * *

Can a leopard change his spots? Not if you are Palestinian Chairman Yasser Arafat. Once a terrorist, always a terrorist. Those on the political Right believe that peace negotiations with Arafat were a foolish and dangerous endeavor. One of those Rightists is forty-eight-year-old Ze'ev Jabotinsky, the grandson and namesake of the founder of Revisionist Zionism and the Jewish Legion in World War I. His grandfather was instrumental in the implementation of illegal immigration of 17,000 Jews from Europe prior to his death on August 4, 1940.

The younger Ze'ev Jabotinsky, who is married, a father of five, and a computer engineer, sat down with me in his living room to discuss the reasons Israel is facing terror today. Ze'ev explained that in December 1992 Israeli and PLO officials met secretly in London, England, to work out terms of reference for mutual recognition and subsequent peace negotiations. The Israeli government did not authorize the meeting, was unaware it was taking place, and considered such talks illegal. An amendment to Israel's Prevention of Terrorism Ordinance in 1986 banned all contacts and meetings with representatives of terrorist organizations. The Israeli government felt that Leftist politicians, academics, journalists, and peace activists undermined its tough stance on terrorism by meeting with PLO representatives. (In 1993 Prime Minister Yitzhak Rabin's[29] government repealed this amendment.)

The illegal meeting in London was initiated by Yossi Beilin,[30] the deputy foreign minister serving under then Foreign Minister Shimon Peres.[31] The premise of the meeting was Beilin's belief that if Arafat had a Palestinian state in Judea, Samaria, and Gaza there could be peace between the Israelis and Palestinians. Beilin met in Tel Aviv with Terge Larsen, at the time a Norwegian academic connected to the Norwegian embassy in

Cairo. Through Larsen's connection, Abu Ala, the financial brains of the PLO, agreed to attend the meeting in London. Since it would be impossible for any Israeli deputy minister to meet Abu Ala, Beilin sent Yair Herschfeld, a historian from Haifa University, as his representative.

Ze'ev said, "You can compare Beilin to former British Prime Minister Neville Chamberlain. Chamberlain met with Hitler at the notorious Munich Conference of 1938 and told his people, 'I believe it is peace for our time.' Chamberlain convinced himself that England could have peace, an eternal peace, with Hitler."

How did Beilin sell his personal dream to his boss, Shimon Peres? Ze'ev explained, "Beilin is a master of politics who uses psychological methods. He managed to harness to his cause the hatred between Peres and then Prime Minister, Rabin. The secret meetings between Israelis and the PLO were unknown to Peres and Rabin. At one point Beilin went to Peres and said, 'The PLO is willing to recognize Israel.' He knew that Peres would interpret this as a win-win situation for him. If Rabin went along with Peres on this peace initiative Peres would be seen as the initiator for peace. If Rabin opposed it, Rabin would be considered a warmonger and Peres as the man of peace."

Yair Herschfeld's illegal meeting and others that followed spearheaded the negotiations in Oslo, Norway. On September 13, 1993, Israeli Prime Minister Yitzhak Rabin and Palestinian Chairman Yasser Arafat signed the Declaration of Principles and the first Oslo Agreement. After more negotiations brokered by the Americans, the Interim Agreement and Oslo 11 was signed by Rabin and Arafat on September 28, 1995.

"The Israeli public was deceived by its leaders," Ze'ev analyzed. "The public's yearning for peace was genuine. It was easy for the Israeli government to deceive the public because it wanted to be deceived. It is my opinion that most of the intelligence community was deceived as well. When I was serving in the reserves, I saw first hand the transformation of the intelligence community. It had been against the Oslo Agreement at first. But an agreement is what the government wanted and the government mocked the intelligence community. The intelligence community became transformed like the people. After being deceived by the leaders, they bought into it. It was mutual deception. This had nothing to do with logic. It was like the followers of Shabbetai Tzevi, the false messiah during the 1600s. Even after his death his believers still thought Shabbetai Tzevi was the Messiah. Overall, the intelligence community refused to analyze the situation impartially and gave obscure interpretations.

"I am for peace, but I was against Oslo. I saw an Israeli news report showing Arafat speaking in Tunis right before the Oslo Agreement signing in 1993. 'Don't be afraid,' Arafat told them. 'Our signature [on the Agreement] only brings us closer to our goals.' Arafat's goals are well defined in the Palestinian Liberation Organization's Charter[32] written in 1964. It was written even before there were any Jewish settlements in Judea, Samaria, and Gaza. Israel wasn't even present in those areas then. Arafat concluded his speech with 'Until Jerusalem.' The crowd joined him and began chanting, 'Until Jerusalem, until Jerusalem.' This has deep meaning for the Muslims. It was a reference to the successful defeat of the Crusaders in 1177 by Saladin (Salah Ad-din Yusuf Ibn Ayyub). And the world heard Arafat's May 1994 speech[33] at a Johannesburg mosque. Israel's biggest mistake was to bring Arafat to Gaza in 1993. He was one of our worst enemies. He hasn't changed. He has proved it with the war he is waging against us since September 2000.

"Many times, Knesset Member Beni Begin, son of former Prime Minister Menachem Begin, would speak up in the Knesset and say that Arafat was breaching the Oslo Agreement. Peres would mock him and say, 'It's not important.' I hope Peres did this because he really believed in what he was doing. He was trapped in a position where he could not go back on his word. Israel was being turned into a political science laboratory whose people were the lab rats. The result of Oslo is more than one thousand Israeli citizens brutally slaughtered by Palestinian terrorists since those agreements were signed. Before the intifada these dead were referred to as 'the victims of peace,' but they are 'the victims of the government's dream or fantasy.' This nation is paying with blood, tears, and war. We are in the midst of the painful payment for allowing our government to make the tragic mistake of signing the Oslo Agreement."

While Israelis were euphoric about 'peace in their time,' the Palestinians' mind-set was undergoing a totally different process. Ze'ev described his grandfather's theory of an "Iron Wall." He explained, "By 'Iron Wall' my grandfather was referring to an Arab national state of mind that will be created by an invincible Jewish military force. It is a state of mind that will cause the Arabs to abandon their dreams of destroying Israel. Only when this 'Iron Wall' is created in our enemy's minds will they be ready to negotiate with us rather than fight us. The Palestinians were utterly defeated in 1948, and it was mainly those who surrendered and stayed in Israel who developed the 'Iron Wall' state of mind. The Oslo process gradually demolished this state of mind and that is the reason why the Palestinians eventually declared war and started murdering innocent civilians in Israel."

Now Israel has to cope with a constant barrage of terrorist attacks. How should the government win this war on terror? "First of all," Ze'ev explained, "the government must declare war against terror. If a country declares war, its rules of behavior are different. The country's legal system is coordinated accordingly when the state of war is declared. That is why President Bush declared a war on terror after September 11.

"Terror is an obscure entity. It isn't your classic enemy. The terrorists hide amidst the civilian population. This contradicts Articles 28 and 29 of the Fourth Geneva Convention.[34] If military personnel hide behind innocent civilians during a battle like the terrorists do today, then those military personnel are responsible for the civilians' safety and not the opposing military force when attacking them.

"In order to win this war against the terrorists," Ze'ev emphasized, "Israel needs to use what is referred to as 'excessive force.' Israel must kill the terrorists one by one, including their leaders. Israel has to dry up the terrorists' economic resources. This is exactly how England won the war against the pirates. It is not a pleasant way to fight, but it is the only way to win this war. Europe and the U.S. do not come out against Israel for fighting terrorism. Instead, they warn us against using 'excessive force.' This is wrong! If a country wants to win a war on terrorism, it must use 'excessive force.'

"Arafat is a product of Palestinian culture. The terrorist problem won't go away when he's gone. Arafat promotes terrorism by totally controlling the educational system's curriculum, TV, radio, and newspapers. These tools are a propaganda machine against Israel and everything Israel stands for. The result is endless suicide bombers murdering innocent Israelis. Arafat has infused his people with the belief that they can compel Israelis to surrender or force them to leave the area. Many Palestinians really believe this is attainable, which fuels their aggression.

"Because of this belief Palestinians see the Israeli security fence, which is being built, as an obstacle to their goal. They are against the fence because it hampers their ability to perpetrate terrorist attacks. They are going to have to be more sophisticated in their methods and it will be more costly for them. The presence of the fence bothers Palestinians more than the actual path it takes. Once the fence is completed they will have to depend on themselves for their own economic conditions. They do not have sufficient resources to live by. They know this and Jordan's King Abdullah knows this. The king does not want them to immigrate to Jordan. After 1967 the Palestinians began to use Israel's resources, such as hospitals, electricity, the water system, telephone, and places of employment. Once the security fence goes up they will either need investments to create their own resources or they will have to start emigrating out of the area until the existing resources become sufficient to support the size of the population.

"From 1948 to 1967, when Israel wasn't in Judea, Samaria, and Gaza, the land could only support around 800,000 people. The population stayed constant even though at the time it had one of the highest growth rates in the world. The stability was achieved by the large number of emigrants. Since 1968, when the Palestinians were given access to Israel's resources, their population increased to 3.5 million and Palestinian leadership intends to bring in 2 to 4 million more from the refugee camps in the Arab world. The security fence will dramatically reduce the size of the population in Judea, Samaria, and Gaza. Until then the Palestinians will increase their military pressure and I'm afraid Arab countries like Egypt might join them."

Ze'ev pessimistically described the reign of Arab terror on the world, not just on Israel. "Al Qaeda will cleverly plan and professionally execute terrorist attacks. They will intervene in Western government affairs by harnessing these countries' democratic processes in order to isolate the u.s. in Iraq. Right now they are restraining themselves. They'll attack only when they have an achievable political target. It is a total war being waged against all democratic Western values and peoples. These terrorists will be defeated only when Western peoples understand the threat and are willing to fight the war until it is won."

Ayelet Bar-On

Lior Sadan

Douglas and Laurie Handelman

Orit Gressel-Raz

Dr. Judith Antonelli

Chapter Four
Crisis: Coping with Life and Terrorism

Ayelet Bar-On's* long golden brown hair swung from side to side with her dancer's walk. Honey, her frisky golden retriever, barked playfully, settling down when Ayelet showered affection on him. The beautiful Israeli spring day, clear, calm, and warm, had the two eager for the sunny outdoors. The manicured front yard and crushed stone driveway were the perfect outlets for cabin fever and the attention Honey craved. Ayelet laughed. Her gorgeous sky blue eyes sparkled as she chased the dog and ruffled its furry head. Mutual admiration between the two gentle souls carried into the office where the interview took place. Honey rested at Ayelet's feet, occasionally looking up as if to give approval to the conversation.

Describing this petite beauty limits one's perceptions. It is her words that reveal a soul, compassionate and passionate. Her inner strength and courage far exceed her build. Devotion to loved ones, championing those less fortunate, and her perceptions and criticisms of Arabs and Jews define the essence of this twenty-four year old. Israel is her home, her heart, and her soul. And she does not always like what she sees or hears.

Politically, Ayelet is to the left. "I know that the Israeli-Palestinian conflict is a very complicated situation," she said. "I'm very sensitive to seeing people suffer on both sides. I think that we should have left the West Bank and Gaza a long time ago. Palestinian children are growing up with tanks in front of their homes. I saw a TV program showing how Israeli soldiers entered a Palestinian house. They told the people that they wanted to use the house to shoot at terrorists from their windows. The people couldn't say anything. They had to leave their home. I don't see how peace can grow in

61

a place like this. I also understand that Israel has the right to defend itself. Suicide bombers are not right. It's the worst thing ever! It's horrible. I would really like the Jewish communities in the West Bank and Gaza dismantled because I don't feel there is any reason for them. I wouldn't want anyone in my family to do their army service in the West Bank or Gaza. I worry about the Palestinian children and who they are going to grow up to be, hating and not accepting of others as if they have blinders on. They won't be able to see Israelis as who we really are: just people. People, for whom hatred is not the theme in their lives; but for many Palestinians it is. They are taught hatred in the mosques and in schools."

Ayelet is a psychology and theater major at Haifa University. She has developed positive, close relationships with Arab Christians and a few Arab Muslims on campus. "My relationship with them since the intifada started has become fragile and tense because their loyalty is split. They are Israeli citizens but they are supportive of the Palestinians and are often blind to any suffering the Jews experience because of terrorism. It has become harder to relate to them." The suffering of both Jews and Arabs pushes Ayelet to keep dialogue open in and out of the classroom. Her conversations with fellow Arab students have been painful yet enlightening. "I took a class titled 'Psychological and Cultural Aspects in Israeli and Arab Political Theater.' Everyone, including the professor, was either a Muslim or Christian Arab. I was the only Jew. The purpose of the course was to read Arab and Israeli plays, then discuss the characters and the issues that were raised in each play. The professor used Greek mythology to explain the Jewish and Arab characters. Israelis were compared to Sisyphus and the Arabs were compared to Tantalus. Sisyphus was punished by Zeus and condemned to push a heavy stone up a hill. As he reached the top the rock would roll back down to the bottom. The professor implied that Sisyphus represents Jews because they work really hard but don't hesitate to roll over others to get what they want. Because the rock perpetually falls back down the hill, the quest for the Jews is never ending. 'Arabs,' he said, 'are like Tantalus,' who was tortured by thirst and hunger. Each time Tantalus (who was condemned to stand in water beneath branches of fruit) tried to drink, the waters would recede and the fruit would be beyond his reach. The professor compared this to Arabs today. There are things that the Arabs want but they don't reach for them. They need to take more action. He wants to see the Arabs in the forefront of science and culture. He said that once Arabs were leaders in medicine and mathematics. He wants this for Arabs today. 'The ideal,' according to the professor, 'is a balance between Tantalus and Sisyphus' – work hard without rolling over people, reach further and attain what is rightfully yours."

Ayelet was angered by the analogy and often spoke up to defend Jews and Israeli positions. "I would go to class and Jews and Israelis were cut down. The professor selected Israeli plays criticizing Israeli actions. By using these works the criticism became a legitimate way for the professor to state that even Jews believe their actions are wrong. For example, we read a play titled, *Security Instructions in the Occupied Territories*. In a small section of the play one of the characters gives instructions on how to tell the difference between a regular Arab and a terrorist. I will paraphrase, but you will get the picture: 'If a man passes by and he looks around nervously, he should be treated as a terrorist. If a man passes by looking forward and he seems at ease, then he is a terrorist with self-control. A man who walks in the street and looks to the sky, he is a religious terrorist.' It continues to list every which way an Arab could walk and look. The play's message was that no matter what Arabs do, they will always be accused of being terrorists by Jews.

"None of the other students questioned the message of this play or any of the other plays. I was the only one who addressed the professor. When the Arab students spoke, their comments were directed to me, attacking me as 'the Jew.' On the second day of class we had a conversation about the right of Palestinian return. As much as I am left wing, I cannot agree with that and I said so. Palestinian right of return will transform Israel into another Arab country. If this is supposed to be a Jewish state, then it must remain that way. My comments made the Arab students very angry. Someone said to me, 'You're not even supposed to be here.' I responded, 'Where do you want me to live? I don't have another country.' He gave me a look implying that I could never understand. Then the class ended. The professor stayed to make sure I was okay. He felt bad that the dialogue had gone too far, reassuring me that it would not happen again. It did, but in various other ways.

"There were many lectures that made me uncomfortable. One time the professor drew a small circle and said, 'This is a Jew.' He then drew a larger circle around it and said, 'This is Jewish society and culture.' Next to these circles he drew another small circle. He said, 'This is an Arab.' He then drew a larger circle around it. He said, 'This represents Arab society and culture.' Suddenly he erased part of the circle representing the individual Arab. He explained that Arabs are more like a tribe, similar to what ancient societies are like. Conformity is a lot stronger. The Arab people make decisions based on what is good for the entire society. They accept what society tells them to accept. The Jew, on the other hand, is ambitious and doesn't see himself as much of a part of society. He makes decisions without necessarily being dictated to by the society. Arabs are more conservative and the elders have more power. He said that we need to be a mixture of both: respect society but still be individuals. I listened to what he had to say, but I did not appreciate his overall representation of Jews, and said so.

"Toward the end of the course I was ready to quit. The professor used architecture to describe Jews. He said something like, 'If there were a hill, the Jew would destroy the hill in order to build a large Western-style building. To build a freeway, the Jew would destroy everything in his path. The Arab, on the other hand, respects nature, respects the hill, and would not destroy the land. They [the Arabs] wouldn't have big roads.' For me, that was the last straw. He implied that Jews use the land for their own needs; that our Western way of thinking is to use whatever and whomever to reach our goals with no respect for nature. This kind of comment drove me up the wall. I left the class in tears. My frustration was bottled up until then. I decided to drop the course. Enough was enough. Later, I saw one of the Muslim girls, an award-winning playwright, from the class. She knew I was upset and calmly told me, 'You shouldn't leave. You raise important issues. It is important that people in the class hear the other side.' She also admitted to me that it is very hard to be a Muslim woman. I thought about what she said and decided to stay. Nothing is simple. The professor is not a horrible person, but there are things that he said that I am very angry about. I think that other people who would hear him could interpret his words and take them too far. He used Israeli architecture just as an example. It implied a lot more than what he said. He didn't hide his beliefs – that Israelis are violent people.

"These experiences and many others taught me that Arabs and Jews have different ways of interpreting what is happening now and in our past. The conflict starts from there. Numerous class discussions made it clear that long before the United Nations decided that Israel should be a Jewish country, Arabs felt that Jews were invading their land. When Israel

won the '67 War, Arabs felt – and still feel – that it was one of the greatest
setbacks for the Arab world. With their larger armies and Israel's smaller
army, the Arab defeat did not make sense to them. The Arab students were
very angry when we talked about it. They feel Jews are occupying their land,
not just the West Bank and Gaza, but all of Israel. We are different states
within the same state. I was on the defensive because they don't see our
right to be here. They do not understand why we are defending ourselves
after terrorist attacks.

"One of the Muslim students said to me, 'If Israeli forces follow a car
carrying their terrorist target and then blow up the car killing not only those
inside, but maybe my little sister, I would go nuts, I would be so upset.' Another person said, 'If someone's house were demolished because a terrorist
may have been there…that would be hard.' I agreed with both of them. I
deplore killing, but can understand why the Israeli government must defend
our people. Unfortunately, the Arabs in my class could not see this point
of view. The class perspective on suicide bombers was infuriating. No one
came right out and said that suicide bombers are legitimate, but they don't
feel that they are bad either. They could understand why someone would
choose to be a *shahid*.[35] They had no problem criticizing my culture, but
were unwilling to see what is wrong in their culture and criticize it. What is
difficult is knowing that these are the more moderate Arab thinkers. These
men and women are being educated in an Israeli university.

"Once, I said to the class, 'Look at women in the Muslim culture. They
are suppressed. The Muslims don't let their women talk. Women have no
say in their society and a lot of these Muslim girls can't go to school. The
women would be a very good influence on the men. They are the mothers, the nurturers, but they have no position of power.' Someone shot back,
'What? There is no suppression of women in Western countries?' No one
in class would admit to me that there is a problem. I am willing to see our
mistakes! The same woman who asked me not to drop the course came up
to me after the class. She's thirty-three, married, and has two children. She
told me that she has a problem at home. She had to fight to go to school
and her opinion never counts. She was willing to say this to me in private,
but would not speak out in class. I am so grateful to have been raised in an
environment and culture that fosters the ability to question and see things
from many different perspectives. If Jews and Arabs can't agree on history,
if we can't agree on what is happening today, and if the Arabs are taught

that Jews are thieves of land, destroyers of nature, and in general are to be hated, no wonder it is hard to make peace."

Sharing ideas, discussing ideology, debating viewpoints – such is the atmosphere of an American college campus. In Ayelet's class at Haifa University there was little sharing, discussing, or debating. Ayelet's eyes have opened to various perspectives because of the university's diverse ethnic mix. She has become an observer and participant in dialogues not just between Arab and Jew, but also between Jew and Jew. "I have a Jewish friend who lives in a community near Hebron," she told me. "We are very different from each other. Family means everything to me. I told her that I can't understand why she would live in the West Bank. She is putting herself in danger, her family in danger – not to mention the soldiers who are protecting her West Bank home. She said, 'The difference between you and me is that I believe that there is something more important than family. The land given by God to the Jews is more important than life itself.' I told her that I don't want my family risking their lives to protect hers. She replied, 'This is our land. We were here long before the Arabs.'"

Challenges on campus extend beyond clashing beliefs. Security is critical and according to Ayelet all students are subjected to the same inspection procedures. Unfortunately, some of her Muslim acquaintances feel security searches target Arabs. She disagreed. "We go through security in every building. The guards have portable metal detectors and search all bags. They ask everyone to open their bags and then they may move the contents around. One day I saw Hasan, a Muslim Arab who was in one of my drama classes. Hasan said to the security guard, 'I was here two minutes ago. You don't have to go through my stuff. Don't you remember me?' The guard told him that it didn't matter. He still had to go through the procedure. Hasan gave the guard such a dirty look. He was so angry. I walked up to Hasan and said, 'They do the same thing to me. I am always checked, even though the guards know me. They look at my ID card and check my bags.' Hasan was not convinced. He was still upset. He kept his head down and wouldn't look at me. He made a motion that meant, 'Leave me alone.' I got into an elevator with him to go to our class. I looked at him and smiled, but he was still angry and turned his head away. At least he knew that I thought he was being treated just the same as me.

"I am positive that Arabs are not targeted. I have a friend with red hair and green eyes. She's thin, short, and looks nothing like an Arab. Every day my friend gets a ride to the university and the routine is the same. The guard checks everyone's ID cards in the vehicle, checks bags, the inside of the car, and the trunk. One day my friend forgot her ID card. The guard told her that she wasn't allowed to continue into the parking lot, even though he knew her. She had to get out of the car and continue by foot."

Even with tight security, safety is not guaranteed. "We had just finished drama class," Ayelet recalled. "It was 6:00 P.M. and I was walking toward the building's exit. Suddenly there were policemen everywhere. Someone had left a backpack near the entryway. We didn't know if it contained a bomb. All exits were shut down. I could see the steel bomb squad robot that is used to detonate bombs. An officer wearing a bulletproof vest directed everyone to the bomb shelter. He had a walkie-talkie in his right hand and was using it to point the way. About forty of us walked quickly down a narrow flight of steps to a room close to the gymnasium. Everyone was relatively calm. The concrete room was dimly lit and there was a small vent opening near the ceiling for air. We sat on the cold floor. Everybody began to call their families on their cell phones. Perhaps it wasn't wise, but we left the bomb shelter door open a crack. We wanted to hear what was going on upstairs and people thought it would help cell phone reception. Many of us knew each other from class, but not well. People passed around candy and drinks. I sat toward the back of the room in a circle with four girls. At first everyone was tense, quiet. But you really can't stay that way for too long. After a while someone cracked a silly joke. He said something like, 'The poor guy who left his bag, now his homework is going to be blown to bits. Can you imagine what he'll say to his professor?' Everyone laughed and relaxed a bit. We talked in hushed voices so that we could hear what was going on outside. Two and a half hours later we heard an explosion. The bomb shelter phone rang and an officer gave the all clear. When we exited the building we saw the remains of the half concrete, half glass walls. The plated glass was completely blown out."

Bomb threats, security checks – routine. It is the suicide attacks that bring the university and all of Israel to a brief standstill. Bombings are the 'Where were you when you heard about…?' moments. What American does not remember where he or she was on September 11? The loss of life from any terrorist attack burns into Israelis' collective memories. One cannot help but pause and take notice. At 2:25 P.M. on March 5, 2003, Ayelet sat in a stadium-style lecture hall with 250 other students. The professor stood in front of the chalkboard and to his left was a large metal door. Ayelet recalled, "I sat in the third row hoping to stay focused on the professor's boring monotone lecture on Freud. Suddenly a student got up, walked to the door, and left the hall. Then another student and another. Every time the metal door shut there was a high-pitched drawn out squeal. *Eerrreeerrreee.* It was a huge distraction. At first we thought people were leaving because the professor was such a bore. I think the professor thought so too. I saw his face and he looked surprised and kind of disappointed. Most of us looked at each other in mild shock. As more and more people streamed out, they were no longer walking, but running! Then a girl stood up and shouted, 'There was a bombing on a Haifa bus.' She had received a text message on her cell phone and asked the professor if we could take a few minutes to let our families know we were okay. Everybody grabbed their cell phones and began to make calls. The circuits were jammed. It took me over half an hour to get hold of my fiancé. There was no TV or radio in the room so our information was limited. Everybody was anxious because we know which buses our loved ones take. Until we had the details of the bus it was hard to relax. My fiancé sent me an internet news update to my phone. The number 37 Egged bus was on its route to Haifa University when a terrorist bomber exploded on the bus. Seventeen people were killed and over fifty were injured. Many of the dead and wounded were teenagers. Since I had the details on my cell phone, it was passed from person to person. I had to follow my phone through the waves of people reading the information on its screen. People were screaming, 'What happened? Where was it? How many people killed?' Many students left, but after awhile we did continue the class."

How is one to react in the face of danger or in the moments before a possible terrorist attack? With courage? With panic? Little Ayelet became a lioness protecting those in her charge. "I teach teenagers MTV-style dancing at a school in Hadera," she said. "Hadera is an hour drive south of Haifa and there have been several suicide bombings there. One particular Saturday I was the only one teaching. There were no security guards. I had shut the school gate but did not lock it, even though I had the key. Sometimes students come late and I wanted to make sure they could get in. I was nervous, listening for anything suspicious. Class had just started when I heard a noise outside the school building. I went to the window and saw two young men who looked like Arabs. They were walking toward the entrance looking around. I had never seen them before and I knew that they did not belong. My mind was racing. Why didn't I lock that gate! I knew that if the men were terrorists I had to keep them far away from the kids. I gave one of the older students the key to the classroom and told him to lock the door behind me. I was screaming, 'Don't leave the room!' I really thought that this was a crisis. I had to deal with it. I went after the men. They were about to climb the stairs to the classrooms. I said, 'What are you doing here?' They told me that they were just walking around. I still couldn't tell if they were dangerous. With as much authority as I could put into my voice I told them to leave. Thankfully, they did. I returned to the classroom, shaking. One of my fifteen-year-old students said that he thought we were all going to die. I didn't tell him that I was thinking the same thing. I just told him everything was going to be okay. It was a close call."

Living in a world fearful of Arabs is deeply distressing for Ayelet. She said, "I think everything comes from fear. It's funny. It's not love first. It's fear first. My paternal grandfather was a Holocaust survivor. I was really affected by this in my childhood. I used to hide food in my bedroom closet. My mom found the food and she was very upset. So I hid bread in my underwear drawer thinking she would not go in there. I was eight years old and terrified. I had recurring nightmares about helicopters with Nazis landing in our backyard and taking over. Even thinking about that fear now, I have tears in my eyes. It was a fear I grew up with. I knew that the Holocaust was something worse than anything I could ever imagine. What the Nazis did to Jews – so inhumane. Where was God all that time? I can't accept it. I had believed in God, but I don't anymore. I envy Christian families who define themselves without religion. They have nobody hating them the way Jews are hated. They have their lives. They can worry about their kids' adolescent problems, trivial things to people living in Israel. For me it would be a blessing to just worry about trivial things. I still have nightmares, but they're different from when I was a child. Now I dream about Arabs. I remember one nightmare where my entire family was in the city of Kiryat Shemona. An Arab came and he put a gun to my dad's head. I woke up terrified. I had another nightmare where I was given a puppy. Because I knew in the dream that Arabs were coming, I put the puppy inside a drawer. I ran away and then the Arabs took over the city. I wanted to go save the puppy, so I dressed up like an Arab and I went back to the house and saved the puppy." Ayelet laughed.

What has life taught Ayelet? She said, "I would like to share something positive, with hope, with a big smile. But I have learned not to trust. I have learned to be very careful, cautious, to always see if there is anyone who looks suspicious. Terrorists can be children, or women, or even someone dressed up as a soldier. I hope to live in Israel when there is peace. I would like to have enough money to do the basic things; you know, home, family. If more, great, if not, then fine. The most important thing in this world is to love your family. Perhaps someday I will be able to do that first, instead of fearing for their safety."

*　　*　　*

He is the son of dreamers who live on the socialist kibbutz Megiddo. And he believes in their dream – to have a family, to live in a peaceful world. Lior Sadan, twenty-six, wants nothing more than to see this dream fulfilled. Part of it will be. Someday he will marry his fiancée and raise a family. The other part of the dream is shattered by the violent world in which he lives. He is left with a wound that cuts so deep that it may never heal. This wound influences the essence of his being – political, religious, emotional, and social. In 1997 Lior's nineteen-year-old brother, Niv, was killed in Lebanon. "I was finishing the army when my brother was in his first year of service," he said. "Niv was in a small prestigious unit. They did the most dangerous and sophisticated tasks for the Israel Defense Forces. His team, which consisted of Niv, his commander, and another soldier, were the front men of their unit. They were out on patrol when they stepped on a landmine planted by the Hezbollah. The three of them were killed and others were injured.

"Losing Niv really changed our family. We became much, much closer. We were a very warm family, very supporting, but Niv's death really made us come together. I think my parents and my younger sister deal with it well. They work. They continued on with their lives. We have to handle the sorrow. Everybody continued on. His death changed our perspective on life, its meaning, and importance." Talking about his brother brings to the surface a hidden pain. Lior unconsciously sighed.

"My brother wanted peace. He was at the peace rally where Rabin was assassinated. At that time there was still Israeli occupation in Lebanon. Politically, our family disagreed with our government's decision to go into Lebanon and fight the PLO [Palestinian Liberation Organization] as a means to create security, and we supported Israel's withdrawal. My brother and I served in Lebanon even though we did not agree with the decision to be there. This created a personal, internal conflict. To support our country we served. We also used democracy to change the situation by going to protests. Politically we always voted for the side that wanted to end occupation. But Lebanon was a totally different situation than what we are experiencing in the West Bank and Gaza today. There were no Israelis living in Lebanon. The army was stationed on a small strip of land. We crossed the Lebanese border to defend Israel. It was pretty easy to pull our troops out.

"The conflict with the Palestinians is different. We occupy territories that do not belong to us and there are 250,000 Israelis living on that land. My family and I feel this is wrong. These settlers force the IDF to remain in the West Bank and Gaza. Their presence does not let the Palestinians live like normal people. The big difference between Lebanon and the conflict with the Palestinians is the solution. From Lebanon we only had to withdraw and I think the majority of Israelis finally understood that we didn't need to be there. In the West Bank and Gaza we have a more complicated problem: We have to take out the Jews who live in the heart of the West Bank and Gaza. The problem over Jerusalem and its holy places is solvable. There is an option of dividing Jerusalem. Perhaps the United Nations will control these holy sites. I really think there is a technical solution for that. Defining which territories will be the Palestinians' and which will be ours can be solved. The big problem with the Palestinians is that they want 'the right of return.' We are talking about millions of Palestinians who would come back to Israel. Israel cannot allow so many non-Israelis into this democracy because it will ruin the country. We will not commit suicide. It is not acceptable even to the radical left wing. The Palestinians don't have much to lose; Israel has almost everything to lose.

"I think it was a strategic decision on the part of Arafat to start the intifada. He saw that we withdrew from Lebanon and he believed that because of the pressure brought on by terror he could use terror and get more than he was offered. On our part, Israel came to the conclusion that Arafat doesn't want to make peace. He wants to be the liberation leader, the revolutionary leader. He doesn't really want a Palestinian state. As long as Arafat is in charge, there will be no peace."

Lior paused, gathering his thoughts. His hazel eyes narrowed, then he continued, "I want to live in peace. I feel a connection to this land because I was born here. I also feel a connection because of the Holocaust. I am Jewish not because I want to be. I was born into it. I don't see myself as a Jew, but as an Israeli. I have never believed in God. God is a fairy tale story. I don't believe in God at all. If I could, I would give up on being Jewish. Perhaps this makes me a little bit radical. Jewish history is full of people everywhere hating Jews. Jews are not wanted. I understand that we need a country. I know that if I go outside this country I will be seen as a Jew and I will have problems. What can I do? I don't like it. I prefer not paying attention to it. I also think Israel is very good for the other millions of Jews living around the world. They know they have some kind of shield, something that gives them security. I don't want to be the Jew who lives outside of Israel."

Perhaps it is because of the death of his brother that Lior is much more cautious and wary than many Israelis. He said, "My fiancée and I are a little bit more extreme. We hardly ever go to public places like restaurants, cafes, or malls. We do not go to the supermarket on Friday mornings anymore because it is crowded. We go on Wednesday nights when it is unlikely to be a terrorist target. We go to friends' houses and to our families' homes. This will be our life until the intifada passes.

"We have already suffered a big loss in our small family. My sister and I are the only ones my parents have. We have no other family in Israel. I don't want to suffer anymore losses. I am afraid of that. My brother's death has made the value of life very clear. I keep my life secure because it is very important for the people who love me. After the army many young Israelis travel around the world seeking adventures and dangerous things, like bungee jumping and rafting. I went directly to the Technion Israel Institute of Technology and received a degree in Computer Software Engineering and now I have a job that I enjoy with a data storage company. My personal goals are the same as they were before the intifada. I want to succeed in work. I want to live nicely. I love my fiancée. I want to start a family. I see a good future for me with what I have now and the course my life is taking. I like to be with people I love. I like to do very simple things like take walks, sit, and drink coffee. I appreciate life."

Lior is both optimistic and pessimistic about the Israeli-Palestinian conflict. "I am pessimistic," he said, "because we don't see the end to the conflict. Everybody knows, however, what the end result will be. There will be a Palestinian state. I am optimistic, on the other hand, because I believe there will be peace one day."

*   *   *

Sitting with Laurie Handelman at her dining room table, I tasted the best flaky potato *burekas*, square pastry puffs of layered filo dough filled with seasoned mashed potatoes. We drank tea and occasionally chuckled. Laurie spoke with an ease reserved for close friends, though we had just met. Sarcasm and brutal honesty was her way of coping with terror. An intense fear gripped Laurie's sense of security and faith in God. A staunch Zionist, she made aliyah with her husband, Douglas, and their one-and-a-half-year-old daughter, Adina, in 1977. The Handelmans have four other children: Naomi, Sharon, Benny, and Ayelet. Hoshaya, a small modern Orthodox community in the Galilee, has been their home for the past thirteen years.

"My philosophy is that 95 percent of the Arab population basically want what other human beings want: jobs, roofs over their heads, food for their kids, food for themselves, to live peacefully with whomever is around them," Laurie began. "People with full bellies and good jobs don't make war. But the remaining 5 percent are squashing the 95 percent who are afraid to speak out because it may be their death. This silent majority are not interested in killing. They are whipped into this frenzy and forced into a public display of unity against the Jews and Zionism.

"After the October riots[36] I consciously stopped buying from Israeli Arabs. I came to the conclusion that the money I give to Israeli Arab businesses may somehow end up in the hands of the Hamas or Hezbollah. Let's say I pay someone for his services and he goes and pays someone else from the West Bank or Gaza for services, and that guy is a member of Hamas. It is just a scary thought that my money may go to pay for bombs, maybe for propaganda, or for the terrorists' salaries, and God knows what else. I am afraid. I am truly afraid. So on one hand I would really like to sound like Sandra Bullock in *Miss Congeniality*, 'I am really in favor of world peace.' But there are people out to kill me for no other reason than my being Jewish. They call me a Zionist, but it comes down to just being Jewish. Zionism has nothing to do with it anymore. It is anti-Semitism through and through. That's it."

Laurie is tired of the suffering. Douglas was out of work for eight months because of downsizing. Then he was fortunate to find an accounting position for an American-based high tech company. "He's just thrilled to work," Laurie said. "Life is crazy, the pressure – money. It's hard for the average person. We just want to get on with life! Enough of the suffering! We're suffering, the Palestinians are suffering. It's enough. How can it be that Arafat has millions of dollars stashed away while his people suffer? You see his wife, Suha, is sitting prettily in Paris with millions of dollars taking care of her. She has been in Paris for several years now. Suha doesn't want to live in Gaza! Suha doesn't want to live in Ramallah! Say one thing and do the other. Power to the people, but let me do it in Paris.

"I think the Western world had better open its eyes a little bit. Even if there were a solution to the Israeli-Palestinian problem, the issue has gone way beyond that. There are no Palestinians, no Jews that I am aware of in Malaysia. There are no Jews in the Philippines to speak of. Why are there such troubles with Muslim extremists in countries where there aren't any Jews, where there isn't any Palestinian problem? Why? No matter where it is, Malaysia, the Philippines, there are Muslim terrorists. The Muslim extremists are making trouble all over the world. The Christians in Europe do not quite understand that once the Muslim terrorists finish with us, they are next. It is not a question of, 'Okay, let them kill all the Jews and it will all be done.' Christians are also infidels according to these extremists. Christians don't realize that this is a threat to them, or perhaps they are too afraid to admit it."

On a day-to-day basis Laurie has had only positive interactions with Arabs. Fear, however, can be enough to destroy any trust. "If you push me up against the wall, I want to get a gun," she said. "I want to protect myself. I need it. This place is empty during the day. I am here all alone – just the neighborhood kids and me basically. There is no gate. You can walk right into this community. There are kids wandering around with no protection whatsoever. On Friday nights all the children are out on the street, sitting, talking, playing. It wouldn't take much for a terrorist to drive in, let off a couple rounds of ammunition, kill easily one hundred kids and be out of here before anybody even knows what happened. The terrorist could disappear into one of the Arab villages nearby without a trace. It is a perfectly plausible scenario. I just go into denial and say, 'Okay, I am okay. It hasn't happened so far.' The government authorities say I can't get a gun. The place where I live is not categorized as a dangerous area and I don't have sufficient ranking in the army to get one. The government has certain criteria for granting gun licenses. They don't just grant one to anybody. I guess I am a nobody."

Though the Handelmans live in a religious community, Laurie struggles with faith in God. "God? He's an extraterrestrial," she said half laughing, yet serious. "I had a major crisis of faith when Nachshon Waxman was killed." On October 14, 1994, American-born nineteen-year-old Corporal Nachshon Waxman was hitchhiking home, at the time a common practice among Israeli soldiers. Douglas explained that Hamas terrorists disguised as observant Jews stopped to pick up Corporal Waxman and kidnapped him. They held him hostage for several days. Then, during an Israeli rescue attempt, the terrorists brutally killed the young soldier. Laurie continued, "The leaders of the religious community called upon everyone to recite Psalms for Nachshon's safe return. The whole country was focused on this young man, praying for him. The IDF knew he was alive and we began the Sabbath with hope. After the Sabbath ended Saturday night we turned on the TV and heard that Nachshon was dead. What good was there in saying the Psalms? Why did I bother? It was a major faith crisis for me, a major crisis."

Laurie's latest challenge involves her eighteen-year-old son's desire to join an elite combat unit with the Israel Defense Forces. "On one hand, I am very proud of Benny for wanting to serve his country. He is very strong. On the other hand, I am not thrilled. He is going into the most dangerous places he could possibly go into. That is what he wants. It has something to do with testosterone and Y-chromosomes," Laurie laughed. "I think at the age of eighteen there is a certain psychological immunity. 'We're all Rambo and nothing is going to happen to me. The bullets are going to bounce off because I am Superman.' The immortality of an eighteen-year-old! It gets knocked out of them pretty quickly. By the time they are nineteen they realize, 'Hey! A bullet could get me too.' It has something to do with the age, which is probably why they draft kids at eighteen and not twenty or twenty-five.

"I am petrified for Benny. I sit here ironing and think about what I would do if I were to see two soldiers walking to my front door to tell me something has happened to my son. I sit here watching funerals and say, 'Am I going to behave like that mother at my son's funeral? Do I do the Ashkenazi bit and bite my tongue and have a stiff upper lip? Or am I going to be my Moroccan self and come out and scream and cry and throw myself into the grave? Am I going to be very low key? I am not going to throw myself in the grave after my son.' Maybe I will, I don't know. I wonder, 'What am I going to say about my son? Am I going to have his pictures on his wall? Oh God! I had better clean his room. If they come in and take a picture of his room like they show on the TV, what are they going to see? They are going to see how my son lived. Oh my God, what a terrible mother!' Have you ever seen these houses where all the pictures are lined up and everything, the kid's shoes, the kid's shirts are still hanging? I think to myself, 'If they come and see Benny's room I will be an embarrassment to motherhood.' I think about these things. We all think about it. Right?"

Part of me is stunned by Laurie's intimate confession. As a mother I realize that the loss of a child is the worst nightmare. I cannot help but think of my two sons. "Let's just pray," I said, "that it will never come to that." Pensive, Laurie replied, "I know."

To break the tension she laughingly tells a joke. "What is the worst thing you could wish a *shahid*? That he should live to 120! If you don't laugh, you cry. It's better to laugh, much better to laugh."

Laurie recalled a time in her life where there was more laughter than tears. When the Handelmans made aliyah they lived in an absorption center in Jerusalem, where new immigrants can get acclimated to Israeli life. They made lifetime friends, the kind of friends who despite long distance and infrequent contact, are a part of you. Rabbi Eli and Dina Horowitz were two of those special people. That friendship came to a tragic end on Friday evening, March 7, 2003. "The Horowitzs lived in Kiryat Arba, which is near Hebron. They were dedicated to Jewish resettlement and Jewish land, but they were not radicals who wanted to go out and kill Arabs," shared Laurie. "They were gentle, kind people who condemned violence. They were encouraging, lovely, lovely people. Terrorists do not care about such things. Dressed as yeshiva students, two terrorists cut through the fence surrounding Kiryat Arba and within a few minutes began their shooting spree. Five were injured. The Horowitzs were sitting at their Shabbat table when the terrorists smashed a ground floor window. I heard afterward that the neighbors heard Dina screaming," Laurie said. "First they shot and killed Eli. Dina tried to escape by running into another room. If I close my eyes I can just about hear her scream. She was shouting, 'Terrorist! Terrorist!' The neighbors heard the last few shots and then there was quiet." Laurie sighed deeply. "That wasn't the first time terrorists had infiltrated Kiryat Arba. It was the third or fourth time. These terrorists were dressed as religious Jews and they were able to get into the community without calling attention to themselves. The terrorists know that on Friday night people's guards are down. People are more relaxed, they are in their homes with their families. That's the terrorists' strategy – to go in when the Sabbath has started, Friday night, and murder." Laurie and Douglas attended the Horowitzs' funeral in Jerusalem. "There were thousands of people," she said. "Then Eli's father,

Rabbi Moshe Horowitz, spoke. There wasn't a dry eye. He was crying out with his soul, 'Why? Why?' It was heartbreaking, very hard."

So much anxiety, tension, fear. "How *am* I dealing with the stress, dear?" Laurie asked her husband sarcastically. Douglas rolled his eyes. A hearty laugh bellowed from all of us. "You just go on," she said. "I sit and iron. I never ironed before." Laurie laughed again and added, "If you like this interview you may send checks, cash, or money order. We will try to accept Visa or Mastercard also." Relief crept over Laurie's face. She had reclaimed her sense of humor. The weight of terror is temporarily lifted with laughter.

* * *

Dr. Orit Gressel Raz, thirty-eight, has a simple philosophy for life: "Be optimistic, or you can't get through it." This lesson permeates her medical practice, which integrates western medicine with a holistic approach. She believes that talking to patients about their emotional health is as important as examining their physical symptoms. Impotence, high blood pressure, backaches and headaches, extreme weight loss and gain, sleeplessness and fatigue are just a few ailments she treats. Each has steadily increased since the intifada began and are symptoms of a problem facing every Israeli today: intense, gut-wrenching stress. No one is immune. Some handle it better than others. One of Orit's patients sought treatment for a reoccurring back problem. She asked him a series of questions: When did you first notice the symptoms? What have you been lifting? How are you sleeping? Did you feel a pull bending down or reaching up? Since none of these questions indicated a cause for the current problem, Orit asked the sufferer if he had any children in the army. Sure enough one of his sons was called to serve in an area of intense fighting. "Stress attacks a person's weakest spots," Orit explained. "This was how this patient dealt with the outside world. A round of massage therapy helped him to resolve the physical symptoms."

Orit rents a home in the Jezreel Valley hilltop community of Timrat. We sat outside drinking cool water under the warm Israeli sun. Lush greens, a large tree, and several catfights caught my attention. Orit, stomach bulging with her fourth child, relaxed in her patio chair. The peaceful scene was shattered at least ten times during our interview. F-16s streaked across the blue sky with deafening speed, a constant reminder of Israel's military defense. Not even the non-stop take-offs and landings at Chicago's O'Hare International Airport come close to the power felt from these air force jets.

The F-16s, soldiers on street corners, guards at restaurant doors, barbed wire fences are constant reminders of the terror facing Israelis. "There is no way we can deal with the stresses, but by putting them out of our minds somehow," Orit said. "You are talking to someone who is emotionally strong. You talk to my patients; they don't feel that way. A car backfires, they can flip. I see people who are emotional wrecks, crying without any reason. We are on a constant emotional rollercoaster. If you are not strong enough, then it is difficult to cope with the day-to-day routine activities like going to buy food and even eating. Some of the problems are caused by the infusion of radio or TV. People have it on all the time. It is hard because you can't work or think that way and the only way to temporarily get rid of the stress is to turn off the radio and TV."

Orit sees a common reaction among many Israelis to a bombing. "You are upset. You are angry with the kids for no reason at all. And you have to be nice. You have to be calm. It is hard when you have to be okay with the kids and you can't cry or be too upset. You have to cope. The routine helps get you through. Making sure that there is food, making sure that the kids have clean clothes, making sure that their homework is done, their backpacks are ready for tomorrow, or that the ballet outfit is washed and ready for the next day. We must deal with those little things. You can't let terror into your ability to function, unless, of course, it hits really close to you."

* * *

Fifty-three-year-old Judith Antonelli, M.D. and department head of the Pediatric Emergency Ward of Ha'Emek Medical Center in Afula, does not have the same optimistic view of the world as Dr. Orit Gressel Raz. "I was not optimistic before, so I can tell you that I am no more optimistic now. I never had illusions about our life," she said. But there was a time in Judith's life when she did live with innocence. She believed that it was possible to live peacefully with her Arab neighbors. This "illusion" was shattered when she was eighteen years old. "I was living in a Haifa neighborhood where Arabs and Jews lived together. The Arabs were the rich ones. My family emigrated from Poland in 1950 when I was one. We were the poor ones. My brother and I went to school with Arab students, we played together, and they were our friends. But just before the '67 War everything changed. One evening I was walking back from school with a girlfriend. Three Arab boys about my age, two my neighbors, approached us. They started to say sadistic things. Things I had never heard them say before. 'Wait, wait!' they taunted. 'In a few days, Nasser will be here, you'll see what we will do to you and your friends.' We didn't answer. We crossed the street and the boys came right up behind us. They were so close to us. So I turned around and I said, 'Fuad, Afu, what are you doing? What has happened to you?' But they continued to make threats. I went home and told my mother. We were all alone. There were almost no Jewish men around because they were preparing for war, my father and brother included. My mother came from the Ukraine and survived the Holocaust. She vowed that she would never be in a pogrom again. So we gathered knives from the kitchen and kept them close to protect ourselves from the neighbors, the people I grew up with, the people I thought were our friends. Fortunately we quickly won the war. Afterward everything on the outer surface went back as if nothing happened. But for me, I will never forget."

Sadness loomed on Judith's face. Wearing her white short-sleeved doctor's coat over a baby blue top, her eyes occasionally glistened behind her gold wire rim glasses. We sat in Judith's cramped office, where there was just enough room for her desk, paperwork, computer, files, and two chairs for visitors. Her door remained closed for privacy.

She married an Italian Jew whom she met while in medical school in Italy. She had told him, "If you want me, you have to move to Israel." They have three sons and one daughter. At Ha'Emek Medical Center Judith works with many Arab doctors, nurses, and secretaries. She likes them, enjoys working with them, and respects their skills. But there are years of pain, stifled to maintain her warm yet professional demeanor. The intifada has made it tougher.

"My parents taught me never to hate or be afraid of anyone. You have to treat each person individually, especially as a doctor. I have two Arab doctors who work with me, nice people as people, but there are some things we avoid talking about, like the intifada. We are trying to work together, but you become more distant. You hear things, you see things, you have to be careful of what you say. If there's a bombing and you want to say what a terrible day, you have to see who is behind you. I can tell you that when we don't touch politics things are pleasant. We have a little kitchen where we prepare our meals and sit and eat together. We talk about our families, about our kids and you think, 'What a pity that it can't be just like this all the time.'"

The majority of children Judith sees are Arab, nearly 80 percent she said. "The Arab kids are sicker than the Jewish children. There are health issues related to intermarriage between relatives. There are more hygiene problems and more diseases. When you treat a patient, you treat a patient. You don't think about him as an Arab, Christian, or Muslim. We do our best without looking where he came from or how he is dressed. We feel what we feel, but we treat all the patients the same. We don't let Arabs wait more than Jews. They get the best medicines, the best care, like everybody else. I have some Arab mothers who come here and even if there are Arab physicians available, they say, 'Oh, Judy, I prayed that you would be here. Do you remember my child being like this or like that?' They say this with sincerity. It's not because they can't avoid me. They can go to another hospital. I know that they are people who just want to live, to survive, to have their kids go to school, grow up, get married, and have kids of their own. It's so terrible: the politics and hatred. And with this hatred another generation, and another one, grows up. This ruins life for all of us. You cannot avoid thinking about this sometimes. If I treat an Arab baby five or nine months old I sometimes think, 'How will he grow up?' The babies laugh, smile at me and I play with them. There is such innocence there and sometimes it hurts me, and I say to myself, 'What a pity that all this innocence goes away with time.' A baby is like a white chart and then the stains are cast."

For Judith, who values the lives of her patients, the loss of innocence is indeed a painful metamorphosis. One experience still hurts deeply. "A few years ago, before I joined the emergency department, we were treating an Arab boy for cancer in the pediatric ward," she began. "For almost five years he came in and out of the hospital. He stayed for very long periods with his grandmother at his side. The nurses always took care of the grand-mother too. They gave her food to eat, things to drink, a bed, and a place to wash. She was always with us, he was with us. The boy learned to speak Hebrew beautifully. He played with us and, like all kids who have terrible diseases, we spoiled him, gave him lots of things. He was the one who was supposed to see that we do not treat Jews and Arabs differently. He is really the one who should come out and say, 'I stayed with the Jews, I know how it is.' When he was seventeen he came to me for follow-up care. He said, "I cannot come on Monday because we have a holiday. Can you see me on Wednesday?" I told him that I could not. I was working in Bet Shean. He was very angry and he slammed the door. Then he opened it and said, 'If I were a Jew, you would receive me on another day.' This hurt me so much and I said, 'Ruchi, if this is what you learned from the age of ten to the age of seventeen, this hatred and these words, you learned nothing. I don't know where you grew up. You are intelligent, you want to be a physician, you grew up with us, and that's what you think of us? Go and find another doctor.' Then a parent of another child said, 'Dr. Antonelli, don't think like that. He's just a boy.' He's not just a boy. He learned to hate and think about us that way from someone. For me it was a terrible day. He was angry and he went away. He did come back and continue treatment. But I couldn't feel the same toward him."

One other pivotal experience in Judith's life has scarred her heart. She explained, "On August 9, 2001, we had an Arab girl, about three years old, in the emergency room. She had drunk a cleaning substance and was brought in by three young men, brothers or cousins. We treated her, gave her an ice cream, and afterward she sat in the reception area watching TV with her relatives. Suddenly the TV turned to the explosion at the Sbarro Restaurant; it had just been hit by a suicide bomber. The young men accompanying the little girl started to laugh. One of the Jews in the room said, 'What are you laughing at?' The men responded, 'No, it's not about what's on TV. We just remembered a joke.'" Judith knew this was untrue and was horrified that anyone could laugh at such a hideous act. She concluded, "It didn't change the way we treated the girl, but you know how you feel at such moments."

Judith is particularly frustrated by the news reports that have accused Israeli soldiers of failing to allow Palestinian ambulances to get through road blocks. "It was like getting a terrible slap in the face," she said, "because we are the opposite of what we have been described as. If sometimes you have to stop an ambulance, you have to stop it. We have seen what the Palestinians are using ambulances for – the transportation of terrorists and bombs. And the whole world is talking about our soldiers like they are Nazis. On the worst day of the fighting in Jenin in April 2002, when our thirteen soldiers were killed, they brought a woman from Jenin into the hospital with toxemia."

Throughout these difficult times Palestinians have been treated at Ha'Emek Medical Center, as well as other hospitals throughout Israel. Judith has treated many sick children from Jenin, a few brought to the hospital in the arms of soldiers. Some children were dangerously ill from poisonous snakebites or scorpion stings. A premature Palestinian baby, weighing 1.5 kilos, was brought to the hospital by an Israeli army ambulance. He was blue and near death. The staff from the pediatric intensive care unit was called to the emergency room, even those who were at home. "Soldiers brought that baby here," said Judith. "That is the strangeness of life. You try to save a life and then you have to go back and fight."

Judith's stories about medical care for Palestinians were not exceptions. At Rambam Hospital in Haifa, where I interviewed terror survivor Orly Virany, I also met Yaffa Perez, the assistant administrator at Rambam. She shared the remarkable story of how a Rambam doctor saved the life of a young Palestinian boy. One of Rambam's doctors was serving in the military in Jenin during Operation Defensive Shield.[37] Soldiers went from house to house searching for terrorists. Families were often asked to temporarily leave for safety purposes. In one home soldiers found a boy too sick to move on his own accord. The Rambam doctor examined the boy, suspecting leukemia. He immediately contacted Rambam and asked to transport the child to the hospital for treatment. Less than twenty-four hours later the boy received free oncology care at Rambam. "We feel that if our doctor is looking this boy in the eyes and if he wants the best treatment for a child of God, we have to help. He is first a doctor, then a soldier," Yaffa said.

The glimmers of goodness described by Yaffa and Judith are often lost in the brutality of war. Even for a trauma doctor like Judith, at times it can be too much to bear. "Sometimes I don't go to sleep at night, because you have to listen, and listen, and listen to the radio. And when I do go to sleep I am afraid of what I might hear in the morning. There's a lot of tension living under a dark cloud. I remember when the bus bombing occurred near Wadi Ara.[38] It was at 7:25 A.M. and I was washing my hair. I quickly finished, and I was so afraid I said to myself, 'Let's pray that there were no kids.' Within ten minutes I arrived at the hospital. The staff nurse said there would be a lot of children. We were very frightened, not knowing what to expect. No children arrived at the hospital, so we helped out in the adult trauma unit. There was an immigrant from Argentina; a girl eighteen years old, like my daughter. She had come to this country before her parents and had already been living on a kibbutz for two years. She could speak Hebrew, but in trauma she spoke only Spanish. I found some people who could converse with her. Her belly, thighs, buttocks, and chest were in shreds. She was unable to hear because the explosion caused tears in her eardrums. So you had to talk at her, face-to-face. Her hair and eyebrows were burned and she sustained trauma to her eyelids. I cared for her like she was my daughter. She was alone without family. I stayed with her for two hours, and then came back to my office. It was terrible." Judith choked, tears filled her eyes. After a few moments she regained her composure and continued. "I was also crying when I was with her, but you try not to show it of course. You are crying a lot more on the inside than outside. As a staff, we talked about what happened, kind of like group therapy. At that time the only patients in the emergency were Arabs. It's very hard to smile at them at such moments – you feel like you are in one world and they are in another. You think, 'Are you happy now?' Two days after the young woman was brought into the hospital she was released. Her parents were on their way from Argentina. That was the last time I saw her."

A good day for Judith is when nothing happens, when patients have pneumonia or tonsillitis. Judith said, "There's a difference when you see illnesses that come from God or from nature versus the pain and suffering caused by the destruction of human beings."

So what has life taught Judith? "My father was one of seven siblings and he was the only one who survived the Holocaust. My parents told me how non-Jews used to call them *Jid* or *Jewid*, 'dirty Jew' or 'bloody Jew,' or say, 'You smell like dung.' I very much appreciate the opportunity to live in Israel. I feel very lucky that we have a state. I know we have to pay for it. We pay a lot, but I think it would be worse for all the Jews if Israel didn't exist. I am convinced we are doing the right things. I am proud about our behavior in this hospital as doctors and nurses. We are human and it doesn't matter what the world says. We are trying every day. Sometimes you know you have to hold yourself back, but I think that we are also succeeding in practicing medicine with the highest standards."

When this interview came to an end, I stuck around for a few minutes. The pediatric emergency ward has a bright, welcoming environment. Balloons gave it a festive birthday party feel, with bright privacy curtains and interesting streamers and mobiles dangling from above. Unbeknownst to Judith, I stood back, absorbed the scene, and watched her from a short distance away. She had gathered an Arab boy in her arms and was reassuring the mother that he would be okay. A smile crossed Judith's face as she comforted the screaming child. Despite all the pain and mixed emotions stirring within her, it was clear that this was truly her element.

Dubi Biran

Shmuel and Orna Lapid

Marion and Daniel Nachshon

Chapter Five
A Historical Perspective: Will Peace Ever Come?

When Dubi (Pivnic) Biran was born, on December 14, 1947, his safe arrival was near miraculous. His father brought his mother to Beilinson Hospital in Petach Tikvah, near Tel Aviv, by horse and wagon, a trip that took over an hour from their tent home in Kfar Shemaryahu. Throughout their rough journey, his parents heard the exploding mortar shells from armed Arabs during the Israel War of Independence. Though the bombing was nearby, they escaped unharmed. "My mother said that with my birth, her first child, there will be no more wars. 'We have come to Israel,' she later told me. 'We suffered terribly in the Diaspora. We will make a new land here and there will be no wars.'" When Dubi became a parent he too hoped that there would be peace. His children are adults now and they have also fought in wars. Throughout Dubi's fifty-two years, battlefields and terrorist deaths have crisscrossed his path.

"Israel cannot afford to lose a single war," states the security doctrine of the Israel Defense Forces. These words echo from the old to the young, from *sabra*[39] to new immigrant throughout Israel. There is either survival and existence or annihilation. Can survival be achieved through war or courageous peace agreements like the one brokered by u.s. President Jimmy Carter with Egyptian President Anwar Sadat and Israeli Prime Minister Menachem Begin on March 26, 1979? For those men and women who grew up under the thunderous dark cloud of war the hope for peace continues to bloom in their hearts and souls as their bodies and minds remain prepared for war.

Dubi Biran sat quietly on a powder-blue faux suede family room couch. He wore a white T-shirt printed with whimsical characters parasailing against an afternoon blue sky. His cell phone, attached to a pocket of his blue jeans, rang occasionally with business and family calls. Steel-blue–gray eyes silently reflect experience, and the smooth creases in his tanned skin show the years of hushed stress. He has a youthful demeanor and build; only the gray, receding hairline reflects his age. His parents illegally immigrated to Israel in 1946 from Constanta, Romania. After surviving a German labor camp in Romania, his father, Ben-Zion Pivnic, met Dubi's mother, Atalia, through a Zionist *gar'in* (a core of people preparing to establish a kibbutz). Together they escaped to Italy. Most of their journey was made on foot, except for a short period in Budapest when they traveled in a covered truck. They walked across the snowy Alps and, once in Italy, boarded the *Enzo Sereni*, a famous ship bound for Palestine. The conditions were near unbearable, the number of passengers far exceeding the ship's capacity. Many were crammed into the belly of the boat. Immediately upon arrival they were removed from the ship and incarcerated by the British in the Atlit detention camp south of Haifa.[40] The camp was surrounded by a fence with armed British guards. After some time the Haganah,[41] the Jewish underground military organization in Palestine, implemented a historical breakout. Dubi's parents walked for hours to their new temporary home on Kibbutz Yagur near Haifa.

Ben-Zion Pivnic joined the Haganah. During military training the British arrested him for illegal possession of arms and sent him to a prison in Tulkarem, where he was detained for several months. Penniless but rich with determination, Atalia and Ben-Zion soon moved to Kfar Shemaryahu, an agricultural village where pioneers lived in tents. They married at the end of 1946. Since the finer things of life were scarce, all the Kfar Shemaryahu brides shared the same wedding dress.

When Dubi was a year old, the Pivnics settled in Allonei Abba, a communal agricultural moshav where the community shared everything except each family's home. Allonei Abba had a profound influence on Dubi's future. He was raised on the stories of the first heroic paratroopers of Israel during World War II. Allonei Abba was named after Abba Berdiczew, one of the thirty-two paratroopers who jumped into enemy territory in Europe during

World War II to save Jews from the Nazis. Abba Berdiczew parachuted into Slovakia with a mission to enter Romania. Though his exact fate is uncertain, Abba never reached his destination. It is believed that he was captured, most likely tortured, and killed by Nazis. Dubi's parents did not speak of the Holocaust. Instead they focused on Zionism, their longing to emigrate to Palestine, and their desire for a Jewish homeland. "Living on a moshav was difficult, yet relaxed and tranquil," Dubi said. "We were farmers. When I was eight my father taught me to drive a tractor. I was surrounded by nature. I was free. It was a wonderful childhood, like in the movies. We did not watch television, but listened to the radio and talked to one another. We went on many bus trips to see Israel, because my parents wanted us to have appreciation of our homeland. There were communal activities. We would get together for parties and beautiful agricultural holidays such as Shavuot. Allonei Abba was surrounded by Arab settlements and we had excellent relationships with them. There was a dirt path that led to their villages. Many Arabs worked with us and I knew all of them. Any Arab worker who got married would invite us to the wedding and we would go. If the Arabs needed help, we would help them. They were setting up permanent settlements and they didn't have running water or any electrical appliances. My mother helped the family of an Arab man who was in charge of the work in the orchard. She gave them a refrigerator and furniture. When I was in high school, I worked on the farm. I had no problems working alone with an Arab in the fields, to go there with him at 6:00 A.M. and come back with him in the evening after a day's work. I learned some Arabic from that close connection."

Dubi finished high school and enlisted in the Israel Defense Forces at the age of seventeen. He joined the Nahal,[42] which combined army service with agricultural training. His unit, Nahal Mutznach, specialized in paratrooper maneuvers; his military service was a difficult one. Dubi explained, "About a year and a half after I enlisted in the army, I saw combat for the first time. It began with retaliation operations in the Almagor area on the waterfront just before the '67 War. And during the '67 War, I fought in just about the hardest battle that the paratroopers were ever involved in. On the first day of battle, our unit was to sever the Gaza Strip from Egypt. Under the command of Rafael Eitan, the paratroopers fought to cut off the Egyptian army's supply lines to the Gaza Strip. During another difficult day of the fighting, we arrived at the battalion's collection station in an area with small, sloping, sandy hills. That was where we evacuated our wounded soldiers. There the one or two battalion doctors gave immediate aid to the wounded and quickly transferred them by army ambulance out of the fighting area to better equipped medical services in the rear. Soldiers surrounded the area to protect the medical personnel and injured. Along with our wounded we brought our dead. That day, we got off the transport and someone yelled, 'A tank is approaching us!' It was an Egyptian tank. We quickly got organized for a circumferential defense. I carried the kind of grenade launcher that fit over a gun's barrel. During battle the grenade is always in the launcher. When you are close to your target, you shoot the grenade like a missile. I approached the Egyptian tank just like the American World War II war hero, Audie Murphy. He would go up to the enemy tanks, open the hatch and throw a grenade inside. The Egyptian tank was trying to run us over. I began to approach the tank when it was fifty meters away. When it got closer to me and its hatch opened, I shot the grenade into the tank and it exploded. Everyone inside was killed. I had only one chance. The tank was going to run me over. I didn't see the Egyptians' faces but I remember the driver's leather helmet. The tank burst into flames and there was intense fire and light."

Was Dubi scared? "Of course I was afraid. Who isn't afraid? There was a feeling – and it's not nice to say – that either you come back in a coffin like a hero or you come back as a hero with a citation. In the paratrooper unit, with its motivation for fighting, it was clear that if you fight, you fight till the end. I think it's a bit stupid now. Even though it might sound like heroism, it was a very, very difficult battle. It was the day I lost fifteen to twenty good friends."

A few days later, during another arduous battle, Dubi was wounded. "I jumped out of an armored troop vehicle when grenades were thrown in by the enemy. Two people were killed. I was wounded by thirty-six pieces of shrapnel. I still have some shrapnel left in my leg. I didn't see a doctor until the end of the day. My leg was bandaged up and then I was sent back to fight." Dubi was awarded the Medal for Distinguished Service and a citation for his service in the '67 War.

After the war, Dubi continued to serve in Nahal Hatzeva, recruiting others to join the Nahal program. In 1969 he returned to his home, Allonei Abba, where he was responsible for the Youth Aliyah[43] groups there. While teaching battle heritage at a summer camp, Dubi met Nurit. They married in in 1970, hebraized Pivnic to Biran, and lived in Allonei Abba until 1973. When the Yom Kippur War broke out on October 6, 1973, Dubi's reserve unit once again went into bloody battle. "It was so much more difficult than the '67 War," Dubi explained. A small grimace crossed his lips. "I was in a battalion of paratroopers in the reserves. We were the first unit to cross the Suez Canal and we suffered many casualties. We got to the city of Suez and were caught in a terrible shooting trap. We were very tired, the only food we had was airdropped to us, but we realized that we were at the end of the war and that the Suez would be the last battle. There was a feeling of competition between the army units to see who would get to the Suez first. My wife just knew that nothing would happen to me, she knew that I would come back alive. I told her that I couldn't understand how she had such spiritual faith. We lost a lot of friends in that war."

With a strong desire to do more for his country's security, Dubi Biran joined the Special Services Arab Department that same year. He studied Middle Eastern studies and Arabic. Much of Dubi Biran's work was undercover, top secret, and dangerous. And at one point he barely escaped death. "In 1983, when I was in Alai, near Beirut, Ron Rozner, an officer in the Golani infantry unit, was sometimes responsible for the soldiers who protected me. One time we went into a house to conduct a search relating to our war on terror and he shouted, 'Watch out!' I didn't see anything. There was a trip wire, a thin nylon wire. Had I stepped on it, I would have detonated a bomb. He saved all of our lives." But that was only one brush with death. Dubi faced many more dangerous situations.

While on duty in Alai, Dubi stood on a porch looking out toward the American Embassy in Beirut. It was April 18, 1983 and he saw the American Embassy blow up right in front of him as the result of a terrorist bomb. The building shattered, spewing concrete into a thick plume of dust that choked the air. Sixty-three people were killed and 120 were injured. American, Israeli, and Lebanese rescue workers rushed to save lives. But Dubi was not one of them; he knew he could not react. At the time of the explosion he was undercover, dressed in Arab garb, speaking impeccable Arabic. The grizzly scene pulled at his heartstrings and his natural desire to aid victims. But one wrong move, one false reaction, and his cover would be revealed.

Dubi's mission was to collect information and to learn about possible terrorist activities. Not even his wife knew where he was or what he was doing. Dubi was a master of disguise, an actor devoted to his role – so connected that he temporarily became his character. At least twice he stumbled across terrorist ambushes while in Lebanon. "It was chaos," he said, "but I was undercover and certainly couldn't expose myself in such situations." And there were other instances. "For example," Dubi said, "if I were driving a Mercedes in Beirut at night with Lebanese license plates to go get a hamburger, I wouldn't expose myself by going up to an American and speaking with him. You can't make that kind of contact, even though we did have certain ties. There was contact between the Americans and the Israelis. They knew part of what we were doing because we had the same common goals.

"When you are living undercover, you don't really feel fear. You don't really understand the fear because you are living the routine of the job. When it comes to the job, sometimes it is no small problem to provide and keep your cover. You can be on a street and see a person with whom you know you have a connection, but it's a secret connection. After many years you sometimes don't remember if it was a secret connection. It's a matter of sensitivity when you don't know how you're supposed to react. It's exactly like the bank manager in Switzerland, who, wanting to safeguard an individual's identity, won't acknowledge the bank customer by saying, 'Hello. How are you?' He waits for the customer to acknowledge him first. He doesn't expose the connection. There are a lot of people out there whose connections with me were totally secretive. Many of those people don't know anything about my undercover work and you have to play the game. You learn and prepare for that part of the job for years."

While Dubi was in Switzerland on an Israeli government security job, he was sent to Lebanon. He stayed in Lebanon for approximately six months. His wife and three children continued to live in Switzerland. "I remember that I used to visit my family once every six weeks. It was very difficult to make the transition between Lebanon and Switzerland. I would fly Swiss Air out of Beirut. After three or four days of crazy quietude, I would return to Lebanon, to the war in Beirut. It was one of the most difficult paradoxes in my life that I can remember."

Sometimes Dubi did not speak to his family for a week or two at a time. Obviously, it was a difficult choice to make. "When you go for that kind of job, you have to know that there is a price to be paid. There's nothing you can do. Sometimes it's a problem. Nurit raised the children by herself until I left the Special Services Arab Department. I realized that I had missed out on a lot of things in life and when I served outside of Israel I didn't even know my children. Every wife whose husband works in this type of job has many worries – silent worries. The last time I was in Beirut there were many terrorist attacks directed at Israelis. My wife would call up hospitals in Israel to see if I had been brought in. She didn't show any outward signs of panic. It was the education and motivation that we received from our parents that placed value on service to this country. I used to carry a coin with Kennedy's picture on it. 'Don't ask what your country can do for you. Ask what you can do for your country.' I believe that this was the atmosphere here during the 1950s and 1960s. We didn't ask questions like the government employees ask today. We asked, 'How can we help? What kind of job can I do?' Today they ask, 'What are the working conditions? What car do I get? How many years of work do I need in order to get a pension or to travel? What's the salary?'

"Such things weren't important to me then, maybe because I was a moshavnik and didn't lack anything. I went to school in Kfar Yehoshua, which is a ten- to fifteen-minute drive from Allonei Abba. I had an important and famous teacher, David Barash, who was once a candidate to be president of Israel. He taught geography and Bible studies and often he combined the two. We would go hiking and he instilled in us a love for the Land. He said that Israel in twenty to thirty years of statehood could not be expected to achieve what America did in two hundred years. You can't have the prosperity that you have in America. He said at the time that if all at once we would have peace, socially and economically Israel would have been in a very difficult situation. He explained: 'Look, what holds us together? It's unity.' During terrorist attacks, during wars, there is more volunteering. This volunteer spirit and the 100 percent reporting for reserve duty – despite the calls for conscientious objection – means that Israel has a number of bonds holding us together."

Dubi worked for the Special Services Arab Department until 1996, serving in and out of Israel, including many places throughout Europe and in Lebanon. Retired from government service, he is now a private investigator for insurance and financial issues within the Arab-speaking sector. For safety reasons, when he travels to Arab villages he is accompanied by an Arab or another Jew who is armed. He has many positive relationships with the Bedouins, Christian Arabs, and Druze who work with him as investigators.

This intifada is the first war Dubi is not directly involved in. What has his experience in military service and undercover work taught him about living with terror? "When I fought in wars I knew that my parents were safe in their home. Now the war is in our homes and Israelis are experiencing feelings of desperation. It's not that we feel that there is no future, but that we have reached a dead end, an impasse. We don't know where we are heading. Many of us thought that we would have had some sort of agreement with the Palestinians by now.

"Two things happened during the last few years that caused me to feel tremendous sadness. One was Rabin's assassination.[44] I never believed a Jew would shoot a prime minister. I was in total shock. Today I can believe anything. The second was the terrorist attack at the Dolphinarium, a disco hall where a terrorist went up to children and blew himself up.[45] That affected me very deeply. I can understand it when it is soldiers, but not children. I don't know with whom among the Palestinians we can speak when they send their people to blow themselves up in cafes or in hotels filled with people celebrating the Passover Seder."[46]

Another area of frustration for Dubi is his feeling that Israel does not control its own destiny. Diplomatic relations often dictate Israel's course. Dubi explained, "During all the wars in which I participated there was a 'big brother,' be it the former Soviet Union or America. We are a small nation. If someone wants to stop the wars, they stop us. Look how the United States puts pressure on us today. In all the wars I have participated in, we were stopped in the middle by that pressure. There were forced cease-fires. I feel as if we're being controlled by someone who is higher up and that our future is not just up to Israel. The British and Americans are bringing us to the negotiating table with the Palestinians. I believe they are dictating the terms to us and taking away our independence. Someone else is determining our fate, not us.

"I was in Bosnia and Croatia. There were roadblocks. This was partitioned and that was partitioned. I believe the solution in the Middle East will be similar. I think we have to make a physical separation between the Palestinians and ourselves with checkpoints. If Palestinians want to come to Israel to work, we have to check them. We live here and they live there. You see a lot of security forces around Israel and at checkpoints. I don't feel comfortable with this. It reminds me of a militant country. But checkpoints provide deterrence. It also causes an unpleasant feeling, a lack of freedom, traffic jams – yet I regard it with complete understanding. But I also believe that anyone wishing to cause a terrorist attack will in the end succeed. It depends only on the person's determination. If he doesn't succeed the first, second, or third time, he'll succeed on the fourth try."

A suicide bomber's determination is only one of Dubi's concerns. As an Arabist, he has a deeper understanding of the complexity of Arab-Jewish relations and the loyalty Israeli Arabs feel toward the twenty-two Arab nations surrounding the Jewish state. Religious extremism is also a major issue. "The fundamentalist Islamic movements that exist have a strong influence on some Israeli Muslim Arabs," Dubi said. "As far as their identity is concerned, they have not yet decided whether they are Palestinian or Israeli Arabs. This is no small problem. An important Israeli Arab deputy health minister, Abdel Aziz Zuabi, once said that they are living in their own country, but not with their own people. These Arabs see themselves as Palestinians. Their relatives live in places like Jenin and Nablus, but the country that is governing over them is the State of Israel. The harsh economic situation is intensifying the friction between Jews and Arabs. It is written in our Declaration of Independence that our two peoples, Jews and Arabs, will live together, but the Israeli Arabs do not buy into this. Besides the problems between Arabs and Jews, there is terrible friction between the Arab Christian and Arab Muslim communities. I feel like we are sitting on a barrel of explosives.

"There are many opinions as to how to resolve this conflict and I'll go to the extreme. There are some who say, 'If we transfer all the Arabs out of Israel, it will be quiet.' I don't believe in this. I think we need to focus on solutions in stages. The peace agreements with Egypt also were in stages. First there was an agreement on the separation of forces. Then a nonbelligerence agreement was signed. Only afterward was there a peace agreement. We live in close and crowded proximity to the Palestinians. Today, if a terrorist leaves Jenin and manages to slip through, he can blow himself up in Haifa within twenty minutes. Therefore, in my opinion, we have to find the solution that first stops all terror. Then, after a certain length of time, when there has been no terror, we continue on. But there are many problems with this. One is the Arab mentality of revenge. If you murder an Arab's relative, then he will kill you in revenge. The Bedouins have a popular saying: 'If after forty years I took revenge but didn't hurt the person, I was rushing. I have time to take revenge.' We are two very paranoid peoples because of everything we have gone through. We Jews have been through Holocaust, the formation of the State of Israel, and all the dangers around us. It is very difficult."

It comes as no surprise that Dubi's beliefs stem from his past experiences. Yet he has spent most of his life pushing the horrors of war out of his consciousness. "I think I have been in denial when it comes to internalization; but that was only a cover. Today I know that I feel the trauma inside from all the wars I participated in. We have no time to go for treatment, which I think is more orderly in America. We have a theory that says, 'Okay. We are living in a situation of war. We have to cope with it. It's a challenge and we have to continue on.' But I have a story. My daughter was present at the rock concert catastrophe in Arad on July 18, 1995, where youth were accidentally injured and trampled to death. I was at the rock festival, but at a different performance. My daughter's girlfriend found me and said that there were a lot of dead people. I went to the area where the ambulances were waiting. People started to come out of the concert area, but not her. I already thought the worst. In the end she was brought out injured. A soldier was supporting her head. She had found herself under a mound of people and didn't understand what had happened. After a long time I said, 'Inbal, I want to talk to you about what happened.' It was a terrible trauma for me. I told her, 'You should know that I was afraid, just as much as when I was fighting in the wars.'"

This experience as well as many recent tragic events caused by terror have forced Dubi to relive his past traumas. As time passes, however, they get placed once again below the surface. He and other Israeli war veterans have survived just fine by coping this way. Asked what life lessons he would like to share, Dubi paused before responding. "I don't see any other solution to our present situation other than talking," he said. "I don't see a solution resulting from the use of force by either side. We are living in a situation where there is no choice but to find a way to make peace. After the very hard battle in 1973 between the Egyptians and us, the cease-fire borders were established. We spoke directly with the Egyptian soldiers in English. They told us that we should only talk and try to find a solution for peace. I didn't go out to kill people and make a mark for each kill on my gun. I spoke with people.

"At one stage of my life I was responsible for the security of Israeli youth delegations sent to Poland. I was in Poland fifteen times. I got really involved in the subject of the Holocaust. That was where I understood why there has to be a State of Israel. We cannot go back in time to the Romania or Poland of the Holocaust. Every time, I learned more and more about the death camps and of the history of the Ashkenazic communities, the cemeteries, the rabbinate, the yeshivas, and the different factions among the Jewish people, and I remembered what Ben-Gurion[47] said: 'When you have no choice, you come to some kind of compromise.' This includes the Arabs. This includes us living amongst ourselves in Israel. You have to be a human being. You have to be a good person. Go to the Ten Commandments. I have a dream that one day we will have peace with our neighbors and I will be able to drive through Syria, Lebanon, and Turkey to get to Europe."

Perhaps Dubi will not live to see this dream come true, but just as his mother did before him, he passes this dream onto his children, and sadly they in turn might have to pass it on to theirs.

* * *

Retired farmers Shmuel and Orna Lapid have not only watched Israel's history unfold; they have lived it. Their experiences could fill a book on Israeli pioneers. The two know each other so well that they often finished each other's sentences. Shmuel spoke in Hebrew, Benay Katz translated, and Orna would lean over to me and add a little background information in English. Captivating, delightful, and attentive to each other, it was easy to feel at home with this remarkable couple.

Their home sits in the middle of Moshav Bet Shearim, where cows need milking and the roosters crow at sunrise. The Lapids' modest ranch home is surrounded by dense flowering trees, bushes, and lush farmland – a slice of paradise in the Promised Land. Harvested from their garden, odd, yellow-orange fruit called loquats graced their dining table. Tea and cake, black-and-white photographs, and old newspaper clippings were passed around as we relaxed.

The stories began. "My father was a Zionist and a *halutz*,"[48] seventy-nine-year-old Shmuel said. "In 1925, when I was two years old, he left for Palestine. My mother, older sister, younger brother, and I continued to live with my maternal grandparents in Lodz, Poland. My grandparents kept writing my father letters telling him that he should come back. They reminded him that he still had a family in Poland. But he didn't want to return. In 1930, when I was seven years old, we joined my father. My mother's father had died. Her family must have said that it was time for her to join her husband. One memory from that time is hard to forget. For some reason I thought children in Palestine didn't need toys. My sister and I gathered up all our toys and I burned them in our stove. From Lodz we took a train to Warsaw and then to Trieste, Italy. It was late at night when we arrived and I was tired. We boarded an Italian boat waiting to transport passengers to Palestine. After several weeks, we reached Palestine and some people disembarked at the port in Jaffa. We continued on to Haifa. There was no port in Haifa, which meant that our boat had to stay far from the coast. Arab workers were sent with rafts to help the Jews off the boat. We were afraid of the Arabs because there had been deadly Arab riots in Palestine not long before our arrival. As the Arab workers approached the boat they made a sign with their hands, two fingers together. This was their way of letting us know that we were equals. They knew we were afraid of them. One Arab picked me up and tossed me to another Arab who caught me on the raft. Everyone from the boat received inoculations against diseases. We spent three days in quarantine, living in wooden huts on the Shemen Beach in Haifa.

"Less than a year after we arrived in Palestine, my mother brought over her sick mother. The British held the mandate over Palestine and if you had a close relative living in Palestine you were given an immigration certificate. My grandmother died about a year later of typhus. Nearly all our relatives were killed in the Holocaust. My mother's younger brother, however, fled Poland in 1920 after he had been attacked and stabbed by anti-Semites. He went to live in New York."

Shmuel's wife, Orna, seventy-one, pointed to an old Jewish newspaper clipping from the United States that told Shmuel's uncle's story. She said, "This article talks about a Polish newspaper report on the attack on Shmuel's uncle. It says that he had died in a hospital. That's not true. The family smuggled him out of Poland. He was nineteen or twenty years old. Jewish boys of that age were conscripted into the Polish army.

"People must realize that things have not changed much since Shmuel's uncle left for the United States. Hatred against the Jews continues to be passed from generation to generation. Today's anti-Semitism is concealed.

It has a different face. Today's 'anti-Jewish' movement is expressed through anti-Israel talk; Israelis – the conquerors. It may not be politically correct to be anti-Semitic, but there doesn't seem to be any issue if slurs are directed to Israel. But one could easily substitute 'Jews' for 'Israel.' This is what I mean by concealed anti-Semitism."

Shmuel continued with his history. "Now this is a story! My father's parents came to Israel in 1933, three years after me. I was ten. My grandfather was a strong Zionist and a follower of a Chassidic rabbi back in Poland. This religious leader forbade traveling to Palestine because he believed that Jews should only come here when the Messiah comes. My grandparents packed their bags and didn't reveal a thing or say a word to anyone. My grandfather didn't tell his rabbi that he was going to Palestine. He knew that the rabbi would tell him to stay and wait for the Messiah. He was afraid that if his rabbi would order him to stay, he wouldn't be able to go. My grandparents didn't receive British immigration certificates. Hitler was already in power in Germany and there were not enough certificates available. So my grandparents left Lodz, Poland, as tourists. First they traveled by train to Trieste, Italy, and then sailed to Beirut, Lebanon. Once they arrived in Beirut everything was organized with guides who were paid to take them by taxi to the Palestinian border. There they were put on two donkeys at night and smuggled across the border into Palestine. My father met them in Nahariyah and took them to Haifa. Afterward he brought them to our shack in Kfar Hasidim. Conditions were rough and we were poor. Our hut consisted of two rooms. There was no stove for heat, but we had a small three-legged brass Primus kerosene stove with a kettle on it. At night we would use a hot water bottle to warm the beds. We used kerosene lamps. The shower and toilet were outside. We had to constantly be on the lookout for scorpions. Within a few days my father arranged for my grandparents to live in Jerusalem, where they remained until they died. They are buried on the Mount of Olives in Jerusalem along with my parents."

Orna leaned over to me and whispered, "Shmuel's story is the most interesting. He wanted to join the Palmach.[49] Religious boys did not go into the Palmach. They were supposed to study. Palmach means 'shock troops' and they were like the partisans of Palestine. I joined the Palmach later, because I am younger than he is." Orna smiled and sat up straight, turning her attention back to her husband.

Shmuel continued. "In 1942 I was in the British police force. All I knew in English was, 'Left, right, left, right,' and 'Go to the right in threes. Right turn! One, two, three, four.' I did guard duty and went out on day and night patrols in Haifa at the Arab marketplace, the railroad station, British Police headquarters, and the city's warehouses. While I was in the police force I was also a member of the Haganah.[50] I didn't get my weapons training from the police. I got it mainly from the Haganah. The British didn't want their Jewish and Arab policemen to be too adept at using weapons; therefore, they gave us pistols. The Italians, Germany's allies, started to bomb Haifa in July 1940, and there were blackouts when this happened. The British feared that the Germans would come to Palestine to fight them. The German army was now in Syria and they also had reached El Alamein in North Africa, 150 miles west of Cairo."

With the ease of a well-read educator, Orna related the experiences of the past to the present. "Every time period has its traumas. The Haganah was an underground army at the time. Its military activities were done in a much quieter way than today because it had to be careful of the British who had the mandate over Palestine. It didn't matter what the facts were or the reasons for the military operations; the British would always condemn the Jews and not the Arabs. This is the same as today. The IDF is always condemned for military actions against the Palestinians, no matter what the reasons. We are always seen as the aggressors against the Palestinian underdog."

"In 1942 Rommel and the German army were near Alexandria, Egypt," Shmuel continued. "Many Arabs hoped for a German victory. The majority of the Arab policemen who were hired by the British were waiting for the Germans to come here in order get rid of the Jews and the British. Many took the pistols that they were given and disappeared. That was when I signed a year's contract to work for the British police force. In 1943, after the year was over, Rommel was defeated and a difficult situation developed. The British were now on the side of the Arabs and they no longer were such good friends with the Jews. I would speak to an Englishman and he would turn up his nose. At the end of my year's contract I had to personally ask to be released from the British police force, otherwise the contract would be renewed automatically. I had had enough. So I wrote a letter requesting dismissal. The Jewish sergeant advised me that when the officer questioned me as to why I wanted to leave the police, I should answer that the salary was too low. Otherwise I wouldn't be able to leave. I gave that answer and I was discharged. A month later I joined the Palmach.

"The Palmach was started in 1941 with British approval. The British were involved because they thought that if Rommel would conquer Palestine, the Palmach would act as the underground force fighting the Germans. The British even paid the Palmach soldier's salary for his first year of service. By 1942 the British were no longer cooperating with the Palmach and outlawed the organization. This did not stop the Jews and the Palmach grew. In the beginning there were six squadrons. Afterward there were ten. In each squadron there were 180 to 200 soldiers. During World War II the Palmach was the mobilized force of the Haganah. There were 80,000 members in the Haganah. The Palmach had no money so we had to support ourselves by working on a kibbutz. There was an arrangement that two weeks out of every month we worked and two weeks were dedicated to training and army matters. We did every sort of kibbutz work, including milking the cows, tending the horses, or working in the fields or orchards. We did military training out in the fields or on the kibbutz. One time we secretly crossed the Jordan River during the day as a military drill and succeeded in coming back without being detected by either the British or the Arabs."

Orna added, "Our fight against the Arabs today is different. During the Jewish War of Independence the Arabs wanted to stop our settlements from growing and the Jewish population from getting stronger. Today the terrorists want to wipe us off the face of the earth. They may not say it in so many words, but we understand this from their propaganda."

Shmuel was energized. There was much to tell and he was anxious to recreate the scene. He continued, "As I mentioned before, the Palmach was set up on kibbutzim. But in order for members to get to know Palestine and the whole region, we traveled a lot. At first I was in a squadron that was in the Sharon area, a zone reaching from Hadera to Tel Aviv. I was stationed on Kibbutz Givat Haim. There were also divisions in Givat ha-Sheloshah and other kibbutzim in the Sharon area."

Orna added, "They moved around so that the British wouldn't know who the members of the Palmach were. The British would ask, 'Are you from this kibbutz? Do you live here? Do you have children?' The British kept their eyes open all the time. They were very frightened of the Palmach because of their military activities. However, the British did allow one or two Jews to guard their own settlements. These guards were called Notrim[51] and they were issued rifles and uniforms by the British."

Shmuel continued. "Around September 1943, right before Rosh Hashanah, our squadron moved to the Jezreel Valley. We never stayed more than a year in one place. One of the biggest obstacles was moving the illegal weapons. Every squadron had its own weapons – rifles, mortars, et cetera. If a squadron would move to another area, its weapons would be transferred as well. A 'slick' was a special container or hole used to hide illegal weapons. For example, if there was a mill or place to make cattle feed, the slick would be under the large engines. They would dig a hole under the engine. If you wanted to get something out of the slick you would have to move the engine to the side. We often used the weapons from the Notrim for our training. But we were always afraid that the British would make a surprise inspection and catch us with the weapons."

Orna said, "Today, Palestinian terrorists hide their weapons from us in tunnels, schools, and hospitals, and other places like that. There is no similarity to our slicks. You must understand that these people are terrorists and that Israel does not want war. Israel wants peace with the Arabs."

Shmuel continued again. "Every Palmach squadron had a gunsmith. He took care of the weapons, making sure they were clean and in working order. Our squadron's gunsmith was Uzi Glass. He later changed Glass to the Hebrew 'Gal,' which means rejoice. At night, he would go into the slick that was dug in the cowshed and take care of the weapons. Years later, when Israel was a state, he invented the Uzi submachine gun. He used to like to play with old weapons and their parts in his free time. Anyway, when it was time to move our squadron, Uzi didn't want to send the old guns and parts in the slick with the other weapons. He kept them with him in a little sack. Perhaps he was concerned that someone would take the sack and throw it away during the transfer. After he put the weapons in a Haganah car, he took all of his belongings and put them in a shoulder bag. He then went back to the kibbutz to catch a ride to his new Palmach posting on Kibbutz Ein Harod. His former kibbutz had a factory for producing fruit jams and every so often trucks with jam would leave for distribution. So on this particular day Uzi caught one of these trucks transporting large containers of jam to a big supply base for British soldiers in the Hof ha-Carmel area near Haifa. This ride would take him part of the way to his squadron's new kibbutz. The driver of the truck stopped at the entrance to the British army's supply base. The British guard wanted to inspect the driver's documentation and to see what was in the truck. The driver explained that he had jam for the warehouse.

"Our guy, Uzi Gal, was sitting next to him with his bag hanging up in the cabin. The British soldier saw the khaki-colored bag and became suspicious. He opened the bag and saw gun parts. The driver and Uzi were arrested. The jam was taken off the truck and soldiers were ordered to search for smuggled weapons by poking holes in the thirty-gallon containers. They destroyed the jam and, of course, they found no weapons. Uzi and the driver were immediately taken to the CID, Criminal Investigation Department – the British secret police. The police questioned the driver about Uzi. He answered that he had never seen him before and that Uzi was hitching a ride to Haifa so he stopped and gave him a lift. They let the driver go. Uzi, however, was put on trial and was sentenced to six years imprisonment. He sat in prison in Acre for more than two years, then was pardoned and released in 1946. Once again, he collected gun parts to build his own weapons. By 1951 the IDF was testing his gun, the now famous Uzi, which for many years was considered the world's most dependable and effective lightweight, rapid-fire automatic submachine gun on the market."

It was Orna's turn to share her stories and she too has memories for the history books. She began, "I was born on Moshav Kfar Yehoshua, which my parents helped to establish in 1927. There were between seventy and eighty families that built the moshav. My parents were Zionists and came from Russia in 1921. They lived a very, very hard life. They worked with their hands from morning until night. And I worked; all the children worked very, very hard. We studied in the morning in the moshav school. I remember my father telling us in the afternoon to help dig up potatoes, pick cabbage, and other hard chores. We raised chickens and cows, and planted vegetables and pears. It was very primitive, not like today. Milking a cow was not so easy.

"In 1946 Shmuel and I met. His Palmach squadron was building a new settlement in the Galilee called Ramot Naftali. They had to plant trees and build houses. In order for the men to have money to buy food, they were sent out to work on other moshavim. Shmuel came to work in Kfar Yehoshua. I was a student and he was a construction worker building the community center that was opposite the school. I used to watch him and he used to see me from the window. That's how the romance started, but it was cut short in August 1948 because Shmuel's squadron was sent to the Negev to fight against the Egyptians. There were so few Palmach soldiers and Shmuel's unit would be transferred to areas that most needed them. At one point the Negev was cut off from the north and Shmuel had to return by airplane.

"In 1947, when I was in eleventh grade, the relationship between the Arabs and Jews was very tense. A war was about to break out between them and Jerusalem was under Arab siege. Many of my older friends from Kfar Yehoshua joined the Palmach then. I, along with a girlfriend, also wanted to serve with them. I did not finish school. I said good-bye to my parents and told them that I was joining the Palmach. They said nothing but, 'Okay, okay. We understand.' There was a system for joining the Palmach: a friend brings a friend. There were no recruiting offices like there are today. A very nice friend of mine told his commander that he brought two girls from Kfar Yehoshua. That was enough to get us in. The Arabs were attacking Jewish settlements all over Palestine. My girlfriend and I were assigned work at a temporary camp set up in an orchard not too far from Tulkarem. The Palmach had to stop the Arab assault near us and my girlfriend and I were assigned to help out in the kitchen. We were to serve an evening meal to forty soldiers who were scheduled to return from the military operation. When nighttime arrived instead of a group of forty, a group of 200 to 250 soldiers arrived. The assault had been very intense and more army troops were brought in. They were hungry and tired. We thought, 'What are we to do? What can we give them to eat?' The salad, the eggs, the coffee that had been prepared were not enough. It was very sad. I said to my friend, 'Give me the sack with the carrots and the sack with the cabbage. We'll put it all in the dining hall and everyone will take straight out of the sacks. So what if they don't drink coffee. They'll drink water.' That was it, very primitive.

"After a while, my girlfriend and I took a course on a wireless two-way communication system. It was similar to walkie-talkies, but much larger and primitive. We'd sit near a huge machine and talk. At first I learned codes so that I could talk and listen to the person on the other end. Then I learned Morse code, which was used when the system became more sophisticated. From the other side they'd say, 'Hello, hello!' and then provide a message for a commander which we would then relay. Just as we finished the course we were sent in a convoy to regimental headquarters near Jerusalem. We took the convoy at night because that gave us the best chance of not getting hit by mortar shells or gunfire. You couldn't get into Jerusalem because it was under siege. There was no food there, no water. How did we travel? We lay on top of sacks of flour and sugar that were on the trucks of the convoy. We were terrified to go through Sha'ar ha-Gai, a point on the road that was very narrow and vulnerable to attacks by Arabs. The Arabs sat on the hills above and among the large forests of pine trees and shot at the convoys. We were very lucky because there was no shooting when we passed through. We arrived at regimental headquarters, which was a resort called Bet Pfefferman between Ma'aleh ha-Hamishah and Kibbutz Kiryat Anavim not too far from Jerusalem. The food went on to help the starving people of Jerusalem. The resort was brand new and had been built by the management of the Dead Sea potash factory. The management wanted a place for its workers to vacation. Everything was ready – the bedding, the kitchen – what a luxury! And then the war broke out. Very quickly the building deteriorated. The Arabs occupied a hill called Radar Hill, which today is called Har Adar. This had been a British radar installation and when the British left at the end of the Mandate, they turned the area over to the Arabs. It overlooked the resort. Every day, boom, boom. We didn't have artillery, but the Arabs did and so, of course, the building was full of holes.

"My job at the regimental headquarters was to work the wireless communication system. My commanding officer was Yitzhak Rabin. He never called me by my rank. He would stand behind me as I received incoming communication and say, '*Nu*, Orna? *Nu*? *Nu*?' which meant, 'So, Orna, what's happening?' He was a very warm person.

"During the summer of 1995, before Rabin was assassinated, he came to Kfar Yehoshua's clubhouse to speak. Besides the local residents, members of our Palmach unit, the Harel Brigade, came to listen. After the speech we reminisced with him. Rabin made sure to maintain a relationship with his former soldiers."

Orna's contributions to the Palmach were similar to the roles young women have today in the Israel Defense Forces. She said, "Then, girls were not in fighting units. We were in communications and other non-combatant jobs. There was no equality between the sexes. Today this is slowly changing. There is more legitimacy for women to serve in fighting units or to fly as air force pilots.

"There was one incident that made me feel very fortunate. I was given a few days off during my service with the Palmach and I had a chance to get a lift to visit my aunt who lived in Bet ha-Kerem, a Jerusalem neighborhood. When I returned to headquarters there was a large artillery shell on my bed that hadn't exploded. When I saw it I was rather pleased it had not detonated. Then I noticed all the holes in the walls from other explosions and I realized that bomb didn't really have my name on it. It wasn't launched with the intent of killing Orna. Today the terrorist attacks are more traumatic for the victims. It is different than during our War of Independence. I didn't take that unexploded bomb personally. No one took these things seriously then.

"Earlier I mentioned that Jerusalem had very little water. During my visit with my aunt in Bet ha-Kerem I said to her, 'Aunt Rivka, I'm so dirty. Maybe I can take a shower?' She said, 'Oy, I'm so sorry, Orna, but there's only a little bit of water left. We're not washing up.' The people of besieged Jerusalem had a system for using and reusing the same water. First the water was used for cooking, then for washing the dishes. After that, to wash the floor and then it was used to flush the toilet. I felt so terrible for asking that I said, 'Oh no. I don't want a shower. Oh, no, no!' A week later I went to see my aunt again and she said, 'Oh, Orna, what a pity. Last night a shell exploded on the water tank and all the water is gone.' The city workers used to distribute water in small tanks on little horse drawn wagons. A long line of people used to go out to fill pots or pails, but there was never enough water.

"During this entire time I didn't know where Shmuel was. We didn't see each other the whole duration of the war. We couldn't contact our parents. There were no telephones and we didn't have mail service because the route to Jerusalem was cut off. One day we said that we have to do something to relieve our parents' worry. But how? Through the Voice of Jerusalem, an underground radio station in Jerusalem, we sent our message. We said, 'All the soldiers from Kfar Yehoshua who are stationed in Jerusalem send their best to their parents.'"

After the War of Independence, Orna waited for Shmuel. She did not know that he had suffered a head wound when a mortar shell exploded during a battle in the Negev. "He has a metal plate in his head," Orna continued. "One soldier was killed next to him and another wounded."

Shmuel recovered. After the war Orna was discharged, but not Shmuel.

By 1950 he had had enough. He said, "After the war people were discharged according to a number of criteria. First were married people and then those who were old. Next were the simple soldiers. I was a sergeant major and was told that I couldn't go home and that I was going to be sent to an officers' training course. I wanted to marry Orna and start a farm, and I knew that if I went through officers' training I would not be discharged. I told my superiors, 'No, I have headaches from my injury and can't go through officers' training.' For eight years I hadn't done anything for myself. I had done things only for the nation. We finally were married in 1950." Orna beamed and added, "We have one son, three daughters, and eight grandchildren."

Orna explained how modern conveniences ease the trauma of terrorism today compared to the stressful war times when she was in the Palmach. "The effect on families during the War of Independence and now during the fight against terrorism is different. Back in 1948 parents, wives, and other family members and friends didn't know what was happening to their loved ones. There were no telephones. Neither Shmuel's parents nor I were informed that Shmuel was wounded. No one knew where anyone was fighting or serving. Sometimes it would take two months for relatives to be informed of a soldier's death. Today it is quite different. Everyone has a cell phone. It's come to the point where the army has had to issue orders preventing soldiers from calling home from sensitive military areas. The enemy has tracking devices that can locate IDF positions from cell phones in use. Once, I called up my grandson who is an IDF soldier. I'm not sure where he was when I reached him, but he said, 'Grandma, it's not really convenient for me to speak with you right now. I have to hang up.' I never did find out where he was when I called."

Orna and Shmuel's past experiences have influenced their perceptions of terrorism in Israel today. "There is no quiet, no tranquility," Orna said. "But we lived through many anti-Jewish riots, wave after wave, and we'll live through this too." Shmuel is not so optimistic. "It hurts to say," he said, "but we might yet miss the terrorism of explosive belts and bombs! We may have chemical and biological weapons thrown at us. I don't think there will be peace or a solution for a long, long time. It's not enough for Israel to want peace. Israelis must also decide how they want to see the country's future borders and present this to the Palestinians. With twenty-five political parties in the Knesset, I don't see us coming to an easy consensus. We are a wagon stuck in the mud with all sorts of groups pulling the wagon this way and that according to their own agendas. I believe most of Israel's problems began after the 1967 Six-Day War when the West Bank and Gaza Strip were taken. We should never have held onto the land. I have a niece and nephew who live in the West Bank and I have never visited them in their homes because of ideological reasons."

Both Shmuel and Orna have lived through incredibly hard times. According to Orna, life's message is: "This is the fate of the Jews and there is nothing you can do about it." Shmuel disagrees: "People were born with evil. They don't acquire it. Because of this there is a need for education and culture from birth on. A person has to learn how to live in a society and how to adapt. If he doesn't become educated and remains as he is, he becomes a barbarian, a scoundrel, a murderer, or a robber. A person has to undergo training and work according to his abilities to make a living and take care of his family. He should not be dependent on charity. I hear people say, there is luck, there is no luck. There is fate, there isn't fate. I don't believe in either luck or fate. Everything in life is by coincidence."

* * *

Hope. With little else to hold on to, Marion and Daniel (Danny) Nachshon rebuilt their shattered lives in Palestine. Both escaped Hitler's hell in 1939, Marion to Scotland and Daniel to Palestine. Marion's delayed journey to the Jewish homeland finally took place in 1948. A few years later Danny and Marion met, fell in love, and married. Both spirited young adults understood loss, courage, and what they called Lady Luck. Luck or a miracle. They are survivors of a past terror, an era of hate and anti-Semitism they never expected to see again. Today they believe that Hitler's hate is reincarnated in Yasser Arafat and Muslim extremists who want nothing less than to destroy Israel and wipe Jews from the face of this earth. Negotiations, peace talks – to Marion and Danny they're just politics as usual. They believe that what matters is not what Arafat says to the Western world, but to his own people. In those words they hear a message of hate and destruction.

A spectacular sweep of bright orange, yellow, purple, and pink filled the evening sky. The air bit with a spring chill. The Bedouin village of Bet Zarzir lay below, where narrow minarets reached above the housetops. Weaving along several descending streets in Timrat, I arrived at the Nachshons'. Their sloped landscape, dotted with meticulous green bushes and trees, led to a beautiful stone entrance and an inviting dark wooden door.

"Come in, come in. Welcome, welcome." Marion whisked me into their comfortable, warm, informal living room, where Danny was waiting. Accumulated knickknacks, books, and plants filled the immaculate room. "Are you hungry, thirsty?" "I'm fine," I said. But like many grandmothers, Marion was prepared. "No? I'll just get some cake and tea." A huge smile warmed her sweet face. Marion returned with freshly baked chocolate cake and steaming dark tea.

Danny's story unfolded like a precious chest of family mementos, revealing the joyous and the heartbreaking memories. Burned in his mind is Friday, September 1, 1939 – the day the Nazis invaded Poland. For fourteen-year-old Danny life would never be the same. Worry and despair filled his parents' quiet conversations. "Many parents thought that Hitler was a figure who would fade away very quickly," he said. "He was a painter, a nothing. They lived with hope that this was something that would pass. But the writing was on the wall. There had been speeches. In 1928, when Hitler was in prison, he said what he was going to do. It's just like Arafat."

Danny's parents recognized that Hitler's power and influence were deepening, his European dominance was growing, and anti-Semitism was booming with electric force. Should they leave Germany? Where should they go? Six of their twelve children had already emigrated, some to Palestine and some to Australia. In the end, Palestine became their only option. Australia had all but closed its doors to Jewish immigration. Having obtained all the necessary legal documents, German passports, and British immigration certificates for Palestine, Danny and his parents journeyed by train to Trieste, Italy, where they boarded a passenger boat headed for Palestine. Left behind were Danny's three married brothers, a married sister, and their families. There were no last-minute tearful goodbyes. The curfew for Jews began at 8:00 P.M. and the older Nachshon children could not risk being caught at the train station. On November 22, 1939 Danny and his parents docked in Haifa's port.

Kfar Hasidim, a religious community ten minutes from Haifa, became the Nachshon family's new home. Danny's strong build and eagerness to contribute to the household led to a blacksmith apprenticeship and eventually a position in the British army during World War II, serving with the Royal Engineers in Holland and Italy. His simple life was tough, but good. Not so, however, for his siblings who remained in Germany. Each one perished. "My sister and her two little sons fled to Riga, Latvia. In Riga there was a massacre and they were killed."

Like Danny, Marion was fourteen years old when she escaped Nazi Germany in 1939. "I always tell my children they should be glad they are here. During the summers my non-Jewish neighbors would throw stones at me. During the winters they would pack the stone with snow and then it would hurt twice as much." Marion's mother "had seen the light" and decided that her two daughters needed to get out of Germany immediately. Marion's two older siblings already lived in Palestine.

Marion continued, "My mother saw the urgency in the situation. She was a courageous woman. We didn't have a car and she did all the running around to the authorities to get papers. They made it difficult for her. She was alone and she had problems with her legs." Passage was secured for Marion and her sister on the Kindertransport to England, set up to save Jewish children.[52] With a tearful goodbye, it was the last time she saw her parents. Marion's mother refused to leave her husband who was near death. He died of natural causes in Germany and soon after her mother was transported to the Auschwitz concentration camp. She was murdered there in 1941.

"I stayed in Britain from 1939 to 1947," she recalled, "during which I lived in Glasgow, Scotland, for five years. In 1948 I came to Palestine." In Britain Marion lived in a place that prepared her for life on a kibbutz. "Our kibbutz group left England illegally.[53] First we traveled to Belgium and then to France. We did all this with forged papers. In Marseilles, France, we went to a camp where we received new identities again. It was all arranged. There were many refugees from all over and from the concentration camps. It was a huge camp. We had to wait there about a week for our new papers so that we could immigrate legally to Palestine. At that time there was a British Mandate in Palestine and they didn't want to let us in. Many ships with illegal immigrants were intercepted by the British and sent to Cyprus or searched in Haifa. We came with forged English papers to Palestine. The night before we arrived in Palestine I couldn't sleep. I had a stomachache. I was nervous because I knew what was awaiting me. They could send us back. Many of my good friends who arrived in Israel a little bit before us were caught by the British and sent to an internment camp in Cyprus. My best friend was in Cyprus for a year. The British sent them back cruelly. Many people died. All through that night it was bothering me that I was being dishonest. There were British on the ship, non-Jews, who were bribed by the Jewish Agency.[54] They looked and looked – and even though the British knew exactly what was going on, they let us in and probably got a lot of money."

What the Nachshons endured seems incomprehensible. Marion disagrees, "No, no. We were the lucky ones. Believe me, we were the lucky ones who got out. The others had a terrible, terrible destiny. I married, I have children and grandchildren and a lot of *nachas*, 'joy.' You see? The others – nothing." The Nachshons have four sons: Shmuel, Yossi, Yaron, and Benny; and a daughter, Nava.

Our discussion turned to anti-Semitism and terror today, and Danny's mood changed from pensive to angry. "Arab demonstrations against Israel and the u.s. are all over Europe now. We see them in Germany, France, and Holland. A friend came back from Amsterdam and told me that there was a demonstration where Muslim children wore fake explosive belts. People watching it just stood there. It's like saying 'Amen' to a prayer; as sure as that. Everything terrorists do here will eventually reach Europe – the belts and the bomb explosions. The first time an El Al airplane was hijacked, people – anti-Semites – said, 'Big deal, El Al. It's only the Jews.' Later on it wasn't only the Jews: hijackings took place all over. It's the same as today. Terror was here in Israel and then it struck the World Trade Center. I watched it on tv. Dear God, what a thing! And now we are experiencing explosive belts. In World War ii we had the Japanese kamikaze, but their attacks were not against civilians. Here, civilians driving a car are shot just traveling along a road in Jerusalem or to Haifa, they are blown to bits in a restaurant, or young girls are murdered in a discotheque. Terrorists with belts of explosives! And then we are the accused because we decide to defend ourselves!"

World opinion. The un. Journalists. These words infuriate Danny. He believes that the world has a double standard: one for Israel and one for everyone else. Misinformation in the media, gullibility of uninformed individuals, and the Arab world's demonization of Israel are what he believes are just a few of Israel's pr problems. "Oil is a very powerful commodity and that is why the Arabs have such an influence over world opinion against Israel. Israel is the victim, but we are the accused!" he bemoaned. "Kofi Annan, the Secretary-General of the un, set up a fact-finding mission to uncover 'atrocities' Israel supposedly committed during the fighting in Jenin."[55] But the UN's Terje Roed-Larson never found the 'atrocities.' He never found the bodies of hundreds of massacred Palestinians because it never happened. Israeli soldiers were killed in Jenin because they didn't want to touch civilians! There was a massacre of our soldiers!" Frustrated and upset, Danny continued, "Do you remember when the Palestinian mob lynched those two poor soldiers who had made a wrong turn into their village?[56] The murderers put their hands in the soldiers' blood, tossed their bodies out the window to the frenzied crowd, and shouted, 'Allah is great!'"

Danny shook his head, and a mixture of anger and disbelief crossed his face. "Terrorism tears you up everyday. You may be occupied by work, but you are going nuts and you can't do anything about it. I bought a copy of the Koran. It was important to me to go to the source to understand Islam. According to the Koran, there are believers and nonbelievers. But this belief goes further and it basically means either you're with us or against us. The Koran tells believers they must respond to the danger posed by the infidel. Even if they are not sure there is a real threat to Muslims and Islam, they must respond. Jews and Christians are considered nonbelievers. They want the Jews out of here. Even if we achieve some kind of agreement with the Palestinians, we are still not a part of the Islamic world that totally surrounds us here in the Middle East. The Muslims want Islamic rule here too. I believe this reflects how most Palestinian Muslims feel. It is a very difficult situation."

Terrorism outside of Israel against Jews worries Danny. He does not believe the Jewish people in the Diaspora are taking it seriously enough. "I do not feel there will be another Holocaust. But synagogues are being blown up, Jewish cemeteries are being desecrated, and Jews are being beaten up, especially in France and Turkey. It isn't the Europeans making the pogroms, but Muslims living in these countries."

Danny wishes Israel could fight terrorism in the all-out way the United States fights it. "But beggars can't be choosers," he said. "We rely on the U.S. for financial support. We have to do what the U.S. government wants us to do. We can't fight the way the U.S. does because we are weak in comparison to them. We are a small country."

Despite all they have endured, Marion and Danny do not dwell on their sad stories of the past or the terror around them. They are grateful for their blessings. With a sparkling smile, Marion said, "I'll tell you what. Live the day. Don't think further."

"We are learning all the time," Danny added. "That's it."

Sadly, Marion Nachshon passed away on November 26, 2003. The photograph taken at their interview became a special memento for the entire family. It was the last picture taken of Danny and Marion together.

Ari Haim

Orly Hadad

Shahar Argaman

Effy Glick

Chapter Six
In the Line of Fire: Military Life

Each year tens of thousands of young Israeli teens prepare for the Israel Defense Forces. Ari Haim,* nineteen, is one of them. Conscripted to the IDF in March 2002, Ari joined a paratrooper unit. We talked at his parents' home in Timrat, a hilltop, middle-class, mostly secular community of 320 families. Timrat sits in the middle of the Jezreel Valley, between Haifa and Nazareth. Along with its spectacular views of the cotton and corn farmland below, and the oak and pine trees that dot the hillside, on a clear day this community offers panoramic vistas of the Hermon Mountains in the Golan Heights, Bedouin villages, Haifa, Migdal ha-Emek, and Nazareth. Though Timrat is not quite the top of the world, the magnificent, austere beauty of the surrounding countryside and blazing sunsets are true assets for its residents. A liftgate and paid community guard provide minimal protection at the top of the only road that twists and climbs around the steep hill to the community's entrance. The sharp hair-raising curves have no protective guardrails. A terrorist in a vehicle could easily crash through the community's pseudo-barrier and proceed with minimal interference.

Ari and I talked in the family office – a converted garage with two desks, white laminate bookshelves filled with manuals and books, a computer, printer, fax machine, phones, television, and small bathroom attached. Some might say that Ari is a Jim Carey look-alike with a sense of humor to match. Tall, thin, but muscular, he walks with a noticeable limp. During the first week of basic training, in full gear, he had sprained his ankle while assisting three other soldiers haul a stretcher laden with heavy sandbags up a steep hill. At our interview he wore his olive green army uniform, consisting of a long-sleeved, button-down shirt, matching pants, and rugged boots. His burgundy paratrooper beret rested on his left shoulder, secured in place by an epaulet. His M-16 was slung across his shoulder, typical of many soldiers you see on Israeli streets.

Ari chose the paratroopers because the unit is known for the diverse background of its soldiers. For most of his life, Ari had been with students from kibbutzim and moshavim. He wanted to meet teens from all over Israel with different ideas and different outlooks.

Mandatory military service in Israel began when the state was first formed in 1948. Today all able 18-year-old Jewish Israeli men and women are drafted. Men serve a minimum of three years, women, two. Ari knew he would be heading to the army after high school graduation, but it was the suicide bombings that solidified his decision to join a combat unit. "I wanted to contribute to the country," he said. "Since the intifada started, most of the teens I know changed their feelings about going into the army. Kids started saying, 'I want to be a soldier. I want to be on the front.' A lot of people know someone who was killed by a terrorist. I'm going to put my life on the line to stop what is going on here. I have the power to stop these terrorists, to be able to protect my family and my people. It's a way of taking a load off my heart."

Before joining the army, Ari went through an extensive medical checkup and numerous routine physical, psychological, and academic exams. The test scores are combined to form a personal profile. Ari received a high score, which opened many respected military opportunities for him. After volunteering for a paratroop unit, Ari's date of conscription was announced, March 15, 2002. Like many soon-to-be soldiers, he went abroad for a holiday, the last fling of freedom before giving three years to the Israeli Defense Forces.

"The months before entrance into the army are nerve-racking," Ari said. "A lot of kids want to join the army and give something back to the country, but you're scared. Are you going to be the one to get injured? Are you going to be the person who dies? I was thinking, 'I am going into the paratroops. We're the guys who go into all the cities and do a lot of the fighting, and I might be the guy who gets the bullet.' It's hard to live with that. It's hard to think that you might be the guy. You think about how you have lived your life. You look back and ask yourself, 'Have I done everything that I wanted to do? Because I might die. Am I okay with my decisions?' I don't know if everyone has sat down and thought about these things, but I have. I have done the things I wanted to do, and I have thought about what I want to do after the army. I also thought about whether or not I was willing to give it all up to save my family, this country. Like me, a lot of kids come to the decision, 'Yes.' But we're still scared. Sometimes you start to shake all over.

"One of the first things you think about when you join the army is how is your mother is going to sleep at night, knowing that her son is out there. And you get that talk, at least I did from my father, that you have an influence on what is going on in the country and that you can make a difference. This is an important thing to hear. My sisters say, 'Take care of yourself. Don't do anything that's too dangerous or too crazy. Don't try to be a hero.' In the end we are all heroes for protecting our homeland. He may not get a medal for it, but in his family's eyes he's a hero."

For many young men and women the fear dissipates once they are armed with constructive information and skill. Draftees are taught to use a weapon only for self-defense – "one of the most important things they teach you in the army," according to Ari. Draftees also learn what to do if someone suspicious approaches them. "First you have to warn him by shooting in the air. If you believe he is about to attack you or he has a weapon and does not stop with the warning shot, then you can shoot him only in the legs. If he runs toward you with a weapon or shoots at you, then you can kill him. If you kill someone who wasn't trying to kill you, then the army is going to put you on trial. A weapon is power. You have the power to take someone's life and you have to use it wisely, and only when you absolutely have to. We can and must differentiate between regular Palestinians and terrorists, between the innocent who want a peaceful coexistence with us and those who want to destroy Israel. There are small Palestinian kids who are innocent, but their parents tell them to throw stones. These kids don't have the ability to differentiate between what is wrong and right. You're told as a soldier, don't point your weapon at children or at women. Men with guns: point it at them."

Army life requires tough physical and emotional adjustment for these young soldiers. Everything is new, tension is high, and in a short period of time they must change their thinking from *self* to *group*. "There is a lot of pressure," Ari said. "You meet a lot of new people. You have to become their best friend and trust them on everything, because when you're in a war situation you need your buddies to watch your back. You must accept people for who they are and you must remember that you're not perfect. It's an important lesson for the rest of your life, especially in the paratroops."

Hearing this, I was curious to find out how Ari and his unit relieve stress. "We sing, even though a lot of the guys can't carry a tune," was his unexpected answer. A smile shot across his face for a moment. "You use someone else's words to express how you're feeling, and if we're not singing, we're listening to music. Music can be calming and make you feel better." Every day his unit sings "Hatikvah," the Israeli national anthem. The song unifies the soldiers and expresses the hope of freedom for the Jewish people in Zion.

Another stress reliever and social activity is smoking. Though Ari does not smoke, many of his tent mates do. He sees it as a form of group therapy. "No one smokes alone. Someone will say, 'I'm going for a cigarette, anyone want to come with me?' As they smoke they'll talk, give each other support, and take a break from reality for a moment." Support seems to be critical for a draftee's survival. Ari explained, "When a fellow soldier says, 'Come on, you can do it,' it is not just a reminder for you; he's telling himself that he can do the run and fifty push-ups too."

The cell phone is an essential stress-relieving tool for every soldier. Ari knows many people, including himself, who have spent half the night talking with someone who isn't in the army. Some cell phone companies offer free phones to draftees with limited free airtime to any two designated numbers. Soldiers often carry at least one additional cell phone for better rates and calling flexibility. Though communication with the outside world is essential for many soldiers' mental health, positive self-talk and muscle flexing are critical to survival in fighting a war. According to Ari, soldiers will build themselves up by acting macho. "They'll say, 'I am not afraid,' when they are. But talking and being bold makes you feel stronger and if you believe it then you feel that you can control your life."

While talk is crucial to release stress, it also builds camaraderie and brotherhood. "You do practically everything with your tent mates," said Ari. "You're on the line with each other, covering each other's backs. It's emotional. You see them in situations of panic and fear, and you see them break in front of your eyes, even start crying. Somehow you connect with them much faster and in the end, you feel for them like brothers."

On May 6, 2002, I witnessed Ari Haim's induction into the paratroops. The ceremony took place after a spectacular sunset at the holiest site in Israel, the Western Wall in Jerusalem. The air pulsed with excited energy as parents, grandparents, brothers, sisters, and friends stood with cameras and video equipment, and jockeyed for positions to see their special paratroopers. Before the ceremony, units spontaneously sang patriotic songs such as "Jerusalem of Gold" and "Hatikvah" – some with arms around one another. Flags rippled in the occasional breeze, top brass spoke, and a band played rousing tunes. Each new paratrooper received an M-16 and a bible. With the ceremony complete, the young men found their families. Some walked over to the Wall to offer a personal prayer. Paratroopers introduced their new "brothers" to family and friends, hugged, and wished them a good night.

We left the square by the Wall and climbed the broad, smooth stone steps leading to the Jewish Quarter of the Old City of Jerusalem. We reached a wide plateau with a stone balcony overlooking the Wall. It led to another set of worn steps. There, a lanky, tanned soldier with his M-16 casually slung over his shoulder called out in Hebrew. "How was it, soldier?" They walked up to each other and began to speak. The soldier reached up and straightened the beret on Ari's head. They talked, smiled, and departed with a handshake. "What was that about?" I asked Ari. "Do you know him?"

The soldier was a paratrooper "watching the line" – on active duty and scanning for possible terrorists. He had noticed Ari's crooked beret and offered to fix it – a big brother looking out for a younger brother. "As a new paratrooper, you have a certain respect for this guy, because he is already fighting in the line," Ari said. "It's like a big family: the guys before you and the guys that come after you. Everyone takes care of each other because in the end you have to depend on one another. My unit has been in the army for only two months. We hardly know anything, so I was grateful for his help.

"The paratroopers were the ones who actually freed the Old City of Jerusalem during the Six-Day War in 1967. As I was walking to the Kotel [the Wall], I wondered what those paratroopers felt when they walked into the Old City for the first time, and when they reached the Kotel after years of Jews' not being allowed there. It touched me. When I walked toward the Kotel before my induction ceremony, I saw Jews praying, including many soldiers. You look at each other and though you don't speak, you feel close, just listening and praying. There's some sort of bond that you're a part of. I said to myself, 'I am willing to go to the army for this.'"

In Ari's nineteen years, he has learned valuable lessons from the constant conflict. "I've learned to cope with problems by stepping back and looking at them from different angles. If that doesn't help, then you should try to figure out what led up to a problem. You can't always resolve it by yourself, so you discuss it with other people. Others have had the same problem, no matter what you think. There are always other people who have gone through something similar and may have different ways of dealing with it. Asking for help isn't a bad thing.

"A lot of who you are is what life has taught you to be. After September 11, some Palestinians were in the streets celebrating the deaths of thousands of people. It's insanity and you can't believe that people could be so heartless. It's hard to see such people dancing in the streets, the adults giving children candy, and burning American and Israeli flags. You start to think about who and what you are up against. It's hard to imagine that parents would endanger their children's lives by encouraging them to throw rocks at soldiers and tanks. Aren't parents supposed to protect their children? We are not going to harm children who throw stones, but rocks can be deadly. I have a friend who is in the army and he nearly lost an eye when a ten-year-old threw a rock at him. If this is what Palestinian children are taught to do, can we make peace with these people?

"Because Israeli kids live with war, with the constant need to survive, we learn how to cope with our problems by standing up for ourselves. When you're eighteen or nineteen and in the army, you are faced with life-and-death situations. You learn how to deal with life – the big problems and the small ones – much faster than regular kids. But we are also taught that you don't go out and kill everyone just because you're hurting inside. It is because of this hurt that people want to go to the army – to stop the terror."

                                    *   *   *

Sadly, military service is as much a part of Israeli life as going to school. It influences relationships between husbands and wives, parents and children, employers and employees. Children and wives often are left alone as the men go off to train or fight. For some this tension could be detrimental, but not for Orly Hadad, who maintains a positive attitude despite many difficulties. At thirty-seven, Hadad is a mother of three, ranging in age from five to thirteen, with another on the way. Married to a career army officer, for the last fifteen years she has built an independent life. Orly is a *sabra*, born to parents who emigrated from Tunisia. Her father came to Israel alone in 1949 at the age of thirteen, through a youth aliyah program organized by the Jewish Agency. His parents did not stop him from going to Israel, but he had to change his birth date on his documents to enter. Only children aged seventeen and older were permitted into the country without a parent. He came with very little money and few possessions and lived on a kibbutz near Safed. Today, such actions seem inconceivable, but Orly explained her father's situation. "Two things happened to the Jews of Tunisia and of North Africa between 1945 and 1950. First, French colonialism in Tunisia was weakened after World War II. Second, there was an awakening of Arab nationalism. Everything changed there. The world itself changed. The encouragement from the Zionist movement's representatives who visited Tunisia and the increasing Arab nationalism together pushed the Jews to leave. Whoever didn't go to Israel went to France. Very few Jews stayed. You have to understand that a boy of thirteen or fourteen in 1949 was not the same as a boy of thirteen or fourteen today. He was no longer a child, but was already part of the workforce. In a poor family, and in his case being the oldest child and the first son, my father had to go out to work. He was already independent before he left for Israel."

Orly spoke quietly, sometimes pausing to think about her answers. Her dark, wavy, shoulder-length hair frames her olive-skinned oval face. In addition to parenting, she works for a health services company managing sales projects. Sitting at her dark wooden dining room table and drinking mint tea, she talked about her life. "I grew up in Afula. Palestinian terrorists and the same PLO run by Arafat as today were part of our childhood. They would go house by house, shooting Jewish families until someone would kill them. They could finish off an entire building by the time the army arrived. It happened in Bet Shean, which isn't too far from Afula. It happened in Kiryat Shmona. It happened in Ma'alot to an entire school group on a field trip. The terrorists went into the Ma'alot school where students from Safed were sleeping and they took them hostage.[57] This is what it was like when I was growing up.

"A girlfriend and I, when we were children, imagined and planned what we would do if terrorists entered our home at night. Where would we go? What would we do? We let our imaginations run wild. We talked about running from our beds to get a knife from the kitchen. Sometimes we thought about hiding under our beds and sometimes running from our rooms to safety. But we never came up with scenarios where we were caught. We were always safe. I thought that I was the only one who did this, but I wasn't. Another girlfriend five years younger grew up in the same atmosphere in the north. So we lived with fear, especially at night. But we got over it and we continued on as usual. This was our reality. There were also bombs. I remember many explosions at the Afula open market. When I was a student in Afula twenty-five years ago, I would sometimes skip school. My girlfriends and I wanted to walk around and the police would stop everyone. They would tell us not to go to a certain street. We would hear the bomb being exploded. Then it was over and we continued on. These are the only things that overshadowed my lovely and good childhood."

The fears of Orly's past are not much different than those experienced by Israelis today. Since she has lived with the fear of terror all her life, she is able to offer understanding. For her close friend, Sarah,* the trauma of terror caused a breakdown. "Sarah has three small children, the eldest is six or seven," Orly said. "She lives in Moshav Aviezer, near Jerusalem. She completely broke down for two reasons. First, Sarah's close friends, Gadi and Tzipi Shemesh, were killed in a terrorist attack in Jerusalem. Tzipi had gone for a prenatal ultrasound. Later that day they were killed in an attack on King George Street.[58] This was very difficult for Sarah because Gadi and Tzipi's orphaned daughters are exactly her own daughters' ages. The second reason for the breakdown was an attempted terrorist infiltration one evening into their moshav. Sarah, her husband, and their daughters went into their sealed protective room, similar to a bomb shelter, to hide. They could hear shots being fired and the Israeli army chasing the terrorist. The loudspeaker blared, 'Stay in your houses, turn off your lights.' Obviously this was for everyone's safety. Sarah and her family waited for the moment when the terrorist would enter their home. There was real fear. In the end they were safe. Israeli army personnel captured the terrorist. But this nightmare left Sarah traumatized."

Sarah later e-mailed Orly and said that if it were up to her, she would pick up and move to Canada. "She doesn't want her children to be orphans. She won't leave them alone. If they get killed, they all get killed together. I started to encourage her and to tell her that we have all gone through something. I also told her that there's no chance it would be better for her in any other country. There is no other place for the children, and that even if the children were to be orphaned, they would continue with their lives. They are the future, not us. That calmed her down. She's okay now. When you continue to live each day and see your family, when you go to work and come back from work, you go back to your regular routine."

Routine is one way that Orly takes care of her family while her husband serves in Gaza. But even with routine, their life is not easy. "It is difficult," Orly said. "There are assignments that require my husband to be away for long periods of time. He has been in Gaza for seven consecutive years. For three of those years there was no war, but there were terrorist attacks against soldiers and Jewish settlers. We didn't feel it here [inside the Green Line], not like now. But it was a difficult period for me because everyone else was going on with their lives and I was sitting next to the radio."

She speaks with Yossi on the phone before he goes to sleep; usually between 1:00 and 2:00 A.M., because that is the only time he has free. She does not discuss her issues, such as a broken dishwasher, because they seem trivial in comparison to his life-and-death work. After a minor crisis is resolved, she will provide a matter-of-fact account for him. Sometimes Yossi asks her for advice, and she gives it willingly.

But the army life is most stressful for the Hadad children, and is eased only a bit by their father's long, cherished weekends at home. "He would usually come home on a Thursday and leave early Sunday morning," Orly said. "But because of the intifada, sometimes he doesn't even come home on Shabbat. Then the problems begin. The children will say, 'Daddy is supposed to come! Why isn't Daddy here?' When he does come home, he is exhausted. On Shabbat he wants to recite kiddush.[59] A little later, without meaning to, he falls asleep and doesn't wake up until 11:00 or 12:00 the next day. Then we just hang out as a family until he has to leave."

Orly feels more than capable of handling things herself, and has made her accommodation to a trying situation. "I want life in this house to be like any other home. I live normally. I have to do all the shopping and taking care of the children, to help them prepare for tests, and also to work. When there are school trips, I go and when there are parent-teacher meetings, I go. I have to do everything. But I don't ask for anything from anyone."

How does this arrangement work within the frame of marriage? Orly responded, "Yossi's my best friend. When something is really bothering me, he's the one who will hear about it. And when something is bothering him, I know that I'm the one to hear about it. I love him. I don't need anything else. We have an agreement. If something happens in his area of Gaza, he calls me before it is broadcast, he tells me that everything is all right, and then says goodbye. That is enough."

There was one intense incident in 1996, however, when she did not hear from Yossi. Orly was eight months pregnant with their third child when her husband's best friend, Nabi, a Druze unit commander who worked with Yossi, was killed. Suddenly, Orly began receiving phone calls from army personnel, including a brigadier general, asking her if she knew where Yossi was. They asked her, "You didn't hear anything? He didn't call you?" By the third call, she was distraught and pleaded for information. "I did not want to understand – and I usually grasp things quickly. That was the first time I was actually afraid for him. My way of coping was to shut everything out. As long as there was no news, the case was closed."

Nearly an hour passed before she finally heard from Yossi. A bullet had hit his boot, but he was not wounded. He was at a coordinating post on the border between Gaza and Egypt. Yossi and his men were surrounded, completely cut off. All night terrorists were shooting at them. Orly could hear the sharp spurts of gunfire over the telephone. Calmly, Yossi asked to speak with each of the children separately. He told them that he loved them. Terrified, Orly took action. "For the first time ever, I called up Army Operations," she said. "It wasn't an official call. It was out of desperation and I think that I was more emotional because I was pregnant. I just wanted someone to put my mind at ease that Yossi would be okay. I spoke with an officer and told him, 'Get Yossi out of there now!' He said that they couldn't get him out. But he promised that the moment Yossi and the other men were safe he would contact me. I didn't sleep at all that night." The next day, the army was able to send in reinforcements and bring the men to safety.

*   *   *

Although it's easy to conjure up the negative aspects of army life, like a husband's absence from his family's daily activities, for many men and women service provides powerful and positive experiences. This certainly is the case for Captain Shahar Argaman of the army reserves. When I met with Shahar, thirty-five, at his workplace in a high tech company in the

Jezreel Valley, security was tight. After passing through the guarded entrance, I left my passport at the front desk and waited in the open, comfortably appointed lobby. An exercise facility was visible from the modular couches centered in the reception area for waiting guests. Shahar exited one of the stainless steel door elevators and escorted me to his office, a room semi-enclosed with glass. He sat behind his desk filled with the necessary ensemble of business equipment. Built like a linebacker, Shahar smiled and leaned back in his chair. A liter of cola sat near his desk and he offered me a glass. Shahar's army reserve unit, Shaldag, was formed in 1974 and is similar to the u.s. army's Delta Force. They rescue hostages, track down terrorists, and searched for Scud missiles in Iraq.

The army must examine approximately four thousand recruits to find the top thirty men who would be eligible for Shaldag. They must endure the minimum twenty months of arduous physical and mental training, which includes high-tech gadgets and weapons, commando fighting, and survival. Only about twenty or so make it through. Their tour of duty is extended to four years, followed by a yearly minimum of forty-five days of mandatory army service in the reserves, up to age forty-five. (Men over forty-five often volunteer.) Unlike regular army units, Shaldag's service is scattered throughout the year, keeping reservists physically fit and updated on the latest technology. Reservists are also involved in numerous classified missions.

Shahar is married with two young boys. His wife, whose father was killed in the Yom Kippur War, served in a non-combat position for Shaldag, collecting information from different units stationed in and outside of Israel. In March 2002, Shahar's reserve unit was called to serve right before Operation Defensive Shield. The call did not come as a surprise to him or to the group of men under his command. Suicide bombings were occurring almost daily and it was quite obvious to many Israelis that the military had to act. The men had two days of practice before moving out to the West Bank. When Shahar addressed his men, he said, "First, I will not force anybody to be here. If somebody would like to leave, please do so. No hard feelings."

No one left. "I knew," Shahar told me, "that no one would leave, because we had 100 percent participation. They had rearranged everything in their lives to come to serve, including canceling trips abroad and suspending job promotions. The second thing I said was that no matter what, I am sorry to say, I would prefer to come back with a dead Palestinian who we killed by mistake than to come back to one of your wives and have to give an explanation."

This statement disturbed Shahar, but he stood by it. "Look, this is a war," he said, "but before we do things, we think. We are not acting like automatic weapons shooting everything that is moving around." Israeli soldiers must live by a high moral code. Soldiers have been killed because they held their fire after terrorists hid behind women and children. To illustrate this point, Shahar related a story told to him by a good friend in the army, which took place in April 2002. "There was a once-in-a-lifetime chance to kill the leadership of the Tanzim – a terrorist organization funded by Arafat – in Nablus. They were all going to the same house. One of our F-16s could have dropped a one-ton bomb on the house and that would have been it. We would not have to risk a lot of our eighteen-year-old soldiers to chase after them. The decision was made not to drop the bomb because we were thinking about the family that lived in that house. I don't have any second thoughts about what we call in Hebrew *tohar ha-neshek*, 'purity of arms.'" Shahar was referring to the high standard of moral conduct that upholds the need to avoid civilian casualties. Even with *tohar ha-neshek*, how could the IDF pass up the opportunity to kill terrorists who were responsible for the deaths of hundreds of civilians, and who could cause more anguish in the future? Shahar responded, "If you ask me, if these leaders kill innocent Israel citizens and fight against our nation in the future, then, I believe, they should be killed. But on the other hand, the Tanzim leaders in that house are our future neighbors and possible partners in peace. You must never forget that."

I asked Shahar if he had to prepare himself mentally for military service, and he responded that he didn't have to. "Sometimes you have to remind yourself that you're not eighteen years old," he said, "and have a realistic point-of-view of what you are capable of doing. But it goes both ways. We were just half a second from killing a very old Palestinian, and the reason we didn't is that we are experienced soldiers." This incident occurred right before the deployment of the Israel Defense Forces' Operation Defensive Shield at the end of March 2002. Shahar's unit was dispatched on a counter-terror covert mission on a main road approximately five hundred meters from the West Bank Palestinian village of Salem (pronounced "sa-alem"). It is west of Shechem (Hebrew for Nablus), and according to Shahar, "Shechem is the

West Bank capital of terrorist activity. Terrorists would leave the town and shoot at settlers driving by, attack their homes, and plant bombs on roads. The terrorists' system of attack was to wait until early morning before dawn or just after dark when people were not on high alert."

Shahar described his unit's operation. "It was evening, pitch black, and we walked into our assigned area by foot. We were directed by army personnel who were equipped with special heavy-duty optical equipment that can be used during the day or night and who stood three to five kilometers away. The equipment is like powerful binoculars, but it also records on videotape. We were in contact with the army personnel by radio and they were directing us to the terrorists' position. We worked together as one group, controlling the area with optical devices. There were two or three groups of six people in the field, including the commander of the whole operation, an emergency backup force, and a central radio station that assists in the control of the area. Three or four groups of soldiers were at a further distance away.

"The road that we had to reach was situated in the middle of a valley and in a flat wheat field. Salem was on a hill about four or five hundred meters away from there. Because of the proximity of the village to the road, it was very easy for terrorists to run back and forth without being caught. On this particular night, two male teens, around eighteen or nineteen years old, were carrying a thirty-kilo bomb. They walked with the bomb between them, each carrying it with one hand. Periodically they had to stop and switch positions to give each hand a rest. Of course, this was very dangerous, because if they dropped the bomb, it would immediately explode. There were enough explosives to take out a bus. Remember, it is dark and we're trying to find these terrorists without alerting them to our presence. We were in full gear with weapons and night vision goggles. We waited for orders from the commander in the field who would give directions on which way to walk. It's very difficult to try and catch terrorists under such circumstances – imagine the dispatcher describing a location when he's kilometers away. He'll say the terrorist is behind a rock six or seven hundred meters away and you can barely see one hundred meters in front of you in the dark. It's a complicated procedure and you need to be specialists in the field to understand the details involved. The young men put the bomb in a drainage pipe under the road and we started running after them. We shot and killed one of the men and the other escaped into a home in Salem.

"Salem is a village with a high concentration of homes in a small area. Families build right next to each other and it's easy for a terrorist to escape in these surroundings. But the powerful optical equipment at the central station confirmed that the second terrorist had entered a home, so we proceeded to 'close the house.' That is the term we use for surrounding a location and securing the area. At this point everyone in the village knew we were there. They had heard the shots and the exploding of the bomb by the IDF bomb squad unit. We shouted to the family to come out of the house. They fully cooperated and we moved slowly. Everyone was calm, there was no screaming or arguing. This could have been a traumatic situation, but the family had seen us approaching through their windows. I've been in other terrorist operations where we had to enter a home in the middle of the night, babies had to be woken, and it was terrifying for the people. We deal with the oldest male member of the family and we try and give him the utmost respect. We ask if everyone is out of the house and then we enter with the head of the household. He opens doors, turns on lights, shows us around. It is an intense situation. We don't know if the terrorist is hiding behind a door, in a closet, or in a cabinet. In this particular incident the terrorist was no longer in the house and we believe he escaped before we 'closed the house.'"

The procedure of soldiers entering a home with the head of the household is controversial. Shahar explained: "We do not use them as human shields. There was a method used by the IDF where soldiers would order men to go to their neighbor's house where a suspected terrorist was and knock on a door or move items in a yard. Some Palestinians were killed this way because of explosive booby traps planted by terrorists, or they were shot dead by a terrorist hiding in the neighbor's house. This method is no longer permitted. We can ask a neighbor if he would be willing to assist us, but if he refuses we must respect that. But it is absolutely normal procedure to ask for cooperation from the head of the household to escort soldiers through his house. We do not ask women to enter the home."

The next night, surmising that terrorists would try again, Shahar and his unit returned to the same area near Salem. "We were expecting a terrorist to come and put a bomb near the drainage pipe," he said. "Right after dark a man came and sat down on the ground and started digging.

This was very unusual. What was a man doing wandering around in the dark? We started chasing after him and as I was running, I thought, 'This is no typical person you are after. If you're not sure, don't shoot.' I relayed this to my men. After we caught him we saw that he was an old man, very confused. He had been digging for grasses that are used for food and he had sat down to rest. He had walked a long way to another village and was on his way home."

Does Shahar, who exuded confidence and calm, ever experience fear? "I normally don't have fear at all," he answered. "The first time I was worried was when we were searching through that home in Salem. Of course, I went into the house with my soldiers. It was just like in the movies, guns drawn. Suddenly I thought of my two boys. It had no connection to what I was doing because I was in the middle of running with concentrated ability. I said to myself, 'Uh-oh, Shahar, hold your horses! Be very careful what you do here because somebody can open the door and shoot you.'"

Shahar had led his men into this house and through many other dangerous situations. I asked him how he defined leadership. "A good leader has to stay focused," he said, "to see what is coming. Even if you are not prepared for a specific situation, you must be prepared to give a quick solution. The other thing is not to lose your strength and your position in front of your team, but to speak on the same level as them. This is the most important thing, because if you want to convince them to stand up with you as the bullet whistles by, then you must make your team understand that you are on the same ground. You are all human beings. You all have families."

Three years after Shahar's military service was completed, he became involved with the Israeli intelligence community. His area of expertise was collecting information about Palestinians within Israel and the West Bank, including details on Palestinian life and terror activities. Shahar was unwilling to divulge classified details of his work. But he did explain that the intelligence business is divided between human resources and SIGINT (signal intelligence) resources. "The first entails getting someone to provide information, which leads to some action. There are a lot of reasons why a person would cooperate with us. As the years have gone by, when it comes to the Palestinians, money has become less important because they cannot take it and buy a house or make life more comfortable without drawing attention. Every person has his weak point that you can exploit to get him to provide the first connection with Israeli authorities. To keep this connection for a long time, this is something else." SIGINT resources include electronic equipment that Israeli intelligence can track, including telephones, cell phones, and other devices.

With all this intelligence, how it was possible for the Israeli government to be blindsided by the failure of the Israeli-Palestinian peace process, which has led to so much frustration and disillusionment on both sides? Had the Israeli government been naive? "First of all, mistakes have been made," Shahar said. "But the people who express frustration, I don't think that they actually understand the thin line we are walking on. The question is not the size of the terrorist nation or organization, or how many rifles they were provided or how many bombs they produced. The problem is the Middle Eastern mentality. The Palestinians think through the eye of force and you can never make them a real partner without providing them with the tools of building a nation. Of course there were signs, and the intifada was very much forecast by Israeli intelligence. We knew exactly what it would be.

"In the beginning, there were almost no suicide bombers and a lot of the activities took place in the West Bank. The Israeli army was well prepared. But then reality hit when terrorist organizations started sending suicide bombers to Israel, and that changed everything. It is a very well-organized, financed war against Israel. Somebody has to provide suicide bombers with bombs. Somebody has to convince the terrorist to act. Somebody has to pay the rent for his family. It is the Palestinian Authority that pays his family $1,000 a month. So intelligence knew, but hope for peace brought Israel back to the negotiating table anyway."

A few months later, I spoke with Shahar again by phone. He told me that terrorist activities have changed. At the beginning of the intifada, suicide bombers came primarily from ultra-religious fanatical groups like Hamas or Islamic Jihad. Their purpose in becoming martyrs is to be rewarded in the next world. "But there has been a shift," Shahar said. "Out of ninety suicide bombers, seventy were Palestinians who were more mainstream and not affiliated with a specific fanatical religious leader. But these mainstream people are Muslims who believe through their religious teachings that there is glory in being a martyr, just like the al Qaeda terrorists from September 11. The Fatah Al-Aqsa Brigades, which is a terrorist organization associated with Arafat, is another one of these groups. Praise for terrorist activities is in the Palestinian streets, in their newspapers, supported by Arafat, and preached in the mosques. Palestinian television has shown families of suicide bombers receiving $25,000 checks funded by Saddam Hussein as if they had just won the lottery. This information is very open and available to the general public. So what is learned from this point is that terrorist fighting has shifted to a battle by regular Muslim Palestinian citizens. This complicates the situation even more.

"The general Muslim Palestinian population has concluded that it is at a point of equalization with Jewish Israelis. Approximately five million Muslims live within Gaza, the West Bank, and Israel. The Muslim population is growing at a faster rate than the Jewish population, and possibly within ten to twenty years will exceed the number of Jews in Israel. The Muslims understand this. This is not a battle for Palestinian statehood, but a battle for the land of Israel. As they wait, they are going to make it hard for Jews to live here in Israel. The only thing that Israel can do is to establish a strong nation and build a fence to separate Gaza and the West Bank from Israel. This fence is deeply opposed by the Palestinians. It will keep terrorists from coming in, and therefore they cannot accomplish their mission of conquering our land. Although it creates problems, such as leading terrorists to use missiles from the other side of the fence, we will defend our country and create a buffer zone. It must be clear, however, that Muslim fanatics are not just targeting Israel and the United States. Intelligence knows this. There is no non-Muslim nation that is safe from being a target."

Though Shahar expressed his support for a fence to keep terrorists out, he cannot help but think of a Palestinian woman who will be kept on the other side. This woman is someone whom he and his family deeply loved. She lives approximately one and a half miles from his house, in the West Bank city of Tulkarem. "She came to our house once or twice a week to clean," he said. "Sometimes she brought two of her three sons, twelve and six years old, and because she was overweight and had difficulty cleaning in some areas, her sons would help her. It wasn't just an employer-employee relationship. She would sit down to dinner with us and we would talk, sometimes even discuss politics. She was not educated, but very involved and aware of what was going on between both nations and the suffering of the Palestinians. We could never forget that she lived there and we lived here and that our lives were very different. There were no economic opportunities or freedom for her in Tulkarem. Her life situation was extremely difficult. Her husband was in Jordan and so was their eldest son who was studying at a university. Though her husband's family lived next door, she was still alone. She was in her early forties, a Muslim with red hair and a temper to match. She wore a scarf and what I remember about her most was her high energy, her smile, and her talkative nature. She often brought us olives or homemade hummus. I think about her a lot, about how she suffers from the situation more than us. She cannot come to my house anymore. Nobody will let her enter where we live. The guards will not harm her, but they will not let her enter. If I were to go over there, Palestinians would lynch me, of course. But this is the way of life. You cannot expect that the Palestinian nation growing up next to you will be like European educated nations, or have some North American way of thinking. But that doesn't mean that I am not frustrated by the situation."

Through all the terror, Shahar wants people to stop and ask themselves how they're treating others. Do they behave like good citizens on the road? Are they good neighbors? Are they polite when waiting in line at the grocery store? He sees value in these so-called "little things" that in the end can mean so much. Shahar has decided to give back to those who are close to his heart. He has established the Shaldag Society to help support families of fallen comrades, to build memorials so that people will not forget their contributions to the State of Israel and for Jews across the globe.

* * *

For Ari, Orly, and Shahar, and for the hundreds of thousands of other Jewish Israelis who serve or are left behind, there seems to be no other way of life. And there are no simple solutions. They deal with mandatory military service, constant fear of imminent attack, suicide bombers, Arab neighbors who seek their destruction. Given the situation, why would anyone remain in Israel? Although some Israelis and Diaspora Jews ask this question, it usually surfaces as a quick flash, a passing doubt that comes and goes in the blink of an eye.

Effy Glick, fifty-five, a retired IDF officer and liaison to the UN, offers these words of wisdom for the Jewish nation: "Young people, our children, search for easy answers during times of pressure and crisis. For some the solution discussed may be to leave Israel and live elsewhere. Our job as parents is to convince them that this is a wrong solution. With the historical experience of the Jewish people, I believe that we must hold onto the land and find the strength to win this conflict, and not to try to find solutions elsewhere. Our people are tired of wandering throughout the Diaspora.

I think it is important for all of the Jewish people to do everything to strengthen Israel. Without a Jewish country, all Jews everywhere in the world are in danger. Therefore, there is no solution other than to stay here. We must take care of Israel and maintain it, despite all the hardships."

Momy Ben-Simon

Renana Laish

Hana Levy

Micha Piran

Omri Krongold

Chapter Seven
Food on the Table: Surviving the Economic Crisis of Terror

Climbing the wide, worn cement steps to the Migdal ha-Emek Department of Social Services was like being on a TV set for *NYPD Blue* or *Law and Order*. The profusely peeling paint and solid creaky door leading to the unknown reminded me of scenes from these cop shows. Once inside, a waiting area and narrow hallways with people lined up against the walls was revealed. Women waited with young in tow; the elderly sat, some with heads down. Guilt washed over me as a receptionist directed interpreter Jeff Katz and me to the modest office of forty-six-year-old Momy Ben-Simon, Director of Social Services. Guilt because of the inquisitive looks and perhaps mild resentment on faces, which seemed to say, "Hey, why does she get to go in without waiting?" I immediately noticed an enlarged photo of the Lubavitcher Rebbe, Rabbi Menachem Mendel Schneerson, above Momy's crammed, but organized desk, and a huge map of his town, Migdal ha-Emek, on another wall. Momy greeted us with a smile; a short salt-and-pepper beard and mustache covered much of his face. A felt-tip pen and what looked like a small rectangular day organizer were visible through the pocket of his white button-down shirt. Social workers Hana Levy, forty-seven, and Renana Laish, thirty-six, joined the conversation. If anyone understands the human toll and the economics of terror, it is these hard working, dedicated social workers.

Before the intifada began, those who lived in poverty needed assistance, the mentally ill and physically challenged needed care, new immigrants entered the country with little more than clothes on their backs, and children went to school hungry. Terror has intensified these social issues. The basic need for the essentials of life – food, clothing, shelter – have increased and resources are more scarce because of the crippled Israeli economy. At the time of this interview, close to 11 percent of Israelis are unemployed. Some statistics go as high as 16 percent.[60] Social workers struggle to meet the demands of this increasing population, and these demands are not the only issues stretching social workers' time and budget. Momy explained how his department's responsibilities have changed. "When a terrorist attack occurs near us, everything that was once planned for the day is dropped. The events dictate a change of agenda. We may be involved in procuring treatment for the wounded, emergency procedures, or informing the relatives of those who were injured or killed. It is extremely difficult work. Our workers have to be so skilled and sensitive when they go into someone's home. It's not something that is taught in any university. That's one level. Then there is the personal level. It is an intolerable situation. You no longer know what you should do. These terrorist attacks can happen to anyone. It doesn't matter anymore if you are an Arab or a Jew."

Then Hana said, "Today people are asking, 'If I go outside, will I come back?' Something has changed in people's general emotional state. There are many people who may not actually be victims of a terrorist attack, but who were in the area of one and now experience post-traumatic stress syndrome. These people may have trouble functioning. Perhaps they witnessed a head flying through the air. Their lives will never be the same. There can be an additional hundred uninjured bystanders who saw all the blood, body parts, and the like. One of our coworkers was present at an attack and she experienced something very difficult. Witnessing such an event changes your emotional state."

Renana added, "The people we deal with here are already considered society's weakest element. They are already in distress. When these people have to deal with terror, they are weakened further. If once we tried to strengthen them using certain methods, today it is more difficult. I work mostly with children. It is very hard to say to parents that their children want them to sit next to them for a long time until they fall asleep. The children are having more bad dreams. The parents want to help but don't always know how."

"This is a battle for their existence as a functioning family unit," Momy explained. "The husband can't support his family because he isn't working. He exists on government welfare. Or the mother of the family is very sick and there are many medical expenses. There are also children from large families who lack many things, both emotional and personal, which need to be supplied. These children are not taken care of or nurtured. Some of them need dental treatment but don't receive it. Some go to school without food. They are neglected. The lists of priorities for these types of families are tremendous. Sometimes the husband only thinks about his needs and satisfying them. What happens to his family is much less important to him. What's left of the monthly income after paying for electricity, water, rent, telephone, and so on, is not enough for the family to get through the month. Therefore, these families come here for help and assistance. We aren't able to supply food here. However, there are many good people who help us out. They supply us with food, clothing, et cetera. We have many private families or businessmen who 'adopt' needy families. Once a week, they give the adopted family a food basket. We have between ten and fifteen families a month coming to us suffering from hunger and distress. Sometimes we have people who are unable to buy baby food for their infants because they're destitute."

Hana added, "This level of poverty didn't exist before the intifada. It's a new period.

"My job hasn't completely changed," she continued, "but it has been affected. We have adjusted to the needs. The problems aren't just with new immigrants either. There are new circumstances and a worsening of circumstances that existed before. There is more anxiety, tension and violence, and other negative effects resulting from terrorist attacks. And we didn't really see hunger beforehand. People don't have food in their refrigerators. This is connected to the economic situation. It is also a global problem. It's everything together. Businesses close because people are afraid to go to restaurants and shop in malls."

Momy added, "Despite everything, we are absorbing new immigrants. I got a phone call on Thursday that three Argentinean families would be arriving that night. I had to get organized. I got an apartment ready for them and provided them with beds, linen, a counter-top stove, a refrigerator, and food. They came with only a suitcase."

Terror acts as a wrecking ball on Israel's economy, therefore the suffering of the poor grows. Momy said, "Take into consideration current governmental decisions that affect the public. The cost of the military operations reaches billions of dollars and the public is asked to cover the costs. The government is also cutting child allowances and increasing taxes. People who had a difficult time coping with the economic situation before now find that they have less income at their disposal. They have more difficulties coping today than they did before the intifada."

Some have found creative ways to keep food on the table. Momy told us, "I have thirty watches. I don't need thirty watches but every week I buy a watch. Who do I buy them from? I buy them from a man who searches for food every Friday for his children. He gets the watches to sell. I don't know from where. He sells them for fifty shekels, thirty shekels.[61] I'll give him fifty to seventy shekels for the watch and tell him to sell it to someone else. He tells me that I have to take the watch. I take the watch and toss it in the house.

"Poor families who live on government welfare do not receive enough to cover monthly expenses. It is our job to find solutions. Part of the solution was the establishment of a food warehouse. Any family that comes to us is directed to this warehouse and once a week they may take a food basket. We established the same sort of setup for second-hand clothing. We receive clothes from good people. We have elderly volunteers who wash and iron the clothes. Then any person who comes to us can go there and buy clothes for a few shekels. When winter approaches we buy blankets and heaters and distribute them to people under our care. In the summer we help out with fans because these people are unable to purchase air conditioners."

The challenge for Momy and his staff is meeting the needs of the ever growing numbers with less government and private resources. Somehow they succeed. In January 2004 his office received the prestigious "City of Volunteers" award from the Israeli government for their involvement in organizing and running various volunteer projects for the city of Migdal ha-Emek. How did Momy do it? He said, "The award was given in recognition of our involvement with and awareness of our community's needs. This ongoing commitment to help people living here started many years ago. We established more than forty volunteer organizations with one thousand volunteers. We are responsible for these volunteers and their contribution to the community."

*   *   *

Hunger motivated a spontaneous trip to Merkaz Horev, a Haifa shopping mall. It led to an unexpected and unforgettable interview with Micha Piran, owner of Broadway Bagel, a kosher restaurant on the mall's ground floor. But first a security guard searched the car, checked IDs, and gave the go-ahead to enter the underground parking structure. Another security guard blocking the mall entrance opened bags and purses, and then moved aside to allow searched people through.

Broadway Bagel was nothing like any deli or bagel chain in the States. Rich wood, chrome, modern art work, bottles of fine wine, and fresh sprays of delicate yellow and red flowers created a warm and inviting space. Yet the place was almost deserted. Despite the lunch hour, less than a handful of customers spelled potential financial disaster for a restaurant with forty-five tables. Waitresses stood around talking to each other. The man behind the cash register rearranged items on the counter. Hard times.

This scene plays out over and over again in restaurants, discotheques, and malls. One act of terrorism might keep Israelis home for a day or two. A series of bombings has disastrous effect. When so many husbands and wives, parents and children mourn, a solemn mood consumes the nation's spirit. This sense of loss has a greater impact on most Israelis than their concern for their own safety.

Fifty-eight-year-old Micha Piran, strong and rugged, understands how the plague of terror affects a business. Walking to the table for the spontaneous interview his presence filled the room. Micha's blue jeans and evergreen button-down shirt matched the casual attire typically worn throughout Israel. Business is something Micha takes seriously. He is a man of action, calculated risk, hard work, and innovation. With another Broadway Bagel at the Kiryon Mall in Kiryat Bialik near Haifa, Micha must rely on hungry shoppers to stay afloat. There just aren't enough of them. I had imagined business would be the focus of the interview. Micha's story, however, began with an unexpected emotional turn.

"I am married with three children," he said. "My son is twenty-eight years old and married. We are expecting our first grandchild. My two daughters are twenty-five and twenty-one. I was an officer in the army. My son is also an officer. He just came home from reserve duty. He was part of a special military call-up, which meant that he had to report to the army immediately. He served for twenty-eight days in Tulkarem and Kalkilya because of the escalation of terror.

"We are around 5 million Jews surrounded by approximately 200 million Muslim Arabs in the Middle East. Suicide bombers have come to kill us just because we are Jews. They don't want us here. This is the main point. Israel is our country and that's why we are here. Whose 'right of return' is it? It's our 'right of return.' I'm ready to start digging anywhere in the Land of Israel, from the Golan Heights down to Sinai. If you find proof that we were not here, I'll get up and leave that day. I understand we have to share the land with the Palestinians. We are ready to do it." Suddenly, distraught and desperate, Micha stood up to leave the table. The microphone attached to his shirt collar held him close. Tears dropped silently down his tanned cheeks, wiped dry before they could reach his chin. He returned to his seat.

"I'm sorry…I'm sorry…Sorry…I wasn't ready…You understand? All the emotions come up," he said. More gentle tears. "I thought that I'm stronger. What can I do?"

It is difficult for many to show emotion in public, and Micha was uncomfortable. His tears represent so much more than a strong man breaking down; they represent a nation in agony and the intense gripping pain brought on by the onslaught of terrorism.

Micha shook his head and continued. "My parents came to Palestine in 1933 from Germany. My maternal grandfather was a senior officer in the German army during World War I. Then, Jews served in the German army. My mother's family lived in a small village near Nuremberg. Her father had a very respectable job similar to a judge in our times. People who had problems between them came to hear his wisdom and they relied on his judgment. Everyone came. He was from a wealthy family and because of this he wouldn't charge money or take any gifts for his work. When Hitler began to rise in power, people could feel there was something in the air. My uncle and my mother said to my grandfather, 'Let's leave Germany. The atmosphere is not good. Let's go to Palestine.' My grandfather said, 'Well you can go. But me? Nothing will happen to me.' The first people in the area who were taken to Auschwitz were my grandmother, my grandfather, and the Catholic priest from the small village close to them. This priest was known as an anti-Semite. He had covered up the fact that he had some Jewish blood in him. So, if you ask about our rights in this country – we have nowhere else to go.

"My father had red hair, he was very slim, and he was not a strong boy. He told me that he had the opportunity to go to the United States of America or to Palestine. He said, 'I wanted to live as a proud Jew in my own country. That's why I came here.' Because of all we suffered and all we experienced in our history, we came back to our own country. That's why we are here. We have nowhere else to go. And that is why we have to fight."

Micha sighed and began to discuss the restaurant business. He had opened this second Broadway Bagel in 2001, less than a year after the intifada started. He said, "Compared to the time when we first opened, which also was not a very quiet time, business has gone down by about 50 percent. We are bringing in money from home in order to survive here. That's not business! And we can't take it much longer. This restaurant has suffered the most because it's in a small neighborhood mall. People are not coming to this mall to window shop. They go to the big malls for that. People come specifically to eat here, which makes a big difference. Our other location is in the biggest mall in the north. There, business is down 20 percent. We reduced the staff and are working fewer hours in the evening. We started to deliver food to businesses." Patrons' safety is a huge concern and a large expense. "I rely on the mall security, but we are paying more for it because somebody has to pay it. The mall can't pay everything.

"I hope that I am not going to lose the business. I hope that I am not going to have to continue to feed it money. I hope that a solution will come. We need the United States and the Arab countries to put pressure on the Palestinian Authority. There is no sense to what is going on here. How much blood will be shed? I don't have an answer to this crisis. I am not a politician. I can't tell you and it is not my decision.

"Very few Arabs come into this mall. Many come into our Kiryat Bialik restaurant, but they are coming less. They are also afraid, because if something happens, they are the first ones, you know, whom people will say something to. Look, I was born into this kind of business. It is very personal. I'm not just coming to take people's money home. I'm always talking with people and I'm always looking at people. It's not easy. In the past when we had a war, it was on the borders and almost nothing happened to civilians. Now terrorists are coming just to kill women, children, and the elderly, and to damage our morale. Once, it was soldier against soldier, which is what you call in war 'a fair fight.' This is not a fair fight. I believe people in the world understand it, but they don't have patience. The European market finds it much easier to deal with 800 million Muslims than with 5 million Jews. You have today in France about 6.5 million Muslims. In Germany there are about 5 million Muslims, who are Turks. In Belgium, there are 800,000 Muslims. The Europeans are afraid because they want support from their Arab populations. They are afraid the terrorist attacks will come to their countries. Of course, attacks have already taken place in Europe, but only in places like synagogues, which means against Jews. So what? The Europeans are afraid that if they support us, attacks will happen on their subways,[62] on their buses, or who knows where else. So, it is political. I know this is the case."

Terror creeps into every aspect of life, attempting to smother any pleasures. Micha explained, "About two weeks ago, I thought I'd take my wife out to see a movie for a change of atmosphere. Her answer was that she was not planning on leaving home until our son came back from the army. I respect that. I understand it. I was not completely in a mood to go out either. Terror affects everybody, mostly on an emotional level. People are afraid. People are not in the mood. 'What, I'm going to eat out while people might be killed in the streets?' The restaurant today is not for food. Everybody has food at home and everybody can order food to be delivered. It's for a change of atmosphere. Going out to a restaurant means celebrating."

Micha Piran and his family lost dear friends, fifty-five-year-old Shimon Koren and his two sons, eighteen-year-old Ran and fifteen-year-old Gal, in the Matza Restaurant bombing on March 31, 2002. "I'm trying to be realistic," he said. "I believe in life on earth and not in life in heaven. They lost their lives, they lost everything. Rachel Koren lost her two children and her husband. She is almost fifty years old. She cannot build another family. What else can you say? This is only one example, one family. This is happening all over the country. Do you know what it means for parents to bury their own children? On television a Muslim Arab woman kissed her son who was going out in the name of jihad to kill himself and other people. The father said on television, 'I have five other sons who can be suicide bombers, and the seventh one will be me.' So with whom can we speak? About what do we want to speak? What kinds of understandings will bring us to a common level? For us, life means everything. So here we are, and still, we hope that outside pressure will bring about something. We don't have other neighbors – I wish we could have other neighbors. I wish we could choose our neighbors, but we can't. We have to live with them. They are trying to push us out of here, but they won't succeed. It's not easy. Israel is not a rich country and Israel's public relations are not the best. We are always coming out a step behind, which is not good. Politicians will be politicians and politics will be politics. Look what happened in Jenin. We lost soldiers there. If any other country had been in a situation like we were in Jenin, they would have given the population five hours to leave their homes and then would have bombed everything from the air. They would have destroyed everything. We didn't do it like that. We told people to get out and then we went from house to house searching for terrorists. We lost a lot of soldiers because of that. No other country would have done it this way. Even the U.S.A., which had support for what was going on in Afghanistan, would have destroyed the whole area without risking any shots at their soldiers. Why should we do it? Because they are Arabs? Because they are sitting on oil? I don't think so."

Micha knows Israel will survive. "For sure," he said laughing. "No doubt. No doubt. The question is how? What it will look like? For sure! For sure! That's why we are here! Where else?"

In a follow-up conversation with Micha in February of 2004 he said that nothing had changed. Regardless of where a suicide bomber strikes, the personal as well as economic impact is painful and swift. He mentioned the suicide bus bombing on February 22, 2004, near Liberty Bell Park in Jerusalem. The murderer had chosen a public bus carrying many school children. Eight people were murdered and over sixty were injured.[63] Micha's restaurants saw an immediate drop in customers and the mood of the nation grew somber, depressed. He concluded our interview saying, "The restaurant business is a barometer for the security and economic situations in the country." How disheartening to know that his struggles remain.

* * *

Hospitality is his business, tourists his lifeline. Terror is the crashing tidal wave sent by madmen to destroy everything he holds dear. Forty-six-year-old Omri Krongold, general manager of the Inbal Hotel in Jerusalem, fights for the hotel's survival and the livelihood of all who work there. It isn't easy. Friendly top-notch service, an outstanding reputation, and tight security are the strong threads Omri hopes will bring customers to the Inbal. The hotel has weathered many storms – terror the most difficult of all.

Omri extended warm greetings as we sat down at a beautiful wooden conference table tucked away in the lower level of the hotel's operations area. Photographs of prime ministers and other notable politicians standing at podiums grace the walls. Numerous service excellence awards fill a glass cabinet. One thing about Omri caught my attention: he wore a dark suit, white shirt, and dominantly red tie. True business attire in a country of casual comfort. His English is very good, a byproduct of a high school education in England, where his father was an Israeli emissary to London. Working his way up in the hotel business has occupied most of his adulthood.

The future of the Inbal occupied Omri's thoughts. "When the intifada first started," Omri began, "the terrorist attacks were very different. We didn't have any bombings. There was shooting at Gilo[64] and shooting on the road to Efrat.[65] Then, on June 1, 2001, we had the Dolphinarium attack and August 4, 2001, the Sbarro attack. At the hotel we felt the effects of the intifada immediately. People didn't want to come to Israel with an atmosphere of war. Somehow, we managed. Whatever happened we found a solution. It was bad for the first couple of weeks, but then we adjusted. First we reduced the rates then we reduced the staff." Before winter 2001 many families came to the Inbal. Now its customers are parents of children in yeshivas in Jerusalem or people on solidarity missions. Jewish holidays, such as Passover, attract large numbers and special events like the Maccabia Games[66] have brought Jewish athletes from around the world. "We thought everything was going to be okay," Omri said. "We thought people were adjusting." Unfortunately, when attacks become more frequent or hit Jerusalem, there is an immediate impact on the hotel's occupancy. "Since the start of the intifada we have had 40 percent occupancy. During the last two months it has even gone down to 20 percent."

The Inbal has three hundred guest rooms with an average occupancy of sixty. Obviously, this has a huge impact on staffing. "Today we have around 100 employees who are working," Omri explained. "Before the intifada, we had 280. Even the ones who stayed on at the Inbal don't exactly make a month's salary. They have reduced hours. You give them vacation time, but after their vacation runs out you start reducing the pay. But, thank God, they have a job, somewhere to go to in the morning, and they are happy. Whoever has a job is happy."

The number of weddings and bar and bat mitzvahs that take place in the Inbal Hotel have decreased considerably. Omri explained, "Celebrations are down because the people from abroad – France, England, the u.s. – are coming less. The Israeli market is pretty much the same. But you can't run a hotel just on events because that's just a sub-income. Those who are interested in holding their events here ask us a lot of questions. 'How many guards are there?' 'How many are armed?' Only yesterday I saw an invitation for a wedding in Jerusalem. It had written, 'All the guards are armed with machine guns.' I asked the bride how she could write this on her invitation, for her happiest day. She told me that people from Haifa and Tel Aviv said that if it wasn't written they wouldn't come to Jerusalem. There is an impression in Israel that Jerusalem is so dangerous that you are going to explode. On the other hand, there are people in Jerusalem who say that they will not go to the Azrieli Tower[67] in Tel Aviv for fear that there might be a bomb."

In July 2001, nine months prior to my interview with Omri, I had stayed at the Inbal with my family. So much had changed since then. You could no longer drive up to the front entrance. Concrete pilings now block the entrance and a guard checks vehicles at the parking lot. Security stands outside. Special visitors and large gatherings warrant even more stringent attention. Procedures are checked over and over again. The hotel's meat restaurant and many of the first floor boutiques were closed: not enough customers.

Omri added, "You were here in July and we were looking and watching. There was one security guard at the entrance. Since then, we have added more and more security. We decided to secure the entrance of the hotel. No cars can park outside because we don't know who might get out of a car. We also moved the taxis to the main street. Lots of people park inside the parking lot, but they are checked twice – once outside the parking lot and once inside. The main idea is to give us a little bit of time, because if someone is going to come and bomb us, we want to see him. There are guards with guns standing at the entrance and hopefully they would be able to stop a terrorist." Only security guards carry guns. "We are still a hotel," Omri said, "and we have to keep up some kind of appearances. I don't know if you'd like it if someone would come and clean your room carrying a gun."

Arabs are important members of the Inbal Hotel staff. Terrorism, however, brings a little scrutiny and some customer suspicion. Omri explained,

"One of our Arab cooks also works at the Emek Cafe in Jerusalem. He was working alongside a terrorist there. So our cook was arrested under suspicion of terrorist activities. But then the police found out that he was not involved. The Arab staff working here today are the same Arabs who worked last year. The only thing that has changed is the attitude of the guests. Their attitude today is not as accepting of the Arab people in general. I believe that if you're nice to someone, you give him a job, don't treat him like a second-class citizen, and keep politics out of the conversations, he will not come back and kill you. But there is no guarantee. It's not a great feeling, but I live with it. I'm nice to them and in return they are nice to me. I keep on working this way. We cross-check with the Secret Service to make sure nothing is being found out about the person. When they come in the morning, we say hello. If anything happened or if something is wrong with the worker, we check him verbally, not physically. I think we'd be able to notice if suddenly something strange were going on with someone who has been working here for ten or fifteen years. I don't believe he would come as he always does to work and then suddenly start to shoot everyone. Something would have happened and we would be able to notice it beforehand.

"The guests who come now are people who have been to the hotel before. They ask if we are sure about our Arab staff, and some have said that they would prefer if we didn't employ Arabs. We get things like that, but in Jerusalem all the hotels have Arab staff. Some guests will request a Jewish taxi driver. One guest told me that he had taken a taxi with an Arab driver at 5:00 A.M. for a 7:00 A.M. or 8:00 A.M. flight. The guard at the entrance to Ben-Gurion Airport stopped the taxi with the Arab driver. Our guest had to ask the guard to let him through. The airport guard should understand that this is a person hurrying to catch his flight, let him through, and keep the taxi with the driver as long as he wants. Let the person get a taxi from there to take him to the terminal. The hotel guest said he had offered to be searched just to be allowed to go in order to catch his flight. He asked why he was being kept hostage with the taxi driver. He told the guard that if he wanted to check him, he should check him. This guest asked me to prevent such a situation the next time, and I said, 'Okay.'"

Fear, no work, and no future prospects for those once employed are overwhelming burdens facing Israelis today. Omri is deeply concerned about the impact of all three. He said, "In the beginning of March 2002 it was terrible, because on top of living with the bombings we had the fear. All of us who live in Jerusalem and all over the country were afraid. I was afraid to go out. I was afraid to tell my son that he could go out. I was worried all the time. We were worried about the hotel. We worried about everything. The whole atmosphere was leading us to ask ourselves, 'How are we going to keep ourselves safe? How are we going to keep our workers safe and the few tourists that are with us?' One of our employees was in the explosion at the Moment Café. She was seriously hurt. An employee of our sister company was killed there. This changed the whole atmosphere for us. There were bombings day after day and it was really bad. There are so many stories about people living in Jerusalem – the oversleeping, the overeating, the inability to sleep at night – because the average person has someone in the army or going into the army: a son, or daughter. They worry. There are no jobs. You have to fire a lot of people and you have to send people who are looking for work away. Some have worked all their lives in the hotel business. What can they do on the outside? There is nothing, no opportunity for them. So we are left with a combination of these three things: fear, no work, and a future where no one can promise us anything. Even when the intifada started, we said, 'Okay. It's going to be like this for a few months.' When a few months passed, we said, 'In the summer it's going to be okay.' And then we said, 'Next year it's going to be okay.' Now we hear from the government and the army that it's going to take five years. So how can you keep people going, help give service, be nice, and tell those who lost their jobs, 'Listen, for five years you aren't going to have a job, you're going to be living in fear all the time, and there is no future for you?' It's very hard to continue. I have to fight the rumors every day. 'Are you closed? Are you open?' What are they talking about? We are not closed. We are here! We are not going anywhere. Jerusalem is *the* place! Some people find a reason not to come to Israel by assuming we must be closed." Omri looked at me and sighed. "You've caught us at a real low point," he said.

"There is a middle class, regular people who do most of the work. They do reserve army duty. Their sons go to the army. But they are now out of jobs. No one is helping them. When the banks had a problem, the government helped them. Nobody wanted the banks to collapse. Who is going to help us? The banks are very strict now. For a few of my friends, the banks have foreclosed on them. They have families and they go to the army, and the banks say, 'We don't want to talk to you.' To the big corporations that are costing the banks many millions they are more considerate. These corporations can get credit from the bank even though they don't have a way to return the money. But the average person who lives in Jerusalem doesn't get the same consideration. I have a friend in Tel Aviv who has a car repair garage. He said to the bank, 'Business has gone down. So understand me.' But no! No understanding from the bank. It's getting harder and harder and harder. There is no response from the government. They are so busy with Arafat. He's legitimate, he's not legitimate. Listen, we are the people who live here. We want the government to be concerned about us. The thing is that nobody cares about the people. Nobody seems to give a damn what we say and what we need."

Talking about the economic situation throughout Israel pained Omri. It is personal because he knows so many who have suffered. He opened his heart. It is not so easy to shut the door on a country and the people he cares so deeply for. He concluded, "At the beginning of the year, in January, my son had a bar mitzvah. Before the bar mitzvah, I had to sit down and think. In this strange world in which we live, how do we convince our son that this is the best place to live, in Jerusalem, in Israel? The more I thought about it, I realized that Jerusalem, that Israel is the right place. This is where we are going to live. I lived in London for four years. It's considered an open country. Yet I saw what anti-Semitism is. I always said to people, 'Anti-Semitism is not a new thing. We are not liked anywhere, nowhere in the world. We have never been liked and it's not something new.' Israel is the only place where you can be proud and you don't have to pay the policeman a hundred dollars in order to keep an eye on your synagogue or your business. From time to time you say, 'Okay, when is the terror going to be over? When are we going to have some rest and peace?' But nowhere else in the world gives you the feeling of being Jewish, of being Israeli. This is your country. You are proud to be in it. You understand the people. You can speak to everyone – the taxi driver and the shopkeeper. You will never be treated like, 'Here is another Jew.' You will not be told there are clubs that you cannot attend, or that you cannot have a position in government because you are Jewish."

Still, Omri struggled to cope with the terror around him. "When you feel down, the whole atmosphere is affected and people know it. How can you keep people smiling? How can you keep a positive attitude? That is the hardest thing for me to do. I say, 'Keep smiling. It's going to be all right.'"

Robin Barasch Permut

Hayah and Marcia Goldlist

Yom Tov Glaser

Michael Lerner

Joe and Sue Freedman

Chapter Eight
A New Life: North Americans Living in Israel

Why would someone move to a country torn apart by terrorism? Many come because they are Zionists. Israel has been a Jewish haven from oppression and anti-Semitism, a ray of hope for those living in poverty, a relief from horrendous living conditions, and in the case of Ethiopian Jews, from the very edge of starvation. Some seek a homecoming to God's Promised Land.

Robin Barasch Permut moved to Israel from New York for love. She said, "I came to Israel for the first time when I was thirty. My husband, who was my boyfriend at the time, had made aliyah and he wanted me to come and see Israel. I came with two suitcases filled with summer clothes. I just figured I would visit for a little while. Instead, I stayed and we married."

Raising two sons and a daughter in a society riddled with terrorism has created a nagging inner turmoil for Robin that is not easily relieved. She said, "Sixteen years ago, when I found out that I was expecting a boy, my first reaction was, 'Oh no, I am going to have a soldier.' But then I thought that by the time my son would reach army age, we might have peace in the region. Right before the Gulf War, my second son was born. I realized that maybe we wouldn't have peace here. I started to really have a conflict with my husband because it was a given that our sons would go into the Israeli army. I wasn't so accepting of this because there was the possibility that my sons would have to fight in an active army. Then Oslo came along and it was, 'Wow! This is okay. I can stop worrying about what happens when the boys are of army age.' When the intifada broke out, I thought, 'Oh my goodness, this is madness.' But I don't think I could live anywhere else and so I accept the fact that my sons will have to go into the army. We live here and somebody has to protect the State of Israel. And if it has to be my sons, well, I'll start praying a lot." Robin laughed, yet her face reflected worry. She has dreams for her sons' futures. Hopes that she will hold as they grow into soldiers.

*   *   *

Rabbi Yom Tov Glaser, an adult education leader for Aish HaTorah in Jerusalem, came to Israel in 1991 from California. At that time he was known as Johnny, a floundering, die-hard surfing, "tie-dyed, long-haired, beaded hippie guy with a guitar on his back." Sam, Johnny's older brother and best friend, believed that Johnny's life needed serious refocusing. Sam arranged for a free trip to Israel. He hoped a positive experience there might give Johnny some direction. Reluctantly, Johnny agreed. "Within nine days I called my parents and said, 'Don't send the surfboards anywhere,'" Yom Tov told me. "I knew I would be here for the rest of my life." His religious connection intensified and Johnny studied to become a rabbi. Soon after, he began to use his Hebrew name, Yom Tov, which means "good day" or "holiday."

Yom Tov believes that there is no better place for Jews than in the Holy Land. "There is a real fear for some Jews that if they come to Israel they might die in a terrorist attack," he said. "These people are making one mistake – believing that they will somehow live forever. We are all going to die. The question is, What did you die for? Or better put, What did you live for? If I have to die, God forbid, in some mindless suicide bomber's scheme, let it be here. If you are going to die for being a Jew, you might as well die for being the best Jew you can be, and that really is my statement about this whole situation. I want to be an amazing Jew. Being the best Jew you can be means that everything is involved, not just ritual, that your emotions and your heart are there. You are doing things with great thought. You are doing things without ego. You are walking with God in your life. Where is your heart? Who are you dedicated to? What is this world about? What is your life about? Is it about the world and then giving some time to God? Or is it about God and then giving some time to the world?" Rabbi Yom Tov Glaser and his wife, Leah, are raising their family in an ultra-religious community in Nachlaot, a Jerusalem neighborhood near Ben-Yehudah Street.

*   *   *

The Goldlist family left their Toronto home and moved to Israel for a one-year trial run in 1995. As their return loomed, the four Goldlist girls pleaded with their parents, "We want to stay! We don't want to leave! Don't make us go back!" Their mom, Marcia, agreed with the girls. "Let's give it another year," she said to her husband, Harvey. He was not convinced. His parents and other family tugged at Harvey's sensibilities. The Goldlist women persisted. With only a few weeks to go, Marcia received a phone call from the renters of their Toronto home. They wished to extend their lease by one year. "Now can we stay?" the girls begged. Sometime after midnight in Israel, Harvey quietly called his parents in Toronto. "We're staying another year," he told them. That morning the girls hugged Harvey and whooped for joy. In 1997 the Goldlists moved back to Toronto vowing to return to Israel permanently. "There was something about Israel that was home," forty-five-year-old Marcia said, "and that never left me." During the three years that followed, the family prepared for their new life in Israel. Money was saved, most possessions were sold, and goodbyes were said to friends and family. The Goldlists made aliyah in July 2000, two months before the second intifada ignited.

* * *

Robin Barasch Permut, Rabbi Yom Tov Glaser, the Goldlist family, and hundreds of thousands of immigrants like them came to Israel for reasons that initially could be summed up with one particular reason: love, religion, Zionism, poverty, anti-Semitism. What holds is their devotion to stay, a connection to Israel that goes beyond words, that is intangible, and perhaps cannot be reasoned with logic. Israel is their soul. It has become home.

* * *

In the heart of New York's Time Square, high school student Michael Lerner and a friend stood in line to buy half-price tickets for a Broadway musical. It was unseasonably warm for early April. The growing crowd was restless and the air vibrated with lively conversation, rumbling car engines, and honking taxis. Soon several market researchers descended upon the corralled public with tempting cold yogurt. The easy targets snatched up the refreshing dollops and a few smacking lips reinforced approval. Unfortunately for Michael, an observant Jew, it was the middle of Passover. Despite his hunger, he refused the yogurt. The experience was a mild form of torture, one that he still has not forgotten. Michael said, "I made aliyah for the free samples at the supermarket. It's my number one and most favorite reason as to why I moved here. I keep kosher and since most of the things sold in the grocery stores here are kosher, I can eat the samples." A wide grin spread across his face and he chuckled. "Life here revolves around Jewish holidays. I love seeing the ads for sales before Rosh Hashanah, the ads for cleaning supplies before Passover, and the ads for dairy products before Shavuot. I smile when a totally secular person wishes me a happy holiday."

Michael Lerner was born and raised in Brooklyn, NY, attended a Jewish elementary school, high school, and then Yeshiva University. The September after his high school graduation he left New York for a work and learn year-long Israel program sponsored by Bnei Akiva, a religious Zionist youth organization. His experience with Bnei Akiva had instilled a love for Israel that grew during his year in Israel and several subsequent visits. Upon his return to the United States, Michael worked toward and received his degree in Computer Science. In 1995 Michael and his wife, Dena, made aliyah with their one-and-a-half-year-old daughter, Naomi. They settled on Kibbutz Merav, a religious community located on one of the hills of the Gilboa Mountain range. Fifty families, most native Israelis, form the tight-knit cooperative. In 1948 the Gilboa Mountain range was divided between Israel and Transjordan. The kibbutz was established in the early 1980s about half a kilometer inside the Green Line, the armistice border established after the War of Independence.

I met Michael, now thirty-six years old, at the Nazareth Illit-Jezreel Technological College where he is the computer systems administrator. Like many Brooklynites, he talked a mile a minute. He often injected subtle, humorous sarcasm, and smiled spontaneously with each quip – an endearing habit.

It is hard to imagine Michael carrying his M-16 automatic rifle during guard duty or climbing tall date and mango trees to harvest the fruit on the kibbutz. This computer whiz with wire-rimmed glasses, a knitted *kippah* on top of his head, a striped button-down oxford shirt, khakis, and a neatly clipped beard and mustache is at ease with these surface contradictions. Actually he does not give them much thought, although he does find the dichotomy of going from city boy to country boy somewhat humorous. "People who live on Kibbutz Merav choose it for the quality of life," he said. "They don't want to live in the hustle and bustle of a city.

Now I can't stand going to the city. It drives me nuts! I go to Jerusalem and I get very tense – all the cars and the noise. I don't drive in Jerusalem. I get out of the car and my wife drives." Trips to Jerusalem are rare, but not just because he hates the city. "We used to drive to Jerusalem by way of the Jordan Valley, which is the quick way. But since the intifada, we drive the long way, through Tel Aviv. That's because there have been various shooting and rock-throwing incidents on the road or coming from the Palestinian village Uja. People have been killed. So instead of a one hour and forty-five minutes trip, it takes us three hours. Through Tel Aviv I just take my regular chances of being killed in a car accident like every other Israeli." Michael laughed at his quip and added, "Statistically, it's probably safer on the Jordan Valley Road."

Several months after the initial interview, Michael once again began to drive on the Jordan Valley Road to Jerusalem. He explained the change: "My sister was getting married in Jerusalem and we were traveling back and forth for all the preparations and festivities. We got sick of the long drive and decided to take our chances on the Jordan Valley Road. We were happily surprised. The army had several road blocks and lookout posts, which made us feel more comfortable and safe."

Michael is all too aware of the nightmares drivers may encounter from Arab terrorists on Israeli roads. On August 9, 2001, roadside terror brought death in the blink of an eye. Like on numerous other days, Michael woke up, checked the latest news, had some breakfast, and headed off to work – nothing out of the ordinary. Later that day, the Sbarro bombing broke the hearts of Israelis, leaving a devastating cloud over the citizens. Michael worked late and headed home. Hungry for additional details from the day's tragedy, Michael turned on his car radio. Suddenly a text message flashed on his cell phone, a message that Michael still has not deleted: "8:33 P.M. Due to gunshots that have been heard in the area, all men should go immediately to the entrance of the kibbutz with their guns. Updates on the voice mail system." Almost simultaneously, Michael heard a radio announcement that shots had been fired in his kibbutz. A wave of fear crashed over him and with a panicked touch he speed dialed home. Dena answered. She and Naomi were fine and Michael could breathe again. Details, however, were still sketchy. Another text message flashed onto his cell phone: "People must go to their emergency locations immediately." Questions pounded in his head. Who was shot? Were there

terrorists still in the area? Should he continue on the road home? Would
he be safe? Michael was on the verge of driving on the most dangerous
part of the road, up the Gilboa Mountain, five minutes from home. Suddenly an ambulance siren screamed from behind. Michael pulled the car
over to the shoulder and he watched the emergency vehicle pass. He sat
there mulling through his options for a few minutes, and then called his
wife again. Still no news, and Dena could not tell him whether it was safe
or not to proceed. "Finally I decided that I would go up to the kibbutz
using the back road," Michael said. "Everyone was milling around by the
office and infirmary. An ambulance was leaving when I got there." Soon
Michael heard the gruesome details. Two or three Palestinian terrorists
who came from the direction of the nearby Palestinian village of Jilaboun
climbed the rocky cliff to the main road leading to Kibbutz Merav. Approximately eight hundred meters from the kibbutz gate, a car with four
female teenagers and one adult driver came under the terrorists' gunfire.
The adult driver had a slight hand wound and continued driving until she
reached the gate. The kibbutz guard called for a nurse, who rushed to the
scene. Another nurse from the health clinic was summoned. Men, M-16s in
hand, scrambled to the entrance. Some piled into cars and began patrolling
the perimeter of the chain-link fence. Their purpose: to guard against a
terrorist infiltration and verify that one had not already taken place. They
checked the weak barrier looking for possible points of entry. None were
found. The army, police, and ambulances surged upon the scene. Intense
adrenaline, fear, worry, and then shock grabbed each member in one form
or another. The teenage girls lived in a foster home on the kibbutz. "They're
children who come from broken homes or are taken out of their homes by
court order due to family circumstances," explained Michael. "The adult
driver was one of their counselors." Vague details soon became a grim reality. Aliza Malka, seventeen, was dead. With no chance of resuscitation, her
lifeless body remained on the kibbutz. Aliza Malka's funeral was the next
day. Another teen was seriously injured and spent four weeks in hospital.
She has undergone additional plastic surgery to correct some scarring.
Two others were lightly wounded and needed hospital care for several
days. The three teenagers received psychological counseling and physical
therapy. They walk with slight limps and their bodies are scarred from the
piercing bullet wounds. With a short pause, Michael reflected, "It was a
very traumatic event, personally and for the community."

The terrorist gunfire had hit on a one-kilometer section of the main road running along the Green Line – a dangerous, easy position for terrorist attacks. Because of its close proximity to the Palestinian village of Jilaboun, murderers could slip in and out of the area quickly. Most sections of the road leading to Kibbutz Merav are between a half and one kilometer away from the Green Line, which offers a small tenuous buffer between Israel proper and the West Bank. This open buffer has had no impact on preventing terrorist attacks. As of December 2003, the Israeli government was in the process of building a security fence to help protect its citizens. "It is not a cement barrier," Michael said. "It's a cleared path about three lanes wide that will eventually have a barbed wire fence in the middle."

The ambush was the impetus for adding security measures. The Israeli government provided funds to repave the kibbutz back road. "Personally," said Michael, "I drive on the main road every day and the people from the kibbutz as a whole do the same. This road makes approximately a two-kilometer semicircle around the kibbutz to the front gate and to our homes. I prefer to drive on the main road because it's a better and easier drive. Also, I think it is important to show a presence. I prefer to enter my home through the 'front door' than to sneak in through the 'back door.' At night I usually choose to turn left and use the back way just to be on the safe side. You never know. It leads into the kibbutz sooner but in order to get to the houses, you have to drive past the fields and cows."

Michael's voice dropped off. He paused for a moment and continued reflecting on community modifications that escalated with each terrorist act. "Two weeks prior to the ambush that killed Aliza Malka, a pipe bomb had been found on our road. In response we added more patrols. A few months after the ambush, we again increased security because a suicide bomber blew himself up right at the entrance of Kibbutz Sheluhot, a kibbutz that is a twenty-five-minute drive from us. We believe he was on his way to blow himself up in the dining hall, which was filled with people eating breakfast. A kibbutz member who had just driven out stopped him. The member started questioning the Palestinian and then the suicide bomber detonated his bomb, killing both of them. We then implemented guard duty twenty-four hours a day. Since I do guard duty, I know that a guard cannot be in all places at all times. The guard goes around the whole community checking the gate and the fence to make sure that no one has cut through it. It has been cut once or twice since we have lived on the kibbutz. Guards need to be aware of who comes in and who goes out. It's not a foolproof method of gaining security.

"The last half of 2002 we received funds from the government to put an electronic fence around the kibbutz. If someone tries to cut or move the wires, a signal is sent to the guard on duty and the army is contacted with the exact location." Michael has had numerous false alarms while on duty. "Sometimes a sagging wire activates the system, which could happen with rain or wind," he said. "Of course, until I'm certain it's a false alarm, I'm nervous. Maybe because I am from New York or maybe because I am in general very aware of terrorist attacks.

"I lock my doors at night. Especially in the summer it drives my wife crazy because I don't allow the windows to be open. It probably stems from a situation that happened to a friend of mine. Her husband was murdered about three or four months before we made aliyah in 1995. She lived in Ma'aleh Michmas, a community in the Jordanian desert near Jerusalem. Terrorists forced their way into her home, killed her husband and wounded her. She lost her unborn child. So I probably would have locked my doors anyway, but what happened there just reinforced it for me. The people in our kibbutz would leave their doors open during the day and night. Now everybody locks their doors at night."

Michael continued to discuss changes on the kibbutz. "Before the ambush, emergency procedures consisted of notification via cell phone, TV, and voice mail, and all men were instructed to go to the gate. Our emergency procedures have evolved since then. Announcements of a security situation are still made via the cell phones, TV broadcasts, and voice mail. There are specific teams of people to handle internal communications to update people, and external communications that include contacting army, police, fire, and medical personnel. The medical team consists of four nurses who live on the kibbutz. They go immediately to the health clinic. We have ambulance drivers who head to the ambulance. The procedure is no longer for all men to run to the gate, but everyone has a specific spot near his house to stand and keep watch. A group of men who served in combat units go immediately to the gate with equipment they keep in their houses – guns, flak jackets, helmets, and grenades. The women make sure that all children and anybody else who may be near their homes are indoors. Though women hold many leadership positions within the kibbutz, they do not participate in guard duty."

Interactions with our Palestinian neighbors were cordial until the terrorist attack. Michael said, "We felt that it was important to have a good relationship with them. They worked in our candle factory and in the fields, and we would see them all the time on the kibbutz. When I had to move my house, I hired some Palestinian workers to help me. All this stopped with the ambush in August 2001. Because the terrorists had come through the village of Jilaboun, we didn't know if they had received assistance from someone who lived there. It turned out that a resident of the village was actually one of the terrorists. I was in that village. I knew some of the men, but we don't have relationships anymore. The vast majority are regular people who want to put bread on their tables, and that's sad. I don't know if life will ever go back to the way it was before. We can't turn back the clock. If the general situation improves, it will take a while to reestablish what was lost. Will that ever happen? I can't really say."

Explaining terrorism to his eight-year-old daughter is a challenging part of his life. He continued, "My daughter asks questions. She watches the news sometimes before bedtime. You can't hide it from children. They have discussions in school and express their feelings. She had many questions after Aliza was killed, like 'Why did they do it? Will they come and do it again?' We try to reassure her without any iron clad guarantees, because there are no guarantees. We also try to reassure her that she'll be okay. I tell her that we do everything we can to keep the children safe. We have guard duty and there are border police that are always in the area. We tell her that we're doing our best."

Michael, with a slight smile curving his lips, continued: "People might wonder why we live here, but it's really a nice place. We are living here for Zionist reasons mainly and we like the rural area. Though we are semi-isolated, we are not completely alone. There is Kibbutz Maale Gilboa and a drug rehabilitation village near us. None of my family or friends from the u.s. would ever ask us to come back. They know better than that. This is a Jewish country, the Jewish homeland, and the only place that I believe that a Jew can really feel at home. And yes, there are very nice Jewish communities in many different places in the United States, but those places do not really belong to the Jews. Here the army is my army, the police are my police, and the holidays that are publicly celebrated are my holidays.

"I work at the Nazareth Illit-Jezreel Technological College, an environment that has many Arabs and Jews. For me that's fine because I tend to look at people as individuals, not as Jew or Arab. I know who's who, but growing up in America I was educated to believe in "truth, justice and the American way", as well as "all men created equal". So I try not to have preconceived notions about others." With a smile, Michael continued, "Some of the students I know by their faces. The ones that I know even better are those who either cause computer problems by erasing files or changing settings, or help me. The Arab students don't cause problems for me because I am Jewish. They don't have issues with me. I think that they respect me because of the position that I have and I also think that the students see that I offer help to all, regardless of whether they are Arab or Jewish. There are students with whom I schmooze and others who come and ask for help. We talk about computer-related topics, but we don't talk about politics. One-on-one, as individuals, we don't have any problems."

It is easy to assume that Israelis' thoughts, actions, and emotions are consumed by terrorism. This perception is false. Michael said, "Palestinian terrorism has become part of the fabric of Israeli life, and life goes on. I guess you can say that we've gotten 'used' to it. Jews have been victims of Arab terror for over seventy years, as the Arabs resorted to terror even before Israel was founded in 1948. During the current intifada, we have seen a dramatic escalation of the terror that we've experienced in the past. Palestinian terrorists have murdered ordinary people going about their daily lives, in coffee shops, pizza parlors, school dormitories, and living rooms. So, you may ask, how do we go on with our lives? I guess we go on because we have no choice but to live. Children must go to school and adults must go to work, because if we stop living then the terrorists will have won. There's always the hope that one day the Israeli-Arab conflict will be resolved and that there will be peace, but at this point I am not sure how that can be achieved. I am not saying that I am a pessimist, but that there are no easy answers.

"Since September 11 I think Americans have a better understanding as to why terror must be fought without compromises. Palestinian terror has been the model for Islamic extremists throughout the world. The situation here is a small part of a growing conflict between two civilizations – the West and the Islamic world. If Palestinian terrorists succeed in attaining their goal, which is the establishment of a Palestinian state upon the ashes of a destroyed Israel, then terrorists the world over will know that 'terror pays.' Global terror, especially Arab terror, is a long-term threat to the peace and stability of every Western nation. Israel must prevail in its fight against Palestinian terror, or soon the West will be faced with a threat to its very existence."

* * *

Joe and Sue Freedman's apartment is located in Gilo, a sprawling hilly neighborhood in southern Jerusalem. Gilo's distinct border stands out against the surrounding area with it's modern Jerusalem-stone buildings and well-orchestrated urban development plan. The pristine area, a five-minute drive from the heart of Jerusalem, is hardly the picture of a community embattled by terror. Yet, a few blocks away, bullets and several mortar shells have terrorized the Freedmans' neighbors.

Two flights of dimly lit stairs lead to their modest, comfortable apartment. With a knock their door flew open with warm greetings. A few steps to the left lead to their living room and a few steps to the right is the dining area. Their kitchen window faces an enormous cement water tank, which obstructs the entire view of neighboring Bet Jala. The Freedmans are not disappointed by this obstruction. The tank blocks potential bullets from hitting their apartment.

With barely a breath, Sue got started. "Where are the American Jews? Why aren't they coming? Do they care about us? Have they forgotten us? Not you, of course," she said pointing to me. Disappointment, frustration, feelings of abandonment, lack of understanding, and anger illuminated her face. She has carried these feelings for a long time, exasperated by family members and friends who do not understand why they live in Israel. She worries most for her four children – Naomi, Aviva, Maya, and Shai. "Wait," I interrupted, "I need to turn on the tape recorder." We laughed. And with that, Sue relaxed. I relaxed. We moved to the dining room table. A spread of various salads, bread, and tea welcomed me. Smiling, Sue looked at her husband, Joe, and said, "You start."

Joe's love for Israel bloomed during his summers at Camp Ramah in Wisconsin[68] and so did a romance with Sue, whom he met there in 1970. The prerequisite to a serious relationship was an agreement to live in Israel. Ten years later they fulfilled this promise. Joe delivered his last copy of his doctorate on their way to the airport. "When we made aliyah we adjusted pretty quickly," Joe explained. "We knew Hebrew and we knew what we were getting into, more or less. The secret was, we came hoping for the best, but expecting the worst. We told each other, 'Let's remember, it is not going to be as grand as we think.' And you know what? It is better than we thought. I know it sounds quaint and Pollyannaish, but you have to have a positive attitude. You have to be able to get up in the morning and say, 'I'm going to make the best of the day.' That has a lot to do with coping with the terror situation as well. Of course, the terror part is the pits. Sometimes, Sue and I – preferably not at the same time – will dip or fall into depression. It can be tough to get out of it when there is a no-win situation at work like needing to let staff go or when another tour group has canceled. Yes, we get down but we have learned to bounce back because it isn't going to help us any." Joe smiled and continued, "The anxiety is not going to be helpful or solve the problem. I can say this cheerfully, because I am not depressed right now."

Sue added, "We manage, we do things, we go places, we cope. It is not like we are in bed clinically depressed" – they laughed – "but we get fatter. There's chocolate, coffee. But there is no question that terror has definitely taken its toll on all of us."

Their two eldest daughters, Naomi and Aviva, were born in the United States and made aliyah with Sue and Joe in 1980. Their three daughters have served in the Israel Defense Forces and Shai, their nineteen-year-old son, is in the middle of his service. There is a strong possibility that Shai will become a commander responsible for training new troops. During the course of our interview, Joe often looked at Sue with loving eyes. There was a comfort between the two, one reserved for soulmates. Sue's eyes often shine with admiration for her husband. A social worker assisting the elderly, her dynamic personality came through with facial gestures and expressions, shaking the beautiful charcoal scarf with thin silver threads that adorned her head. Throughout the interview Sue listened closely to Joe's comments, then added her perspective.

When the Freedmans moved to Gilo in 1983, terrorist attacks and imminent danger never crossed their minds. It was a safe, lower-middle-class neighborhood of Jerusalem. Joe explained, "Gilo was built after 1967. You have to imagine that Jerusalem between 1948 and 1967 was wedged into a corridor with an apex. The city was divided in half. What people don't realize is that there was East Jerusalem and West Jerusalem. But East-Jordanian-Jerusalem extended north and south of West-Israeli-Jerusalem. Thus,

West Jerusalem was surrounded on three sides. During the Six-Day War in 1967 all of East Jerusalem was liberated from the Jordanians and the city became united. Israel started building new neighborhoods in former East Jerusalem, primarily in areas not previously inhabited. There was virtually nothing here in Gilo. There had been some sort of Jordanian army base here, an outpost. We did not uproot people in order to build here. The evidence that we didn't kick people out is that on that borderline between Gilo and the Arab village of Bet Safafa, there are a number of Arab homes clearly in Gilo. The Arab owners refused to sell. What our contractors had to do was to simply build around their homes. The Arabs were not evicted. Gilo is on top of the hill that was virtually a barren area. Bet Safafa is down at the bottom of the hill."

Gilo is a neighborhood that has been periodically mentioned in the media because of shooting from Bet Lehem (Bethlehem) and Bet Jala. Joe explained why Gilo was an easy target: "The reason the terrorists shot from Bet Jala is because it's in Area A, which means it belongs to the Palestinian Authority. So the terrorists knew they could shoot from there and be at low risk of soldiers coming in and invading. The Israel Defense Forces did that eventually, but it was only after the constant shooting went on for a long time. Bet Jala is a very quiet Christian neighborhood, very peaceful. What happened was the Tanzim, the militant wing of the Fatah, which is Arafat's faction, would go to the homes of these nice Christian Arabs and say, 'We are using your roof to shoot into Gilo.' The poor home owner could either say, 'I rather you would not,' or, 'How do you take your coffee?' They really had no choice. If they said they'd rather not, then they wouldn't be around to object anymore. So these terrorists go on the roof and they shoot at Gilo. What are the Israelis to do? The army shoots back at the source of the shooting. So what happens, of course, is that the homes of these innocent people in Bet Jala are being wrecked. Then the Israelis get blamed for shooting at the homes of these innocent Arabs."

According to the Israel Embassy of Public affairs, "Gilo is a residential neighborhood of about 40,000 which lies within the municipal boundaries of Jerusalem and of Israel as defined by Israeli law."[69] Sue put this into perspective: "Whenever there is shooting on Gilo it is not like you are shooting out in the West Bank, which I do not justify either. You are shooting in the capital of the State of Israel. Let's call a spade a spade! It is like shooting into Washington, D.C. The poor people who are living on the side facing

Bet Jala, which is a few blocks from here, have sandbags around their houses and their windows blocked. These are people who are really in a nightmare situation. We hear the shooting, but it hasn't hit us directly." To protect its citizens the Israeli government ordered the army to erect concrete blockades in Gilo. The barriers are in front of schools, synagogues, homes, and roads facing the area under Palestinian control. Mural artists have painted scenes on many of the barricades to improve the view.

Joe has four siblings, three on the West Coast of the United States and one in Florida. "None of them have any idea why I came to live in Israel. They can't understand it," he said. His siblings are not alone. It is difficult for many to rationalize why anyone would give up the comforts of the United States for a land where terror is common. But it is the Freedmans' religious, spiritual, and historical connections that bind their hearts and souls to Israel.

Joe continued, "I think our Jewish memories are very short; our memories of the Holocaust and of other less drastic anti-Semitic outbreaks. I think that perhaps taking Israel for granted over the years led to a certain sense of Jews not having to worry about Israel. Israel was a thriving state. Up until a few years ago, the economy was booming. We saw Israeli tourists in every country of the world traveling around. I think at some point Diaspora Jews became ambivalent toward Israel. Israel is not a buzzword. When I was growing up, if I heard the word Israel my eyes would start to water. I would feel proud. I went to the first showing of the movie *Exodus* in 1960 or '61 in St. Louis. I was just bursting with pride. There was a zeal that was there. I didn't belong to a Zionist youth movement, but it was definitely a part of my identity. Where it came from I am not sure. Maybe it was at Camp Herzl. Maybe it was at Camp Ramah. Maybe it was from my former first grade Israeli Hebrew school teacher. But I wouldn't be here in Israel if it weren't for faith in God and I wouldn't stay here if it weren't for my faith in God. For me, that is where everything stems from. The faith factor is a part of the motivation, part of the whole theology of why I am here and why I am a practicing Jew. I have questions of faith just like everybody has, just like the greatest philosophers in the world, the greatest theologians, the greatest rabbis. Everybody has doubts. The best marriages are not necessarily beds of roses all the time. If we have faith in each other, faith in being a couple, you know you will make it through. That is how I see my relationship with God. The Talmud is filled with statements of how the righteous suffer and the wicked prosper. This is the odyssey. How do you solve that problem? There is no solution. The rabbis 1,600 years ago could not solve it. I don't know why I should feel able to solve it either. When faced with incredibly challenging theological problems like the Holocaust or terrorist attacks, someone could say, 'If God exists, how could He possibly allow this to happen?' Like during the Passover massacre at the Park Hotel – innocent Jews were there to celebrate the holiday of freedom, and they were blown to bits. I say it flippantly now. Obviously at the time and still now it disturbs me greatly. But my whole theology is not a tit-for-tat theology where every little thing I do has cosmic effect and that I or any human being has a way of understanding how God acts. I am morally outraged by rabbis who give theological responses to tragedies by saying they know why God did this. Like they know the reason. Between Rosh Hashanah and Yom Kippur 2000, a rabbi, who does not live far from Gilo, said in a sermon that the reason this whole uprising started again is because the Israeli government decided that a giant turbine had to be moved on Shabbat. That is why the violence started! Hearing this upset me and I said to everybody sitting around me, 'How does he know? Did he call God on his phone to find out what the reason was for the outbreak of terror?' I don't build my theology on knowing what motivates God and what doesn't motivate God. A lot of my theology comes from the fact that with all of our travails, the Jewish people survive after 4,000 years and that, to me, averages everything else out. No matter how terrible things have been, God is not a computer, that if you put in the right data you get the right answer back."

Sue added, "I remember when my daughter, Naomi, was working in a restaurant in Nahalat Shivah on Yoel Solomon Street, an area near downtown Jerusalem. It was before this intifada. There was a terrorist shooting attack near where she worked and I was so nervous. I couldn't get hold of her. She didn't have a cell phone. I said to an Israeli friend of mine, 'Oh my God, I just hope Naomi is okay.' This friend said very fatalistically, 'Sue, if the arrow is meant for you or the bullet is meant for you, it will find you.' I have often thought of this. If things are meant to be, they will happen. I guess I believe in God. I think I believe in God. I do believe in God.

"Our children in their young lives have been to more funerals than I have gone to in all of my life. On the day of the terrorist attack at the

Sbarro Pizzeria, I went to the hospital to see if I could help out. On the way, I dropped Shai at Mount Herzl for the funeral of a young French boy who lived in our neighborhood and who went to the same high school. These young kids are exposed to terror and they have to deal with it. Another of Shai's friends was one of the five boys killed in Atzmona. When we were eighteen we were going to proms. The children here have such a serious life and you know when they finish high school they aren't going to check out colleges and fill out scholarship forms like our nieces and nephews in the United States. Like my friends say, 'When we were growing up, we went to college, got married, and started life.' Here it is a different roadmap, a whole different rite of passage. It makes me cry sometimes. A lot of the young people here make it their goal to go into elitist army units. They're not trying to get out of the army. They want to serve. It is hard for me. It is very hard for me. How do I cope with it? When mothers and fathers take their kids to the army for the first time, they say they wear sunglasses because behind the sunglasses they are crying. I remember taking each of our girls. It is hard. It is very hard. I am not going to minimize it."

The conversation shifted to Joe's work. He is the director of Ramah in Israel, the same organization that operates the camp he attended in Wisconsin. He runs youth programs through the Conservative branch of Judaism sponsored by the Jewish Theological Seminary of America. "Since we moved, I have been involved in a profession directed toward bringing Jews here from the Diaspora. So my work is Zionist work. I became a certified tour guide because I love being out in the field. I love the country. I love the history. I love everything about it. We, as a couple, had and still have a lot of enthusiasm for being here and we're proud. As time goes on, even with the intifada, the more certain we feel that this is where we belong. It is not, 'Oh my gosh, maybe we made a mistake, let's go back to the United States.'"

"I feel very proud to be here at this difficult time," Sue interjected. "On one hand, we received e-mails from friends, which are very nice and express support. On the other hand, we get e-mails saying, 'When are you coming back home? Aren't you packing your bags already? Isn't it enough already? Don't you realize the problems? Why aren't you coming home?' Our answer is, 'This is home.' I find these e-mails insulting. I find they negate everything we've tried to do here in the past twenty-one years."

The conversation changed to tourism, since Joe's livelihood depends on it. "Tourism," he said, "is in the toilet. We have seen a decline not only since the beginning of the intifada but particularly after September 11. I have had to let key staff go. It was really, really sad. I have spoken with other tour guides and travel agents, and the general consensus is that the economic damage since the intifada started will take eight to ten years to get back to where we were in 2000. In 2000, when tourism was one of the best years ever, the statistics were that 80 percent of the tourists coming to Israel were not Jewish. That was in a good year."

Joe's primary focus is not general tourism, however, but teens who come to Israel through Ramah programs. Can he blame parents for not wanting to put their children in possible harm's way? Joe answered, "We, of course, try to reassure parents that we would never do anything to put their children in danger. Now, can we guarantee anything? This is a question I get at Ramah orientation sessions all the time. The answer is, absolutely not! I say to parents, 'I can't guarantee anything, no more than I can guarantee at the end of this orientation that you are going to get in your car and return home safely. You hope so, I hope so, and statistically it's probably true. But I can't guarantee it. Can you?' One of the parents said, 'Life is full of risks and you have to calculate the risks you are willing to take.' Another parent said, 'It is a risk when I let my sixteen-year-old get in the car and go out at night. He might drink and drive and then get into an accident. He might lose his way and wind up in a dangerous neighborhood. Look at all the risks involved in that.' What can a parent do? You can't lock your kid up forever. Part of growing up is facing those risks and taking them. I might be a nervous maniac, but as a parent I have to face that risk. Is going to Israel something these teens have to do? No. No more than going out at night and driving to a party. Their lives aren't depending on it. Parents have said in these sessions, 'If I'm going to broadcast to my kid that Israel is important, then I'm going to take the risks for the important things that I want to teach my kids, for the right values.' So what are those values? What is the important message? The answer is, 'We stand by Israel whether it is in good times or in bad times.' If you can trust the organization, whether it's Ramah or Young Judea or any other reputable organization, to take the proper precautions, then be willing to take the risks. A lot of parents can do that. They see and feel the need to be here. They understand why Jews need to visit Israel and why we need a strong Israel. On the other hand, I have also heard from parents: 'I know intellectually that what you are saying is correct, but emotionally I can't do it.'"

Although the numbers of students attending Ramah programs in Israel are still down compared to the years before the intifada, the current participants have more than doubled since 2002. Joe said in a follow-up interview, "So far we have rehired one staff member. We could use more staff, but we have to take it a step at a time. Tourism throughout Israel has increased slightly, but there is still a long way to go."

Joe's desire to instill *ahavat yisrael*, a love of Israel, was influenced by Theodor Herzl,[70] the visionary for modern Israel. "Herzl teaches us the power of being an individual. In 1890 he said that in fifty years there would be a Jewish state and everyone laughed at him. He was off by eight years. He teaches us to strive even if the goal seems like an impossible task. I tell my tour groups that the message of Herzl is the message of every person in this country, whether a new immigrant or a native Israeli. Every person here has a potential for making this country even greater and better than it is. To me this is the magic of this country. It is the power of what one individual person can do. If you put that together with many other people who feel the same way, then you have this tremendous power. The big question is, How do you sustain the vision of Herzl? This question is the motivating force behind living in Israel and bringing people here whether it is for two days, two years, or a lifetime. I don't say every Jew must come and live in Israel, but every Jew must have a relationship with this country. You can carry on a love relationship with letters and through e-mails, but only for a certain amount of time. After a while, it is going to wane. How do you keep a love relationship going? You have to meet occasionally, right? You can't sit in Milwaukee, or Minneapolis, or Memphis, or any other city and say that you love Israel, that you support Israel, and you're all for it, and not visit. That is what it comes down to. You can't carry on a love relationship vicariously."

Since the initial interview with the Freedmans, the Israel Defense Forces has had a steady presence at an army post between Gilo and Bet Jala. Terrorist sniper fire is almost non-existent now and most residents have removed the sandbags from their windows. The concrete barriers remain. Joe is certain that the army's presence has made a difference.

Sue is full of optimism. She hopes and prays that families will come back soon and visit them in Israel. "I'm not referring to my own immediate family, but to the global family of Jews. We need you and we want you."

Arik Schahaff

Avi Borovoy

Chapter Nine
The Loss of Innocence: Children Facing Terror

Twenty-odd years ago, I went with my high school political science class to the Ethan Allen Correctional Facility for Boys in Wales, Wisconsin. We entered through a barbed wire fence and instantly freedom versus incarceration burned a lasting impression on my unexposed, naive world. The teens housed at Ethan Allen were behind bars to protect the public at large. Ha-Emek ha-Ma'aravi, the high school I visited in Israel, also had guards. It had an eight-foot green metal fence with a chained door for the school entrance, and various security procedures including ID review. The difference was that the Ha-Emek teens had committed no crimes – no drug busts, no assault or battery, no theft. The prison-like exterior was the precautionary measure to keep terrorists out and teenagers safe. Perhaps the comparison between a boys' correctional facility and this Israeli high school may seem extreme, but the common security elements were duly noted. The teens at Ha-Emek ha-Ma'aravi regional high school on Kibbutz Yifat do not appear to give their situation much thought. This is what must be done to survive, there is no other way. But, it is a heartbreaking commentary on growing up with terrorism. I don't even want to imagine what one or more terrorist attacks on our schools in the United States might force us to do to protect our children.

Arik Schahaff, principal of Ha-Emek ha-Ma'aravi, has done everything in his power to create an enclosed paradise of learning for students and teachers. "One of the biggest things that influenced my life was that I hated my high school. My high school felt like a prison, because the teachers and principal made our lives miserable. My eleventh- and twelfth-grade scout leader got me thinking about going into education. Then, when I was a scout leader I decided to be a teacher. I was sure that someday I would be a principal. I wanted to change the system. And if you walk around our school, you will see that it is very different than the typical school."

Arik was not alluding to the metal or stone fence surrounding the high school or the armed guard stationed at the locked entrance. I immediately recognized "the difference" Arik referred to. I saw students strolling on gravel paths surrounded by lush grass and freestanding buildings. Laughter filled the air. Teens sat on benches talking with each other. There was a casual, peaceful openness – a dichotomy to the world beyond the wall of twisted wire and old worn stones. The tension of the Israel outside faded away on the inside. School was a refuge.

Arik likes it that way. Though the school may be a shelter from terror, he does not hide reality from the students. Israeli life is embraced openly. Discussions about bombings and terror take place frequently, memorials are in place to remember the fallen, and items are collected for soldiers protecting their country. Practice drills for emergency situations are common, and juniors and seniors prepare for mandatory service in the Israel Defense Forces.

Even with these activities, Arik never loses sight of a collective dream – peace between Israelis and Palestinians. He knows there are many obstacles, but whenever he can, he extends the olive branch to those who might be willing to hold it with him. He does this by encouraging teacher and student participation in outreach programs between Jews and Israeli Arabs and Jews and Palestinians. For this, Arik is an unusual man. He does not give lip service to building bridges between Arabs and Jews. He lives it and models moderate views in an environment of high tension, black and white thinking that often comes with being young, and feelings of despair over the helplessness terror creates. He understands the fears, confusion, frustration, and anger because he has experienced all of those emotions and more. But he has built an environment where all ideas are welcome for discussion, even if they are what he perceives as extreme, standing firm in his convictions while encouraging others to voice their opinions. "I know what I think about war today," he said. "War is ugly, it stinks, it's very bad. I see hope. I know it is difficult to say this because Israel is going through trying times. I believe that we always have to talk with our enemy. This is what I am trying to tell everyone. I am not afraid of saying it. I wanted to make a bumper sticker: *The Hell with the Consensus*, but I am not going to do it."

He strives to always put the interests of the children and school first. Teachers, students, and parents know that he is accessible. He gives respect and receives it. His laid-back yet professional style wins the hearts of both staff and students. Some of the teens described their salt-and-pepper-haired, fully bearded, secular fifty-four-year-old principal as, "Hip!" "Cool!" "Fun!" When Arik talked about taking a year sabbatical, a number of high school juniors protested, "Not until after we graduate!" Principal Arik agreed.

As in the United States, education in Israel has taken a huge economic hit. Reduction of services is a necessity of more than just economic woes. Terror's repercussions have forced money once used for enhancing the quality of education to issues of security. Armored school buses, fences, safety shelters, armed guards, and special training for social workers and educators drain the budget of the Ministry of Education. The Psychological Counseling Service (pcs) provides teachers and students with psychological support in coping with terror. It offers guidance to rebuild a sense of security, hope, peace, and tolerance, along with grief counseling and therapeutic intervention. These high priorities have depleted many man-hours previously used to diagnose and treat students' learning disabilities, behavior, and social problems.

Like many educators throughout Israel, Arik takes this situation unhappily in stride. There is nothing to be done and there are no immediate answers to resolving the education crisis. He and thousands of others work with whatever assets they have available. What Ha-Emek ha-Ma'aravi has is the open campus environment, which offers a little breathing room and space to roam. Not many schools, especially in the big cities, are so fortunate.

I met Arik in his office. Secretaries worked in a room semi-enclosed with glass, with a sliding window that stayed open for easy access to students, teachers, and visitors. To my left was the staff lunch room. A computer waited for someone to check the latest Internet news or sport scores, and a warm coffee pot sat half full on a counter. Following directions, I walked down a narrow corridor and made a sharp ninety-degree turn to Arik's modest office. His desk formed the top of a T with a dark wooden table creating its leg. Seven chairs were situated around the second table, perfect for impromptu meetings with a few staff members or students. Natural light streamed through a window onto the sparsely decorated white walls. Sunshine yellow paint brightened the space behind his desk. Notices engulfed a cork bulletin board and folders, paperwork, a telephone, and computer took up most of Arik's work space. A black-and-white photo of Herzl, the father of Zionism, hung above his chair. My eye caught a certificate for ten years of participation from IPCRI – the Israel/Palestine Center for Research and Information. With pride, Arik pointed to the framed paper and explained that Ha-Emek ha-Ma'aravi has been involved in a pilot program called Education for Peace. "I have many Palestinian friends through IPCRI," Arik said, "teachers like me, who I know want peace. They want me to live in peace here and they want to live in peace on the other side. I know about this personally because until October 2001, along with eight of our teachers, I attended a series of seminars in Antalya, Turkey, for Palestinian and Israeli teachers. Forty Jewish and Arab Israeli and forty Palestinian teachers came together for the purpose of discussing peace. We talked about what we will do at the end of the intifada, what we will tell our children, and how will we teach them.

"The Palestinian teachers I know who want peace are afraid to speak out because they have no democracy. This is the problem. But they are there. I am in touch with them, if not by telephone, by Internet, and we share information as to what is going on. It is very difficult to talk with them because their telephone lines don't work so well. Of course, most of the Palestinian schools in the West Bank and Gaza are teaching hatred and destruction of the Jews. I know this. But if you have one small seed, you have to plant it and help it grow.

"Since the intifada, only teachers have met with Palestinians. In the past we visited a school in Bet Lehem and they came to us. But because we can't meet with the Palestinians anymore – the danger is too great – we asked volunteers from our school to meet with volunteers from an Israeli Arab school in Ibillin which is in Lower Galilee. We have a long-standing relationship with them. We had a two-day seminar between our Jewish teens and the Arab teens from Ibillin at Neve Shalom. Neve Shalom is a community where Jews and Arabs live together.[71]

"The program mostly focused on how to solve problems. First we talked about resolving problems between friends, and then between neighbors. Only at the end of the program did we talk about the Arab-Israeli conflict.

There were very intense discussions between the Jewish and Arab students at Neve Shalom. The Arab village, Ibillin, was involved in demonstrations against Israel on Rosh Hashanah and Yom Kippur, October 2001." Arik explained that at one of the demonstrations a sixteen-year-old Arab student from this Ibillin school was killed by Israeli police. The student had been standing outside holding a protest sign. "The students are very angry, not only because of this boy's death," Arik said, "but because they feel that they are not treated as equals by the Israeli government. There are many complicated problems between our different populations. The Neve Shalom experience was very interesting. Kids from here who hate Arabs continue to hate Arabs. They didn't change their point of view very much. But they saw that the Arabs behave like us, they love the same movies, and the same music, and that they are people."

The seminar was a beginning. The intifada has created thick walls between Jews and Arabs. Arik knows this. But still, he believes wholeheartedly that any effort is better than none at all. "I can tell you that not everyone agrees with this program and we do not force students to participate. We know that parents are afraid and that's why we ask for volunteers for the program. Those who object say, 'Why are we talking about the Arabs? Why should we talk to them?' Many say that this is not the time."

Students who attend Ha-Emek ha-Ma'aravi regional high school come from nine kibbutzim, moshavim, and small communities throughout the Jezreel Valley. In the 2001–2002 school year, 815 students enrolled for seventh through twelfth grades. The school has 810 Jews, 1 Bedouin Muslim, and 4 Circassian Muslims. Why would Muslims attend a Jewish high school? According to Arik, "The Muslim parents chose to send their children to Ha-Emek ha-Ma'aravi not only because of the high level of educational excellence, but also because of the relationship between teacher and students and our education of tolerance."

Barriers may be difficult to overcome, but Arik believes that communication is one of the most important steps to understanding. He said, "In my class we talk about pluralism, we have debates and everybody has the right to speak and give their opinions. Everything can be discussed. Students are not afraid to say, 'Transfer the Arabs out of Israel,' or to ask, 'Why didn't we destroy everything in Jenin?'[72] I have a teacher here who tells the kids, 'I believe that you shouldn't go to the army.' She can say this at our school even though I believe that it is very, very important for the students to go into the army and to keep the morale high. This is what pluralism is about."

Intense discussion about the conflict is not the only change at the high school. The school employs two guards instead of one and students may not leave the premises without parents coming to get them. While students are on break, teachers walk the grounds, carefully scanning the area for anything suspicious. There are drills for terrorist attacks and in case of war. "Of course, if something happens in Israel, like a bombing, we watch TV and make an announcement on the loudspeaker," Arik said. "We have to do this because otherwise the students run out of class asking more and more questions. They can go to the library and open the Internet to see what is going on. The children are much more afraid. We have told them that they can speak with their advisors in school any time. We have also given the students a hotline number to call if they need to talk to someone when they are not here. The teachers are very afraid too. They worry because their sons or daughters are in the army. They worry about being away from their small children who are in different schools. What if something happens at their school? It's very difficult, so we talk with the teachers."

A particularly emotional and stressful time for all Israelis was during the spring of 2002. Between March 20 and April 4 there were seven suicide bombings throughout Israel. One of the most horrific was the Park Hotel bombing in Netanya on March 27. A suicide bomber detonated a bomb strapped to his body in a banquet room filled with 250 guests who had gathered to celebrate the Passover seder – children, parents, grandparents. He killed 30 unarmed celebrants and injured 140. The trauma of this murderous event and the numerous other bombings required special assistance to help students and staff cope. Arik explained, "The day before the pupils came back to school after the Passover holiday break, we brought all the teachers together with the school psychologist to discuss with them how to behave, how to talk with each other and the kids, and how to recognize the pupils who might have problems. Most important was that teachers had to find a way to discuss the situation in a lesson, not by going into the classroom and saying, 'Okay, now let's talk.' It wouldn't work. For example, during the lesson I taught on pluralism, the students were talking about their fears. They get on a bus and they don't know if they will live after that. So we talked about it. One of the kids said, 'Why do we have to be afraid and the Palestinians don't have to be afraid?' So we talked about this too. I told my class that when my son went into the army, I didn't know what would happen to him and that I worried all the time. Of course, the students know. We don't have to tell them that we are concerned. They can see it on our faces."

Teachers and students must be prepared for the worst-case scenarios: a terrorist bombing, a shooting spree, or conventional, chemical, and biological warfare. "We talk about what the teachers need to do in case something happens at the school. They are the leaders in the classroom. They have to get over their fears and tell the class what to do." In March 2002 the students and staff of Ha-Emek ha-Ma'aravi had to use their training for a real-life and terrifying experience. Arik recalled, "The police told us that there was a terrorist in the area and we were told not to send the kids home. The youngest kids were already on the bus. They closed the roads and we had thirty buses standing in line. The police understood that this was a problem, that if someone wanted to kill kids, this would be the way. So the police let the buses go out. Here in school, I announced over the loudspeaker that everybody was to stay in their classroom. We locked the gate and a group of emergency volunteers from Kibbutz Yifat came to help guard the school. We told the kids to stay calm and the teachers talked with the students about the situation. It was very good training for us so that we could see where there were holes. We have trained groups of students – a fire group and a first aid group – and we didn't tell them what to do in this particular situation. They came to their positions and stayed in case someone needed them. The shutdown was only for half an hour and then the kids were allowed to go home. The next day we told the students what had happened and why."

Arik pointed to a folder and said, "This is my bible. If something should happen, I can open it and have in front of me all the addresses, phone numbers, and other important information on all the kids. And it's not only for if something should happen at the school: I have to be ready for everything." Arik pointed to another folder. It held the school's security procedure, adapted and pared down from a massive stack of rules and regulations into a user friendly manual intended to meet the needs of immediate action. Though neither folder is far from Arik at any time, a small glance and a pause of apprehension or perhaps hope was noticeable. I can imagine Arik's silent prayer: "May I never have to use these folders and the information contained within."

One of the biggest differences between American teens and Israeli teens is what they face after graduation. Arik supports the necessity of the mandatory army service that faces the majority of Israeli high school graduates, and preparation for the army is an integral part of the eleventh and twelfth grades. Arik said, "American children are thinking about dating, college, and parties – good for them. But here teens lose their childhood. The army is part of our lives. I did it, my children did it, and the pupils here will do it too. Students meet with soldiers who tell them what the army is like and they help them choose a unit. They meet with army psychologists. The army believes, and I also believe, that if you come to something that you recognize and it is familiar to you, then it's much easier for you to ac-climatize. In our school almost 100 percent of the students go into combat units. There are some kids from our school, two in the past year, who have chosen not to go into the army. One is a pacifist, and one is ill. The pacifist is working in a hospital for the disabled. He doesn't want to have a gun. Out of the 122 seniors of 2002 just a few are talking about not going into the army. Of course, everyone has to make the decision on their own to go or not to go." Conscientious objectors will be jailed for refusal to serve. There are, however, many reasons why a teen can be exempt from serving in the army, including health or religious beliefs.[73] My own thoughts drifted to September 11 and how schools throughout the United States canceled field trips, especially those to Washington, D.C., New York, and abroad. With terror nearly an everyday occurrence, I asked Arik if he had eliminated school outings. The answer was a resolute "*No!*" "We continue to take our kids on field trips, we didn't stop it. We have to continue with our routines. The ninth grade went to the Arbel, the mountain over the Sea of Galilee. The students told us that the trip was great because they were the only group there and didn't have to wait in line for another school to go down the mountain. Our eighth grade is going for three days to the Galilee and we are waiting for permission slips from the parents. We will go even if only 50 percent of the kids can participate, because we believe that they need to go. Every year the eighth grade goes to Jerusalem. At the beginning of the year, we send a letter to the parents explaining that we are planning a trip to Jerusalem. This year, 60 percent responded, 'No, we don't agree to a trip to Jerusalem, but you can take the students elsewhere.'" Arik explained that many parents felt that a trip to Jerusalem was a greater risk, more dangerous. Numerous terrorist attacks have occurred there, but the Galilee has been safe. "Before we take a group on a trip," Arik continued, "we check with the police to make sure an area is safe, and if the police tell us that it's okay, of course, it's okay. We take more armed escorts with us nowadays. We have to be much more conscious. We have to look at everything around us, but we have to continue. The students' safety is my responsibility. I don't sleep on these field trip nights. I have the cell phone next to me. I constantly call the staff to see what is going on there.

"We have to continue. This is our life. I don't believe that terrorism can win a state. The aim of terrorism is fear. I don't believe that when the terrorists flew the planes into the Twin Towers that all of the United States came crashing down. Terrorism can't take us as a state. We have to watch everything around us, but we have to continue."

Arik has four adult children. "Of course, I will tell my children, 'Don't go on the bus, I will take you in the car.' My youngest son – he doesn't listen to me. He's twenty-one now," he laughed.

Despite worries about terror, Arik has a simple approach to life. "Life is fun," he said. "And you have to find a way to live it. You have to go and find the way so that it will be nice for you and for those around you. I'm trying to be very calm, and I believe if the principal of the school is very calm, it will spread all over. And I see that it's working. I believe that we should continue with everything. If we have planned a lesson, then don't stop the lesson. Teach the students. There may be an abnormal situation on the outside, but inside school we try to keep it as normal as possible. I am a simple soldier in the army of God. I am not a philosopher. I believe that this is life. This is our life in Israel."

*   *   *

At Ha-Emek ha-Ma'aravi high school, sixteen-year-old Avi Borovoy* bounced her way to a small one-story rectangular structure for art class. Her long, straight dark brown hair swung back and forth against her dark blue T-shirt. "Please Save the Animal Kingdom" in bold white letters blazed from the front center of her shirt with a giraffe striding in the middle. The words: "If people care, the world and its wildlife can be saved," formed a border. Avi loves animals and has been a vegetarian like the rest of her siblings for most of her life. We entered her art room and with a critical eye she showed me the black-and-white photographs she had snapped and developed from her school trip to Poland. Ominous images of concentration camps, abandoned rooms with spider-webbed window frames overlooking an eerie pathway, and memorials to those who were murdered in death camps. This class trip made a huge impression on Avi, leaving her with a greater appreciation of life. Though Avi was acutely aware of the terror in Israel before her visit to Poland, she became more sensitive to the loss of innocent lives. "Your point of view about life changes after you come back from seeing the concentration camps," she said, "and you see that people died there for nothing." The experience invoked a strong desire to help others and reinforced her belief that killing, regardless of the cause, is wrong.

Avi and some of her classmates at Ha-Emek ha-Ma'aravi had traveled to Poland for a week in March 2002. The trip was the culmination of four months of elective study about the Holocaust.[74] For Avi, it was a journey into her family's history. Her beloved paternal grandfather was a Holocaust survivor. She walked through the Plaszow[75] concentration camp, where her grandfather was held captive. In memory of those who died, her great-grandparents, cousins, and seven great-aunts and great-uncles, Avi recited kaddish, the prayer for the dead. Her namesake, Yital, was one of the great-aunts who perished.

As Avi talked about her experience, this normally cheerful teen grew serious. "Once a week, on Fridays, I went to school to learn about the Holocaust as a prerequisite for our trip to Poland. Emek ha-Ma'aravi is a kibbutz high school and Fridays are working days for junior high school kibbutz kids. From grades nine through twelve, kibbutz teens must give one day of work to help their kibbutz." (Jewish schools typically run from Sunday to Friday, with only Saturday, the Sabbath, off.) Avi continued, "Each grade has a different scheduled day off school. But since I and many other kids from my high school don't live on a kibbutz, we are required to do volunteer work on our day off. Some kids work in libraries, kindergartens, first-aid stations, or help troubled youth. Since the trip to Poland was optional for the eleventh grade, the Holocaust class was held on our volunteer day. Kibbutz kids who went on the Poland trip had to make up their lost work hours. We prepared for our trip through study and class discussions. Then we traveled for a week to the northern part of Poland. We visited several ghettos. We saw concentration camps, including the place where my grandfather was. Every day I was there, I cried more. I cried like a year's worth of tears. It was really hard.

"At first when I came back, I didn't know if the experience really changed me. It didn't seem like it did on the first days back. Then there were some suicide bombings and when someone died, the people were no longer strangers. It was like losing family. You think about not only the people who died, but also everyone else. What if it was someone you know, or if it's you?"

Avi values family and friends, plays the drums, piano, guitar, and other instruments that she told me are too numerous to name. She enjoys taking photographs and hanging out with friends. Math is her least favorite subject and she looks forward to never opening a math book again. The latter was exclaimed with a big grin and a drawn out whoop. She is outgoing, delightful, and funny. Like many of her Israeli peers, living under the constant threat of terror has forced her to mature perhaps faster than her North American counterparts.

"Living with terror makes kids like me, and those even younger, grow up faster than we should," Avi said. "And I refused to grow up until now. I didn't make the decision. It just came, without knowing, especially after I saw a different view of life in the ghettos and concentration camps."

Though school is a place of learning and personal growth, it also represents a safe haven to relieve the overwhelming burden shouldered by Israeli youth. Avi explained, "We get updates in school, talk about what's going on. You just learn naturally by living here how to try to survive and what to look for. And you try not to be scared. It's kind of hard to express all of your feelings in front of thirty kids, especially when you just want to cry. I actually did it – started to cry – and I went out of class. I just couldn't sit. I felt like I was choking. Luckily, I found a teacher who was with my group in Poland. She sat outside with me and we talked for an hour. There's so much emotion because of these terrorist attacks – all the death. There's so much you don't share with other people. It just chokes you up. That hour freed me. It changed me. Expressing everything, just sitting there, without caring what was around me. It's school – but so what? I sat there and cried. I didn't mind. I told the teacher what I felt, how I had changed since I came back from Poland, and the way I look at life differently now."

School is not where Avi feels the most secure. "I feel safest at home," she said. "I didn't really think about it until a few months ago, when someone saw a suspected terrorist running around a few kilometers from our school. We were locked up in our classes for what seemed like an hour. Everyone called their parents on cell phones to tell them what was happening and to find out if they had any information. Once the police caught the guy, we were able to go home. I just know school would not be the first place I would run to if there were terrorists walking around. You don't really feel 100 percent safe. It's a door in a fence between you and the outside world. It's not that good a door."

Throughout all schools in Israel, changes in policy, behavior, and surroundings have forced students and teachers to adapt. Avi explained, "Teachers have to keep their mobile phones on all during class in case something happens. Cell phones are really popular in Israel because of the intifada. I'd say 95 percent of the kids at school carry a mobile phone. I share one with my younger sister, but mostly I have it. It makes me feel better. You know that if something happens you can call someone.

"We used to walk to a gas station nearby. There is a little restaurant there. You know, you'd just go out of school for fifteen minutes during a break, get yourself a sandwich, a coke. And now students can't leave school property."

Terror is not a common subject of conversation between Avi and her friends. She said, "We know what's going on. We don't have to be reminded. I don't want to sound that way, but we are just kids and we are trying to have fun and live a normal teen life in Israel. Everything has changed for us. You can't really go into a restaurant now without being scared. There are guards all over, but we still go out to movies. Sometimes we take buses, but it's scary, and now our parents mostly give us rides. The parents are more scared than we are. I hope that I won't have to worry about my kids the way my mom worries about me. That is why I don't go out a lot, not even once a month. I try to stay as safe as I can, taking my time in order to make sure that I am not in a situation where I might get hurt or killed by a terrorist. Part of it is that I know my parents trust me when I go out. They trust me to do the right thing. The other part is that I want to be the best person I can be, and that means making good decisions.

"I was supposed to go with my friends to a concert of famous singers in Rishon LeZion. It's about a two-and-a-half-hour bus ride from here. I had been with friends in 2001 and it was really a lot of fun. My mom said, 'I'm not going to tell you no, but I don't want you to go.' I told her, 'It's okay.' All she had to do was say no and I wouldn't go. My mom said, 'If you go, I'll just stay up all night and listen to the radio hoping not to hear any horrible news.' And I decided that one night of fun for me was not worth that one night of worry for her. Another friend couldn't go either 'cause her parents wouldn't let her. So we all hung out here and we had a great time. I would have gone if my mom hadn't said no, 'cause my dad was okay with me going. He looks at it from a different point of view than my mom. They both are afraid. It's just that my mom shows it much more than my dad does."

Some of my conversation with Avi had taken place in her school art room, but most of it took place in her bedroom. Both of us sat on her steel gray carpeting. Her drum set, desk, bunk beds, CDs, boom box, and homework almost consumed the room. Avi leaned against a white wall filled with posters from favorite movies such as *Galaxy Quest* and *The Usual Suspects*. She wore no makeup. Several multicolored braided string bracelets adorned her wrists – one she made, two were bought.

Throughout our intense conversation, Avi threw out quips that made me laugh. While we talked about her being a vegetarian, with sparkling eyes and a slightly higher pitch, silly voice she said, "I've been clean for most of my life." Smiles and giggles followed. Her quick wit was a refreshing reprieve from the seriousness, but it dissipated quickly.

Avi told me, "In Timrat, the community where I live, we have a new volunteer program that provides courses to learn CPR and survival techniques. So I volunteered for the training. I want to be prepared so if a terrorist attack happens, I can help. I want to do something so that others can live. When a suicide bomber comes, he believes he is doing something to serve his country. They shouldn't do it! I don't find death a solution to anything. No one should die before they should die. One should die old with grandkids, not young. We haven't even lived life yet. That's why I don't support what the terrorists are doing. We need to talk it out."

Awareness of one's surroundings is a key element to safety in Israel. Avi talked about how she goes about being cognizant of potential danger: "Well," she said, "you have to look for someone that looks suspicious. I hate to say it, but you have to look for Arabs. Not the nicest thing to say, but you have to see if there are any Arabs around you. If I think that I just saw a few people who look suspicious, I just go the other way. It may take a bit longer to get to where you want to go, but you feel safer. That extra minute you take going the longer way is worth everything else you could lose in the short run. And that's one of the things I learned growing up here. From the first glance, you've got to read people. What are they doing there? Do they fit into your environment? Like, if you're going shopping, is someone standing around staring? You learn to examine people and see if they are dangerous without even knowing them. It's about comparing people. This is something you learn from experience and common sense. They don't teach us this stuff in school. Sometimes you're scared to just walk around. I know how to look out for guys that look dangerous and I try to stay away from a lot of people when it's crowded. And yet, I'm not giving in to the situation. I still go out to movies and stuff. For now, I'm just hoping that one day I'll be able to go near an Arab and not be scared that I'm going to blow up or something."

Avi's not afraid of all Arabs. "I met some Arab kids where I study music, three boys and one girl," she said. "They're Christians who live in Nazareth. I'm really close with the girl. They're nice and I'm not scared of them. They are all pretty good friends of mine and I trust them. It can take a lot for me to trust someone. I probably would have been afraid of them if they were not in my class, and I didn't know them. When we are in music class, we act like youth are supposed to act, having a great time playing instruments and learning together. We try not to involve our outside life in our music world. We try not to mention anything that happens, like a bombing. We just focus on then and there and try to have fun. You have to know how to forget all the bad stuff for a minute. I can easily do it. I don't know how or why, but I can do it fast. I come back to reality when I see my dad watching his news. Then I hear what I've missed that day and how many more numbers have been added to the list of people killed since the intifada started."

Avi uses her music as a refuge to get away from this stress. She said, "Usually, before I go to bed, I stay up half an hour or an hour listening to songs and I try to figure out what they are telling me. I also play the drums or the piano. I close my eyes when I play. When you close your eyes you look into yourself. You become a combination of self and the instrument. It's so amazing 'cause you don't even pay attention to whatever is around you. Even if thousands of people were looking at you, you wouldn't care. It's just you." Later I heard from Avi that once the music course ended, she no longer had contact with her Arab classmates.

I asked Avi if she had anything in common with her Palestinian peers. She gave a quick response: "Yeah, we probably have the same thoughts sometimes. We are basically going through the same things in growing up. They're old enough to make their own decisions. That's something I've got in common with them." Avi paused for a short time. "Actually, the more

I think about it, we have less in common. They are brought up to believe that killing us is good. And we've grown up to know that they want to kill us and we should be careful. We know that we have to defend ourselves. It wouldn't make sense though if they all felt that killing is good. And still, fourteen-year-old Palestinian kids are coming here to blow themselves up."[76] Avi recently offered her condolences at the shivah house for a terror victim not much older than herself, the son of her mother's college friend.

The fundamental differences between Avi and Palestinian teens leave her uneasy. How could anyone hate so much that they would die in order to kill Jews? As incomprehensible as this hatred is, Avi has no problem understanding what it means to love something so much that she would be willing to put her life on the line to defend it. Since our initial interview, Avi has graduated from high school and will join a tank corps unit in the Israel Defense Forces. She will carry the memory of her paternal grandfather who, after surviving the Holocaust, fulfilled his dream of raising his family in Israel. She holds the memories of her trip to Poland and her pledge to remember that life is sacred.

She will soon take on responsibilities too unclear as yet to know how they will change her. Through it all there is one constant that she can count on – her family's love. "They've given me tools to handle this world," she said, "and ways to walk in this world so that I don't have to worry about a lot of other things except making good choices. They have given me trust, patience, tools to be a better person. I've learned how to take my time, instead of always being in a rush to finish things or go somewhere. Respect people, but be wary of strangers. Speak your mind, but be willing to listen to others. I wish I could say that I do these things all the time. I'm working on it. What more can I do?"

Benay Katz

Jeff Katz

Chapter Ten

Holding a Family Together: A Message of Hope

Traffic came to a dead stop on the Tel Aviv–Jerusalem highway. Horns blared with five long beeps followed by two quick blasts. No, these were not frustrated drivers releasing anger over the snail's pace, but celebrants of a national soccer tournament which had let out fifteen minutes before. Yellow and green flags waved from car windows, men selling ice cream and souvenirs stood in the middle of the freeway, and emanating from open car sunroofs and windows, teenagers gave out whoops of joy.

Benay Katz and I were on our way to Jerusalem for a few last interviews before my return trip to the States. For the previous hour she had shared her experiences of living with terror. With the honking horns and wild enthusiasm, I turned off the recorder. We sat in her car dazzled by the amazing spectacle. This was an Israel rarely seen by the outsider's eye – a breath of fresh air, a reminder that life is not always so bleak, even in the face of terror. Soon traffic began to flow and we returned to reality. Luckily, Benay had accounted for traffic and the interviews in Jerusalem took place on schedule. There was also enough time for last-minute gift shopping and dinner in a vegetarian restaurant on Jaffa Street in the heart of Jerusalem.

My last hours in the city echoed the rapture and uplifting spirit of the happy spectators we had seen earlier on the freeway. This time, however, the celebration was not over soccer. Instead, we stood with thousands who commemorated Yom Yerushalayim, Jerusalem Day, overflowing Jaffa and Ben-Yehudah Streets. What an experience! The site where numerous suicide bombers had murdered the innocent, where the spirit of a nation once filled with despair, was now filled with hope. Floats, performing youth groups, motorcycles, and flag wavers paraded the streets and traditional music filled the air with an electricity similar to Fourth of July celebrations throughout the United States. On June 7, 1967, during the Six-Day War, Israeli paratroopers battled their way to the Western Wall, the holiest site for Jews. For nearly twenty years, Jordanian rule had prevented Jews from entering the area. Garbage and other unimaginable means were used to bury and desecrate the sacred Wall. Today, with tight security, anyone may approach the hallowed ground.

Jerusalem was the fulfillment of Benay's Zionist dream. Over twenty-nine years ago, she came to Israel after enrolling in the Hebrew University. "I came to Israel from Milwaukee, Wisconsin, as a nineteen-year-old idealist," she recalled. "Like so many teenagers, I saw my world in black and white. There was absolute right and absolute wrong. I was raised in a Zionist home. To me, being a Zionist meant living in Israel. At the same time, I felt deep gratitude for having been born in the United States. I felt I had absorbed the values of a great culture, which I brought with me to Israel.

"Today I often think about how my choice to live here has impacted my five children. Before the start of the intifada, they experienced a sense of freedom and safety. Our front doors remained unlocked. I didn't give a second thought to letting the kids roam the streets of our village at any hour of the day or night. There was never a reason to be afraid. This leniency, however, took some conditioning because American parents are used to being more protective of their children. But times have changed. We no longer allow our children to wander as freely as before. The fear of terrorist attacks unconsciously influences my thoughts, if not my actions. I don't fall asleep at night until my children are safe at home. I still let them go to movies and restaurants, and even to take a walk at night. After all, I do the same.

"On February 13, 2004, our youngest, Eliraz, celebrated her fifteenth birthday at a restaurant in Herzliyyah. She had two requests: first, Italian food and second, that the restaurant must have a security guard at the entrance. Unfortunately, the guard showed up as we finished our supper. Initially Eliraz was distraught when she saw no guard. Quietly the two of us made a plan of attack. I would sit facing the entrance and visually check everyone entering the premises. We decided that if someone looked like a suicide bomber we would throw things from our table at the person. It made us laugh. We envisioned throwing forks and saltshakers at a suspicious person only to find out he was the innocent restaurant owner. Kidding aside, during Eliraz's celebration, I spent the entire meal 'on guard duty.' Actually, at any restaurant I am constantly on the lookout and always sit facing the entrance. At the same time, I reassure my family that we are safe.

"I do the same thing when we travel by bus. I look at each person before he gets on. Does his waist look thicker than normal? Does he have weird expressions on his face? On one bus trip, Eliraz and I were on our way to attend a family celebration. Suddenly she squeezed my hand and I saw that she was near tears. I asked her what was wrong. We were sitting in the front of the bus and she said, 'Mom, we should move further back so that when the suicide bomber blows himself up we won't be blown to bits.' I felt a chill run down my back. I knew for her sake I needed to keep my composure. I responded, 'Eli, the people closest to the driver are the safest. The terrorists usually keep walking toward the middle of the bus.' This seemed to reassure her a little, but of course it was hard to relax. When I think about this conversation and the one in the restaurant, I cannot help but wonder what kind of mother I am. How can I subject my children to this type of danger and fear? It's too surreal and it's too sad."

Several other experiences have been burned into Benay's memory. She told me, "During the summer of 2002, I took Eliraz and three of her girlfriends to a Haifa mall to see a movie. As I turned into the mall I saw a number of policemen were patrolling the area. I didn't think anything of it because their presence is not unusual. I also wasn't alarmed by how long it was taking to get into the mall's parking lot. Traffic stopped and I was preoccupied with getting the girls to the movie on time. After fifteen minutes of little progress, I told the girls to get out of the car. I gave them instructions to go into the mall and buy the tickets. As soon as I parked the car I would join them. Ten minutes later I was in. When I approached the mall guard, I asked him if he knew why there had been a traffic jam. What he said made my heart sink. 'There are terrorists in the area,' he said, 'and the police are searching for them.' I felt dizzy. What had I done? I had sent four young girls into a mall where terrorists might be hiding. I was engulfed by panic and ran into the mall to find the girls. It was almost completely empty. I found them on the third floor, near the theater. They wanted to look around the mall, but there was no way I was going to let them. I spent the next two hours staring at the theater's exit door. With the police protection, I felt it was safer to remain where we were than to go back to the parking lot or outside. In the end, the police caught the terrorists and another disaster was averted.

"Though this was nerve-racking, it wasn't the worst experience I've had since the intifada started. The most traumatic incident occurred in the beginning of October 2000. A few hours after the intifada started, Israeli Arabs started rioting in support of the Palestinians. That same day my husband, Jeff, had left for Ben-Gurion Airport in Tel Aviv for a business trip to Canada. It's almost a two-hour drive from our home and he had at least five hours to make the plane. Four hours after he left, he called from his cell phone. He wasn't going to make his flight. Israeli Arabs were rioting in Fureidis, a coastal village about half an hour's drive from our house en route to the airport. No one could drive past the village because the Arabs were burning tires on the roads and throwing rocks at cars. Traffic was at a standstill. Since Jeff should have been on the plane, I called our travel agent for advice. In turn, she contacted the airline and informed them of the situation. A few hours later, Jeff managed to get to the airport safely, even though he had to pass another rioting Israeli Arab village on the way. The plane was waiting. Because of the riots, Jeff wasn't the last passenger to board.

"The next few days were terrifying for me. I didn't drive Eliraz to gymnastics practice because we would have had to travel on a road through Manda, an Israeli Arab village on the way to the facility. My girlfriend's car was stoned on that road by angry Israeli Arabs. She was fortunate not to be hurt: her windshield was shattered and her car sustained some other minor damage. I was not going to take the risk. Ten minutes from my house, Israeli Arabs were also rioting in Nazareth. I didn't want any of us to leave our hilltop community. I relented, however, when Aryeh asked to visit a friend in Migdal ha-Emek, three miles away. It was a decision I later regretted. Close to midnight I received a phone call from Aryeh. He had heard there were riots somewhere near the center of Migdal ha-Emek and he wanted to come home. I told Aryeh I was on my way. I had to get him away from there as quickly as possible. I was shaking. I had no idea what I was heading into.

"Since Jeff was gone, I considered walking over to my neighbor to see if he would drive me to Aryeh. I stood next to his door debating if I should knock. I couldn't bring myself to do it. I got into the car and started the five-minute drive to Migdal ha-Emek. I cried the entire way. In a few minutes I reached the fork in the road where one way led to Nazareth and the other to Migdal ha-Emek. The police had closed off both roads and they were turning cars away. I started to panic. I had to get Aryeh no matter what. A policeman stopped me as I started up the road. Between my tears I managed to tell him that my son was trapped inside the city. He was very understanding and told me to stay safe and to get my son. Since the riots were contained to a few blocks in the center of the city, I had no difficulty reaching him. I hugged Aryeh and took him home. This experience left me shaken for days.

"It is my job as a parent to ensure my children's safety. Have I let my personal ideals and beliefs come between motherhood and Zionism? I think about what living with terror has done to my children. None have voiced a wish to leave and emigrate to North America. Each one firmly believes Israel is his or her home. Learning about the Holocaust has had a profound impact on their worldview and defines their reasons for continuing to live in Israel. Their paternal grandfather, Wilfred, was a Holocaust survivor and living in Israel was his dream. At my in-laws' home my children ate Shabbat dinners beneath the photographs of three of their grandfather's seven younger siblings murdered by the Nazis. Tzviya was given the middle name Esther, in memory of one of the siblings, and Avital was named after another. Jeff and his brother and sisters carry the names of other family members murdered by the Nazis. The memory of the Holocaust is a part of our lives. It is a part of the collective consciousness of every Jew living in Israel.

"Sometimes parents do not realize the psychological effect traumatic experiences have on their children. Jeff and I had no idea of the impact the first Gulf War had on Tzviya and Lianna. They were thirteen and ten years old when the first Scuds hit Israel on January 18, 1991. For the next six weeks we were under daily attack. The government had prepared the country for this possibility and called on everyone to create a sealed room in their homes. We used the master bedroom on the top floor. Our bedroom windows were sealed from the inside with thick clear plastic. When everyone was safe inside the room, we filled in the gap between the bottom of the door and the floor with a towel soaked in water and baking soda. These measures were to prevent deadly chemicals from missiles from seeping into the room. When the first Scud hit we didn't know if it was chemical, biological, or conventional. We ran to our sealed room and put on gas masks. Eliraz was a preschooler, too young for a standard gas mask. Instead she went into a clear collapsible plastic tent with an air filter. One side of the tent was equipped with built-in gloves for parents to insert a comforting hand. I put candies inside the tent to entice Eliraz to crawl in. We also had the dog with us. Then the children remembered our parakeets downstairs. They became distraught, but we were too afraid to open the door to our sealed room. There are no explosions when a chemical bomb drops. Not a sound. At least that was what we were told. We had no idea if we had been hit or not. The children stared at the door and cried for their birds. When the all clear signal was given over the radio, the kids ran down to see if they were still alive. Of course, they were all right because no non-conventional weapons were dropped on us.

"Within a few days, Jeff and I came to the conclusion that our family would be safer in our very small bomb shelter on the ground floor than in our upper bedroom. Saddam was firing conventional weapons and against that the bomb shelter was our best protection. To play it safe, however, we closed off the air vents and hoped the air supply would last the duration of a Scud attack. Jeff's parents came to visit for a day during the second week of the war. They too joined us in the bomb shelter during an attack. Jeff's mom, Doris, told me afterward that she wasn't worried about a bomb, only about a lack of air! We were eight people wearing gas masks, one toddler in a tent, and a dog in our tiny bomb shelter. There was no room in which to move and after twenty minutes our air supply was dwindling. Luckily, the all clear was soon sounded and we were free to leave the shelter. Saddam's Scuds were usually fired during the night. During the day we went to work and the children went to school. Everyone in the country carried gas masks and collapsible tents with them. Stores sold colorful plastic boxes for students to carry their masks and life continued in a fairly normal state of business as usual. When evening arrived people became basket cases. Once it was dark in Iraq, we knew we would be attacked. The anxiety resulted from not knowing when or where. Jeff was working at the high tech company Intel. With just a few exceptions, almost everyone anxiously left work early and headed home to be with their families. The country just sat and waited. We slept with the radio turned to the quiet station, a silent channel that would blast a loud, blaring siren each time a Scud was launched against us. Awaking with a jolt, we'd hurry to the bomb shelter and wait for the all clear signal from the TV in the room. During every attack I called my in-laws to make sure they were all right. They lived ten kilometers north of Ramat

Gan, where many Scuds fell. My father-in-law told me that his bed shook with each explosion. We talked through our gas masks and it was hard to hear each other. Our conversations were brief.

"My mother, Miriam, who lived in Milwaukee, also called during the attacks. She spent the first four weeks of the Gulf War in front of the T V watching and waiting for news about Israel. One evening, when we were still retreating to the master bedroom during the first few days of the war, we looked out the window toward Haifa and saw two U.S. Patriot missiles flying toward an incoming Scud. We couldn't believe what we were seeing. Just then my mom called and I told her about the Patriot missiles. She said, 'Yes, I know. I see it on CNN too.' My jaw dropped, as if that was really possible in my gas mask. I said, 'Mom, it's out my window!'

"Experiencing the war via CNN was too nerve-racking for my mom. She wanted to be with her family and so joined us for the last two weeks of the war. Landing at the airport she was handed a gas mask by the army. Like many other able men, Jeff was called to army reserve duty during the last few weeks of the war. The tension and stress caused by the war was everywhere. A few days before the end of the war my father-in-law suffered a heart attack. I called Jeff's army unit and he rushed to join his siblings at the hospital. Doris brought plastic sheets and tape from home and sealed the Intensive Care Unit against chemical and biological attacks. The hospital staff had forgotten to do so. I left the kids with my mom and traveled the two-hour drive to the hospital in Tel Aviv to be with them. I alternated between looking at the road and at the sky for Scuds until I arrived safely. The war proved too much stress for my father-in-law, a man with a heart condition. He was scared for his children and grandchildren. On the last day of the war, he died. His premature death was hard on all of us.

"I didn't quite realize the full trauma of his death and the war on my children until a few years later, when we were in France. A fire station siren blared while Tzviya and Lianna were sitting in our rented RV. They started to cry hysterically. The siren sounded just like the one we heard during the Gulf War. They were inconsolable, hiding under the table, sobbing and covering their ears. It took us a long time to calm them down.

"The effects the first Gulf War had on our children were unexpected. We had spent those six weeks living in terror, but when it ended, we thought it was over emotionally for the children as well. The extent that the terror of the intifada has an effect on our children will become evident only in the years to come. Right now they try to cope on a daily basis. They all know people who have been killed or maimed by terrorists, and they all experience the initial fear of not knowing if their loved ones have become victims. My children live with stresses and traumas few Western children experience. Our country is at war with an enemy not always seen. I dreamed once that Israel encased itself with a magic bubble providing protection from its enemies. No missile could penetrate the bubble and no army could attack. Maybe my bubble is the much maligned security fence of today. I can only hope so.

"One day there will be peace here. One day the shattered trust between Jews and Arabs will be rebuilt, even if it takes a hundred years. We need to show our children Arabs with whom they can live in peace and security. Our future depends on it, just like the Arabs' future depends on teaching their children to strive for peace and coexistence. We are in constant contact with Israeli Arabs out of choice and because we live near Nazareth, Haifa, and many Bedouin villages. Our dentist, orthodontist, general practitioner, home builder, and many storeowners are Muslim and Christian Arabs. We also employed several Arabs when we had a clean room company for the high tech industries.

"Our ex-foreman, Wisam, is Muslim. He comes from Umm el-Fahem, a very large Israeli Arab village. He stopped working for us four years ago when we finished a project. We never lost contact with him or with his family. After the Israeli Arab riots we invited Wisam and his family to our sukkah during the Jewish holiday of Sukkoth. We told him it was our 'peace tent.' Many official 'peace sukkahs' were put up throughout the country that October 2000 as a means to reestablish communication between the Arab and Jewish communities. The riots dealt a crushing blow to coexistence. Jeff called Wisam and asked him to join us with a promise that we wouldn't talk politics. Wisam and his father came. We avoided politics, but somehow the conversation turned to the United States. They expressed intense hatred toward America. 'America,' they said, 'is a racist and evil country and we would never set foot on its shores.' They told us they would only travel to Muslim countries. Aside from comments such as these, we shared a pleasant evening with them. More important, we proved to each other that coexistence was still possible.

"In May 2003, Wisam invited us to his engagement party. We didn't know if we should go. I was scared to drive into Umm el-Fahem. The mayor of the city had just been arrested for allegedly supporting a terrorist organization and I wasn't sure Jews would be safe in the village. Jeff decided to go alone. A few minutes before he was going to leave, I changed my mind. I set my fear aside because I wanted Wisam's family to know that we care about them. I also felt that our presence would make a statement: Arabs and Jews can coexist. Avital and Eliraz came with us. As we approached Umm el-Fahem our apprehension grew. To cut the tension, Avital pointed to an Arabic sign that she couldn't read and quipped, '"Kill the Jews." Hmmm, that can't be good.' We burst out laughing. Her humor reflected our fears.

"Wisam's family greeted us with hugs and kisses and our daughters were made to feel welcome. We were the only Jews invited. For a while we sat in the small crowded apartment with the extended family. Pictures of relatives adorned the walls as did a Palestinian flag. Then we left with the family procession to the bride's house in the Muslim village, Arara. As we left Umm el-Fahem, there was a demonstration against the Israeli government. Signs declared, 'Democracy – not just for the Jews' and 'Supporting an orphan is a step toward peace.' The government had stated that Israeli Arab citizens could not give financial support to Hamas families – the 'orphans' are the suicide bombers' children.

"At the entrance to Arara there were protesters. The girls and I felt nervous, vulnerable. Once in the village, some of the drivers in our procession honked their horns to announce our arrival. At the bride-to-be's home the men stayed on one side and the women on the other until the ceremony began. There were a few hundred people and most of the time the girls and I stood watching the women dance with Wisam's fiancé, a student at Haifa University. Food was brought out by the fiancé's female relatives and distributed among the two families. For the most part, we were ignored by other women and not offered anything. We felt out of place. One elderly aunt, though, must have seen our discomfort and came over to us. She smiled and gave us food. After a while Wisam was brought in by the men and he danced with his fiancé. Other members of the family danced too. Wisam's sister grabbed Avital and Eliraz to have them join the dancing. I could see the shock on many of the fiancé's family's faces. Avital and Eliraz didn't notice. They had a wonderful time and quickly picked up the dance moves of the other women. Wisam's mother took my hand and we joined the girls dancing in a circle. We stayed three and a half hours.

"It was an amazing experience for all of us. I was thrilled that the girls saw a part of Israel's society that few of their friends have experienced or know about. Though we did get plenty of uncomfortable looks at the party, many people were friendly and no politics were discussed. Four of our Muslim ex-workers were invited to the celebration and Jeff had the opportunity to speak with them. They said that the two years building the clean rooms for our company was the best experience they had ever had. It was also the first time they had lived among Jews. Jeff had rented an apartment for the men in Kiryat Gat, a Jewish town close to our work site. Every weekend Jeff drove them back to their villages.

"On the way home from the engagement party, Eliraz asked me, 'If I don't want any Arabs killed, does this mean I am a Leftist?' This question made me so sad. I explained to her that people on both political sides don't want to see Arabs killed. We don't believe that killing is the answer and killing Arabs is not what the political Right stands for. The Left and the Right want the same thing – they both want to live in peace with the Arabs.

"Wanting to live in peace, however, is a distant dream. One of the biggest conceptual differences between Israelis and Palestinians is in their maps of the region. One only needs to look at these maps to see the crux of the problem. Our maps show Israel, Gaza, and the West Bank. The Palestinians' maps show the land with no Israel. This denial of our existence and our rights to any of this land is the whole story without words."

Benay concluded, "I have changed in the almost thirty years since I moved to Israel. I saw my world through the eyes of a nineteen-year-old idealist. Now I see everything through the eyes of a mother of five. I have mellowed over the years. My children's physical and mental wellbeing take precedence over everything else. So why do I stay here? Why do I still feel this is the only place to raise my family? The answer was and still remains: Zionism. I want to be part of the Zionist dream, to build a safe and secure Israel, a place where Jews everywhere can find refuge and a Jewish homeland. I want to help preserve the Jewish culture and the Jewish people.

"The world today is not unified. It is still divided and defined by ethnic, nationalistic, and religious differences. This will not change in coming generations. The world is too fragile for worldwide peace to take hold. In the meantime, I want to make sure my family stays safe in the one country where we Jews can protect ourselves and proudly be ourselves. Israel is the only place where I truly feel a sense of belonging. This land is where my ancestors lived before they were forced to roam in the Diaspora. I feel the line of continuity as I walk in my garden and look down upon the Jezreel Valley. I am a proud Jew in the Galilee like those Jews who walked here before me over three thousand years ago. Israel will persevere and remain a strong democratic country despite the many obstacles placed in her path by the Muslim world and by European nations who continue to condemn Israel for its right to self-defense. I want to be a part of this country and help it realize its continuing central place in history. Israelis want nothing more than to turn this jewel in the Middle East into a vibrant country dedicated to enriching the lives of all its inhabitants – Jews, Muslims, and Christians. We will continue to respect religious differences as stated in our Declaration of Independence. We envision a future of mutual trust and coexistence that can truly be a light among the nations. Until that time we are and will remain a people waiting for peace."

Endnotes

1. "Do me a kindness and a truth." (Genesis 47:29) A kindness done to the dead is a true kindness, for one does not expect a favor in return. (Rashi) The Midrash relates that when God desired to create man, Truth argued that "he should not be created, for he is full of lies." Kindness, however, said, "He should be created, for he is full of kindness." To this, Truth might have replied: "But that, too, is just another of man's lies. Yes, man does acts of kindness to his fellows, but not because he is 'full of kindness' – only because he expects them to be kind to him in return. However, there is one act of kindness that proves Truth wrong: the kindness done to the dead. This "kindness and truth," as the Torah calls it, shows that man is capable of a truly altruistic deed, thereby attesting that all our acts of kindness – even those superficially tainted by selfish motives – are in essence true, deriving from an intrinsic desire to give of ourselves to our fellows. (Rabbi Menachem Schneerson, the Lubavitcher Rebbe)

2. This was the demarcation between the 1967 borders of Israel and the West Bank territories captured in the Six-Day War. "The reference came about because someone used a green pen on the map of the armistice agreement with Jordan to draw the border." Source: American-Israeli Cooperative Enterprise. "Glossary." The Virtual Jewish Library. http://www.us-israel.org/jsource/gloss.html#g

3. August 9, 2001, "15 people were killed, including 7 children, and about 130 were injured in a suicide bombing at the Sbarro Pizzeria at the corner of King George Street and Jaffa Road in downtown Jerusalem. Carrying the explosives in a bag strapped to his body, the terrorist entered the restaurant just before 2 P.M. and detonated the bomb. The 5 kg.–10 kg. bomb, which was packed with nails, screws, and bolts, completely gutted the restaurant, which was full of lunchtime diners....Hamas and the Islamic Jihad claimed responsibility for the attack." Source: Israel Ministry of Foreign Affairs. "Suicide bombing at the Sbarro Pizzeria in Jerusalem." State of Israel. http://www.mfa.gov.il/mfa/go.asp?MFAH0kb90

197

4.   On December 1, 2001, two suicide bombers detonated in the pedestrian mall on Ben-Yehudah Street. Eleven people were killed, ranging in age from fourteen to twenty-one. Another 180 people were injured. Hamas took responsibility for the attack. Source: Israel Ministry of Foreign Affairs. "Victims of Palestinian Violence and Terrorism since September 2000." State of Israel. http://mfa.gov.il/mfa/go.asp?MFAH0ia50

5.   On 7 March 2002, five eighteen-year-olds were killed and twenty-three people were injured when a Palestinian gunman entered a yeshiva in the Gush Katif community in Atzmona. Source: Israel Ministry of Foreign Affairs. "Victims of Palestinian Violence and Terrorism since September 2000." State of Israel. http://mfa.gov.il/mfa/go.asp?MFAH0ia50

6.   In addition to the shots fired on the road, bullets continue to fly into Kadim. On April 29 at 3:30 P.M., a terrorist shot at a resident as he gathered his mail from his box at the Kadim office. Fortunately, he walked away unharmed.

7.   On October 14, 2001, a terrorist dressed in an Israeli paratrooper uniform opened fire at the Afula central bus station. Three Israelis were killed and several others were injured. Source: Israel Ministry of Foreign Affairs. "Victims of Palestinian Violence and Terrorism since September 2000." State of Israel. http://mfa.gov.il/mfa/go.asp?MFAH0ia50

8.   On March 5, 2002, a terrorist blew himself up on the number 823 Egged bus at the Afula central bus station. An eighty-five-year-old man was killed and numerous people were injured. Islamic Jihad took responsibility. Source: Israel Ministry of Foreign Affairs. "Victims of Palestinian Violence and Terrorism since September 2000." State of Israel. http://mfa.gov.il/mfa/go.asp?MFAH0ia50

9.   On June 28, 2001, terrorists shot and killed twenty-seven-year-old Ekaterina (Katya) Weintraub while she drove on the Jenin bypass road. Source: Israel Ministry of Foreign Affairs. "Victims of Palestinian Violence and Terrorism since September 2000." State of Israel. http://mfa.gov.il/mfa/go.asp?MFAH0ia50

10. The first intifada was during 1987–1993. "The intifada…was triggered, though not caused, by a car crash in which four Palestinians were killed by an Israeli vehicle on December 8, 1987. Hundreds of Palestinians turned on Israeli troops stationed in the Gaza Strip's largest refugee camp of Jabalya, and demonstrations and riots spread like wildfire to other refugee camps throughout the Gaza Strip and the more affluent and secular West Bank. In December, the riots spread to Jerusalem." Source: The Department for Jewish Zionist Education, The Pedagogic Center.

"Israel and Zionism: The First Intifada, 1987–1993." The Jewish Agency for Israel. http://www.jafi.org.il/education/100/maps/fintifada.html

11. Lehi is the Hebrew acronym for "Fighters for the Freedom of Israel." This secret militant group of young men and women fought against the British before Israel became a state. The British nicknamed Lehi the "Stern Gang" for its founder, Abraham Stern. Out of the approximately 840 members, half were in British prisons. Many were sentenced to death and hanged. The British murdered a few members, including Stern. Source: Gad Nahshon, "Amir: Freedom Fighters of Israel," *Jewish Post*, July 2002, www.jewishpost.com/jp0807/jpn0807g.htm

12. Akko is a Mediterranean port north of Haifa.

13. Ariel Sharon is the current prime minister of Israel.

14. "Jenin was entered by Israeli forces in early April 2002, as part of Israel's Operation Defensive Shield…23 Israeli soldiers were killed in the street fighting, 14 of them in a single day from a charge carried by a suicide bomber that triggered the collapse of a building and from shooting done by his accomplices. Overall, Israel said that its forces had killed 47 militants and 7 civilians." Source: "Jenin in the News." WorldHistory.com. http://www.worldhistory.com/wiki/J/Jenin.htm

15. Tefillin: Phylacteries containing four biblical passages that are reminders of God's covenant with the Jewish people.

16. Yasser Arafat, president of the Palestinian National Authority.

17. "On September 13, 1993, a joint Israeli-Palestinian Declaration of Principles (DOP), based on the agreement worked out in Oslo, was signed by the two parties in Washington, outlining the proposed interim self-government arrangements, as envisioned and agreed by both sides. The arrangements contained in the DOP include immediate Palestinian self-rule in Gaza and Jericho, early empowerment for the Palestinians in West Bank, and an agreement on self-government and the election of a Palestinian council. Additionally, extensive economic cooperation between Israel and the Palestinians plays an important role in the DOP." Source: Israel Ministry of Foreign Affairs. "The Israel-Palestinian Negotiations: Background – Israel-PLO Recognition." State of Israel. http://www.mfa.gov.il/MFA/Peace%20Process/Guide%20to%20the%20Peace%20Process/Israel-Palestinian%20Negotiations

18. "At the urging of Israeli Prime Minister Ehud Barak, U.S. President Clinton announced on July 5, 2000, his invitation to Prime Minister Ehud Barak and Palestinian Authority Chairman Yasser Arafat to come to Camp David to continue their negotiations on the Middle East peace process." On July 11, the

Camp David 2000 Summit convened. The summit ended on July 25, without an agreement being reached. At its conclusion, a Trilateral Statement was issued defining the agreed principles to guide future negotiations." Source: American-Israeli Cooperative Enterprise. "The 2000 Camp David Summit." The Virtual Jewish Library. http://www.us-israel.org/jsource/Peace/cd2000.html

19. Ehud Barak, Israel's prime minister between May 1999 and February 2001.

20. The 1967 lines were those delineated following the 1967 Six-Day War, and included in Israel the West Bank and Gaza Strip.

21. Literally "kingfisher"; a classified elite unit in the Israel Defense Forces.

22. Ramadan is the ninth month of the Muslim calendar, when it is believed the Koran was sent down from heaven. During the entire month of Ramadan, Muslims fast during the daylight hours.

23. A suicide bombing at Café Moment on March 9, 2002, killed eleven people. Fifty-four were injured, "when a suicide bomber exploded…in [the] crowded cafe at the corner of Aza and Ben-Maimon Streets in the Rehavia neighborhood in the center of Jerusalem. Hamas claimed responsibility for the attack. The bomber walked into the cafe, located…about 100 meters from the prime minister's residence, and detonated a powerful explosive charge that completely gutted the restaurant." Source: Israel Ministry of Foreign Affairs. "Suicide bombing at Café Moment in Jerusalem March 9, 2002." State of Israel. http://www.mfa.gov.il/mfa/go.asp?MFAH0lb10

24. "On April 30, 2003, a suicide terrorist blew himself up at the entrance to Mike's Place, a pub/cafe on the Tel Aviv promenade. Three civilians were murdered and over 50 were wounded in the attack." Source: Israel Ministry of Foreign Affairs. "Details of April 30, 2003 Tel Aviv suicide bombing." State of Israel. http://www.mfa.gov.il/MFA/Government/Communiques/2003/Details+of+April+30-+2003+Tel+Aviv+suicide+bombing.htm

25. "Nine people - four Israelis and five foreign nationals - were killed and 85 injured, 14 of them seriously, when a bomb exploded in the crowded Frank Sinatra cafeteria on the Hebrew University Mt. Scopus campus shortly after 13:30. Hamas claimed responsibility for the attack." Source: Israel Ministry of Foreign Affairs. "Terrorist bombing at Hebrew University cafeteria: July 31, 2002." State of Israel. http://www.mfa.gov.il/MFA/MFAArchive/2000_2009/2002/7/Terrorist+bombing+at+Hebrew+University+cafeteria+-.htm

26. The Lebanon War. Source: Mitchell Bard, American-Israeli Cooperative

Enterprise. "The Lebanon War." Jewish Virtual Library. http://www.us-israel. org/jsource/History/Lebanon_War.html

27. On April 22, 1979, "Danny Haran, 28, and his daughters Einat, four, and Yael, just two, were killed in the attack along with policeman Eliyahu Shahar, who was called to what was originally thought to be a burglary and was shot dead by one of the (PLO) terrorists...Danny Haran and Einat were killed in cold blood by the terrorists. Yael died of suffocation in the arms of her mother, Smadar, who was trying to keep her quiet while they hid in terrified desperation from the terrorists who had invaded their home." Source: Jpost.com staff, "Senior officer: Kuntar was sent by Palestinians, not Lebanese," *Jerusalem Post*, November 11, 2003, http://www.jpost.com/servlet/Satellite?pagename=JPost/JPArticle/ Printer&cid=1068525554710

28. Shabak is a Hebrew acronym for Sherut ha-Bitachon ha-Klali, General Security Service, which is also known as the Shin Bet.

29. Yitzhak Rabin was a Labor Party politician and member of the Knesset. In June 1992 he was elected prime minister of Israel. Rabin began peace talks with Yasser Arafat in 1993. He was assassinated in November 1995.

30. Yossi Beilin is an Israeli politician who has held various positions during Labor governments.

31. Shimon Peres has served as a member of the Knesset since the 1950s. He helped form and has belonged to the Labor Party since 1968. Besides serving as prime minister and various other ministerial positions over the years, Peres was foreign minister under the Labor government of 1992–1995.

32. The PLO Charter. Source: "The PLO Charter." Information Regarding Israel's Security (IRIS). http://www.iris.org.il/plochart.htm

33. On May 10, 1994, at a mosque in Johannesburg, South Africa, Arafat declared, "The jihad will continue...You have to understand our main battle is Jerusalem...You have to come and to fight a jihad to liberate Jerusalem, your precious shrine...No, it is not their capital. It is our capital." (Israel Radio, May 17, 1994; *Jerusalem Post*, May 1994) Arafat also compared the Oslo Accord with the truce between Muhammad and the Quraish tribe, which later was annulled: "This agreement, I am not considering it more than the agreement which had been signed between our prophet Muhammad and Quraish, and you remember that the Caliph Omar had refused this agreement and considered it a despicable truce...But the same way Muhammad had accepted it, we are now accepting this peace effort." (*Ha'aretz*, May 1994) Source: Israel Ministry of Foreign Affairs.

"Incitement To Violence Against Israel by the Leadership of the Palestinian Authority." State of Israel. http://www.mfa.gov.il/mfa/go.asp?MFAHocogo

34.   "Geneva Convention relative to the Protection of Civilian Persons in Time of War – Adopted on 12 August 1949 by the Diplomatic Conference for the Establishment of International Conventions for the Protection of Victims of War, held in Geneva from 21 April to 12 August, 1949." Source: "Geneva Convention relative to the Protection of Civilian Persons in Time of War." Office of the United Nations High Commissioner for Human Rights. http://www.unhchr. ch/html/menu3/b/92.htm

35.   *Shahid* is the Arabic term for a martyr.

36.   In October 2000, Israeli Arabs in Nazareth rioted by throwing stones and block-ing roads. The riot was a show of support for Palestinians in the West Bank and Gaza.

37.   This operation took place during March 28–April 17, 2002. "Operation Defensive Shield – the Israel Defense Forces' (IDF's) counterterrorism operation in the West Bank – aims to confiscate illegal weaponry and bombing materiel; destroy factories producing bombs and missiles; constrict the environment in which terrorists plan, prepare, and execute terror attacks; and, most important, ap-prehend the operatives behind the current terrorist offensive." Source: Matthew Levitt and Seth Wikas. "PeaceWatch: Defensive Shield Counterterrorism Accomplishments." The Washington Institute for Near East Policy. http://www. washingtoninstitute.org/watch/Peacewatch/peacewatch2002/377.htm

38.   On March 5, 2002, a suicide bomber blew himself up on the number 823 Egged bus traveling from Tel Aviv to Nazareth. The bus was near Wadi Ara, which is close to Afula. Seven people were killed and approximately thirty were injured. Islamic Jihad took responsibility for the attack. Source: Israel Ministry of Foreign Affairs. "Victims of Palestinian Violence and Terrorism since September 2000." State of Israel. http://www.mfa.gov.il/mfa/go.asp?MFAH0ia50

39.   *Sabra* is a Hebrew term for someone born in Israel. It is derived from the name of a cactus fruit, which is prickly on the outside but sweet on the inside.

40.   "The British issued a policy document [the White Paper of 1939] to limit Jewish immigration to 75,000 over the following five years. This White Paper also ended Jewish land purchases." Source: "*A History of Israel.*" Mark Schulman. http://www. multied.com/Israel/1939WhitePaper.html

41.   "Three Jewish underground movements operated during the British Mandate period. The largest was the *Haganah*, founded in 1920 by the Jewish community

as a defense militia to safeguard the security of the Jewish population. From the mid-1930s, it also retaliated following Arab attacks and responded to British restrictions on Jewish immigration with mass demonstrations and sabotage. The three organizations were disbanded with the establishment of the Israel Defense Forces in June 1948." Source: Israel Ministry of Foreign Affairs. "History – Foreign Domination – February 3, 2004." State of Israel. http://www.mfa.gov.il/MFA/Facts+About+Israel/History/HISTORY-+Foreign+Domination.htm

42. Nahal is a Hebrew acronym that stands for *Noar Halutzi Lohem* (Fighting Pioneer Youth). Nahal units combine military service with agricultural work in moshavim and kibbutzim.

43. Youth Aliyah (Aliyat Hanoar) was an organization initiated in the 1930s that brought young persons from all over the world to Israel and helped them settle in institutions and villages.

44. Yitzhak Rabin was assassinated on November 4, 1995, after attending a rally in support of the new peace process.

45. On June 1, 2001, "21 people were killed [including 16 teenagers] and 120 were wounded when a suicide bomber blew himself up outside a disco near Tel Aviv's Dolphinarium along the seafront promenade just before midnight…The terrorist mingled with a large group of teenagers, who were standing in line to enter the disco. While still in line, he detonated the explosives strapped to his body. The explosive charge contained a large number of metal objects – including balls and screws – designed to increase the extent of injuries…The 'Palestinian Hizbullah' claimed responsibility for the attack." Source: Israel Ministry of Foreign Affairs. "Tel-Aviv suicide bombing at the Dolphin disco – June 1, 2001." State of Israel. http://www.mfa.gov.il/mfa/go.asp?MFAH0k0g0

46. Thirty people were killed on March 27, 2002, "and 140 injured – 20 seriously – in a suicide bombing in the Park Hotel in the coastal city of Netanya, in the midst of the Passover holiday seder with 250 guests. Hamas claimed responsibility for the attack." Source: Israel Ministry of Foreign Affairs. "Passover suicide bombing at Park Hotel in Netanya." State of Israel. http://www.mfa.gov.il/mfa/go.asp?MFAH0le00

47. David Ben-Gurion was an Israeli statesman and the first prime minister of Israel.

48. *Halutz* is Hebrew for "pioneer."

49. Palmach (a Hebrew acronym for Plugot Machatz, "shock companies") was the elite fighting division of the Haganah, established in May 1941.

50.   Haganah was a secret military organization founded in June 1920 put together
       to protect Jewish residents in Palestine from Arab attack because the British
       did little to protect Jewish settlements. After the 1929 Arab riots the Haganah
       "became a large organization encompassing nearly all the youth and adults in
       the settlements, as well as several thousand members from each of the cities. It
       initiated a comprehensive training program for its members, ran officers' training
       courses; Established central arms depots into which a continuous stream of light
       arms flowed from Europe. Simultaneously, the basis was laid for the underground
       production of arms." Source: "*Haganah*." History Learning Site. http://www.
       historylearningsite.co.uk/haganah.htm

51.   *Notrim* is Hebrew for "guards" or "monitors."

52.   "Following Kristallnacht, the Night of the Broken Glass, on November 9, 1938,
       groups of children were transported to Britain for sanctuary via a program called
       'Kindertransport.' The children had to be between the ages of 3 and 17 and they
       had to leave Germany alone, without their parents. Ten thousand children were
       transported to the UK on trains via Holland. Only about 20% of these children
       were reunited with their families." Source: A Teacher's Guide to the Holocaust.
       "Children." Florida Center for Instructional Technology, College of Education,
       University of South Florida. http://fcit.coedu.usf.edu/holocaust/people/children.
       htm

53.   "In the 1920s and 1930s, the British capitulated to Arab demands to limit Jewish
       immigration to Palestine and they issued a series of 'White Papers' rendering
       Jewish immigration illegal. The White Paper of 1939 limited Jewish immigration
       to Palestine at 10,000 people per year for five years. The Haganah and other
       agencies established a secret, underground network to continue the flow of
       Jews to Palestine." Source: Anti-Defamation League. "Immigration Since the
       1930's." Anti-Defamation League. http://www.adl.org/Israel/Record/immigra-
       tion_since_30.asp

54.   "The Jewish Agency was established by the World Zionist Organization at the
       16th Zionist Congress, on August 11, 1929, as a partnership between the WZO and
       non-Zionist Jewish leaders…As the de facto government of the state-on-the-way,
       it was recognized as the official representative of the Jewish community and world
       Jewry vis-à-vis the League of Nations, the British Mandate government, and
       foreign governments…The Jewish Agency was also responsible for the Yishuv's
       internal affairs: immigration – allocating certificates supplied by the Mandate
       Authority – and resettlement of new immigrants, the building of new settlements,

economic development, education and culture, hospitals and health services." Source: The Jewish Agency for Israel. "History." The Jewish Agency for Israel. http://www.jafi.org.il/about/history.htm

55. Jerusalem, August 1, 2002: "The UN Secretary General's Report on Jenin, released today, came about as the result of false Palestinian propaganda regarding an alleged 'massacre' in the Jenin refugee camp during the course of Israel's Defensive Shield counter-terrorist operation of April, 2002." Source: Israel Ministry of Foreign Affairs. "Israel's Reaction to the UN Secretary General's Report on Jenin." State of Israel. http://www.mfa.gov.il/mfa/go.asp?MFAH0m5r0

56. "On October 12, 2000, two reserve army drivers were apprehended by Palestinian police after they mistakenly entered the Palestinian controlled town of Ramallah. They were brought to Palestinian police headquarters in the center of Ramallah, where a violent mob of Palestinians stormed the building and tortured the soldiers to death, mutilating and defiling their bodies beyond recognition." Source: Israel Ministry of Foreign Affairs. "First Cpl. Yosef Avrahami." State of Israel. http://mfa.gov.il/mfa/go.asp?MFAH0ik20

57. On May 15, 1974, in the city of Maalot 27 Israelis were killed, "21 of whom were children, and 78 wounded by PFLP [Popular Front for the Liberation of Palestine] terrorists in a school, after an unsuccessful rescue attempt by the IDF." Source: Israel Ministry of Foreign Affairs. "1967–1973 Major Terror Attacks." State of Israel. http://www.mfa.gov.il/MFA/Facts+About+Israel/Israel+in+Maps/1967-1993-+Major+Terror+Attacks.htm

58. "Gadi and Tzipi Shemesh were killed by a suicide bomber on King George Street in Jerusalem on March 21, 2002. Eighty-six people sustained injuries and three individuals were killed." Source: Israel Ministry of Foreign Affairs. "Victims of Palestinian Violence and Terrorism since September 2000." State of Israel. http://www.mfa.gov.il/mfa/go.asp?MFAH0ia50

59. Kiddush is a prayer over wine traditionally recited on the Sabbath and holy days.

60. Source: Ruth Sinai, "Unemployment is 6% higher than official figure, report claims," *Haaretz*, February 9, 2004.

61. Fifty shekels is equivalent to about twelve U.S. dollars at the time of writing.

62. Micha's prediction of terror in Europe came true on a wide scale on March 11, 2004, in Madrid. "Ten bombs explode[d] on four packed early-morning commuter trains in Madrid, killing 191 people and leaving at least 1,800 injured"

Source: "Timeline: Madrid Investigation." April 28, 2004. BBC News, UK Edition. http://news.bbc.co.uk/1/hi/world/europe/3597885.stm

63. On February 22, 2004, a number 14A Egged bus was destroyed by a suicide bomber near Liberty Bell Park. Eight people were killed and over sixty were injured, including eleven school children. Source: Israel Ministry of Foreign Affairs. State of Israel. http://www.mfa.gov.il/mfa/go.asp?MFAH0ia50.

64. "Gilo is a residential neighborhood of about 40,000 which lies within the municipal boundaries of Jerusalem and of Israel as defined by Israeli law...it has been subjected to indiscriminate sniper and machine gun attacks from neighboring areas under the control of the Palestinian Authority." Source: Embassy of Israel. "What is Israel Doing about the Attacks on Gilo?" Embassy of Israel, Washington D.C., Public Affairs. http://www.israelemb.org/public_affairs/FAQ/currentFAQ.html#14

65. Efrat is situated 8 miles south of Jerusalem over the Green Line in the Etzion Bloc. "Since the Intifada began, cars driving on the tunnel road from Efrat to Jerusalem, built to bypass nearby Palestinian villages, have become targets for Palestinian drive-by shootings." Source: Jessica Steinberg, "Boom in the house of the rising sun," *The Jerusalem Post*, November 13, 2001. http://www.jpost.com/Editions/2001/06/20/RealEstate/RealEstate.28684.html

66. "The Maccabia is a series of athletic competitions for Jews throughout the world. Like the International Olympics, the Maccabia is held every four years. The goal of the Maccabia is to promote the physical strength of Jews while fostering a sense of nationalism among Jewish athletes...The first Maccabia was held in Palestine in 1932. 390 athletes from 14 countries participated in the event." Source: "Homeward Bound: The Maccabia." http://www.wzo.org.il/home/dev/maccabi.htm

67. The Azrieli Tower is a tall office building that houses a shopping mall in Tel Aviv.

68. Camp Ramah is the youth summer camp of the Jewish Conservative Movement. It offers educational and recreational programming for the campers. Source: Camp Ramah of Wisconsin. www.ramahwisconsin.com

69. Source: Embassy of Israel. "What is Israel Doing About the Attacks on Gilo?" Embassy of Israel, Washington D.C., Public Affairs. http://www.israelemb.org/public_affairs/FAQ/currentFAQ.html#14

70. Theodor Herzl was the father of modern Zionism. He outlined his vision for a

Jewish state in his magnum opus *Der Judenstaat* (*The Jewish State*), which was
published in February 1896.

71. Neve Shalom-Wahat al-Salam is a village located between Jerusalem and Tel
Aviv. Its name is the Hebrew and Arabic for "oasis of peace." There is an equal
number of Arab Israeli and Jewish Israeli residents living together in the village.
The kindergarten and primary school have approximately 290 Arab and Jewish
students, around 90 percent coming from places outside of Neve Shalom-Wahat
al-Salam. This is the only school with a bilingual education program, where Arab
Israeli and Jewish Israeli teachers speak in their native language. In addition to
the primary school, the village has a "School of Peace," where Jewish and Arab
tenth through twelfth grade students can come together from schools throughout
Israel and discuss their similarities, differences, peace, and conflict resolution
during a two to three-day seminar. Source: Neve Shalom/Wahat al-Salam. www.
nswas.com

72. Arik's comment is in reference to Israel's Operation Defensive Shield, where
soldiers went into the Palestinian town of Jenin to combat terrorism in March
and April 2002.

73. "A soldier may seek an exemption from service or a deferment for special
reasons under Article 36 et. seq. of the Defense Service Law (Consolidated
Version) (1959) as amended. Special reasons in this instance include educational
requirements, economic hardship and extenuating family circumstances." Source:
Israel Ministry of Foreign Affairs. "Israel's Policy on Selective Conscientious
Objection." State of Israel. http://www.mfa.gov.il/MFA/Government/Law/
Legal+Issues+and+Rulings/Israel-s+Policy+on+Selective+Conscientious+Objecti.
htm

74. Each year 14,000 to 20,000 Israeli high school students participate in organized
trips to Poland. 4,000 of them participate in official Ministry of Education
delegations. The other students are parts of independent delegations organized
by educational networks, local municipalities or by individual schools in con-
junction with private companies which provide flights, ground assistance and
educational instruction. Source: Israel Ministry of Education, Culture and
Sport. State of Israel. http://www.education.gov.il/mivzak/DOVERETMSG/
DOVERETMSG_msg_item.asp?cd=3138&category_nm=&mode=

75. The Plaszow concentration camp was located ten kilometers outside of Krakow,
Poland. Many Jews from Krakow were sent to Plaszow, first as a work camp and
then as a concentration camp.

76. On March 26, 2004, for example, the IDF caught a teenage Palestinian boy wearing an explosive belt at a checkpoint.

About the Author

Waiting for Peace: How Israelis Live with Terrorism is Liza M. Wiemer's second book. She is a freelance writer, public speaker, and has been a Jewish educator for over 25 years developing award winning curricula. Along with her husband and two sons, Ms. Wiemer resides in Milwaukee, WI.

For more information go to www.israelbooks.com.